Florence Greenberg's
JEWISH
COOKBOOK

Florence Greenberg's
JEWISH
COOKBOOK

In association with the Jewish Chronicle

CHARTWELL
BOOKS INC.

The author and publishers would like to thank Ann Harris for her advice,
and also the following for sponsoring the color photographs:
Tomor Margarine, Van den Berghs : page 60
Carmel Fruit and Vegetables : pages 70–71

COOKERY CONSULTANT : STEPHANIE BLASBERG

Photography by Robert Golden *(pages 20, 32, 97, 98, 128 and 155 by
John Miller; page 125 by John Lee)*
Line illustrations by Freda Miller

Photographs on pages 1 and 2 show a traditional
Shabbat dinner of roast chicken with roast potatoes
and broccoli, and dried fruit casserole with kichals
and lemon tea.

Menorah on front jacket kindly loaned by Jerusalem the Golden,
Golders Green, London; plates on page 60 by Polonez, Shepherd's Bush
Centre, London

First published under the title *Florence Greenberg's Jewish Cookery Book*
First edition 1947
Eighth edition, third impression 1975
This edition published by Chartwell Books Inc.,
A Division of Book Sales Inc.,
110 Enterprise Avenue, Secaucus, New Jersey 07094

© Copyright text Jewish Chronicle Publications and The Hamlyn Publishing
Group Limited 1980
© Copyright illustrations and color photographs The Hamlyn Publishing
Group Limited 1980

ISBN 0-89009-301-6
LOC Catalog Card Number 79-53995

Phototypeset in England by Tradespools Ltd., Frome, Somerset
Printed in Italy

Contents

Useful Facts and Figures

Notes on metrication

In this book quantities are given in metric and Imperial measures. Exact conversion from Imperial to metric measures does not usually give very convenient working quantities and so the metric measures have been rounded off into units of 25 grams. The table below shows the recommended equivalents.

Ounces	Approx g to nearest whole figure	Recommended conversion to nearest unit of 25
1	28	25
2	57	50
3	85	75
4	113	100
5	142	150
6	170	175
7	198	200
8	227	225
9	255	250
10	283	275
11	312	300
12	340	350
13	368	375
14	396	400
15	425	425
16 (1 lb)	454	450
17	482	475
18	510	500
19	539	550
20 ($1\frac{1}{4}$ lb)	567	575

Note: When converting quantities over 20 oz first add the appropriate figures in the centre column, then adjust to the nearest unit of 25. As a general guide, 1 kg (1000 g) equals 2.2 lb or about 2 lb 3 oz. This method of conversion gives good results in nearly all cases, although in certain pastry and cake recipes a more accurate conversion is necessary to produce a balanced recipe.

Liquid measures The millilitre has been used in this book and the following table gives a few examples.

Imperial	Approx ml to nearest whole figure	Recommended ml
$\frac{1}{4}$ pint	142	150 ml
$\frac{1}{2}$ pint	283	300 ml
$\frac{3}{4}$ pint	425	450 ml
1 pint	567	600 ml
$1\frac{1}{2}$ pints	851	900 ml
$1\frac{3}{4}$ pints	992	1000 ml (1 litre)

Spoon measures All spoon measures given in this book are level unless otherwise stated.

Can sizes At present, cans are marked with the exact (usually to the nearest whole number) metric equivalent of the Imperial weight of the contents, so we have followed this practice when giving can sizes.

Oven temperatures

The table below gives recommended equivalents.

	°C	°F	Gas Mark
Very cool	110	225	$\frac{1}{4}$
	120	250	$\frac{1}{2}$
Cool	140	275	1
	150	300	2
Moderate	160	325	3
	180	350	4
Moderately hot	190	375	5
	200	400	6
Hot	220	425	7
	230	450	8
Very hot	240	475	9

Notes for American and Australian users

In America the 8-oz measuring cup is used. In Australia metric measures are now used in conjunction with the standard 250-ml measuring cup. The Imperial pint, used in Britain and Australia, is 20 fl oz, while the American pint is 16 fl oz. It is important to remember that the Australian tablespoon differs from both the British and American tablespoons; the table below gives a comparison. The British standard tablespoon, which has been used throughout this book, holds 17.7 ml, the American 14.2 ml, and the Australian 20 ml. A teaspoon holds approximately 5 ml in all three countries.

British	American	Australian
1 teaspoon	1 teaspoon	1 teaspoon
1 tablespoon	1 tablespoon	1 tablespoon
2 tablespoons	3 tablespoons	2 tablespoons
$3\frac{1}{2}$ tablespoons	4 tablespoons	3 tablespoons
4 tablespoons	5 tablespoons	$3\frac{1}{2}$ tablespoons

An Imperial/American guide to solid and liquid measures

Solid measures

IMPERIAL	AMERICAN
1 lb butter or margarine	2 cups
1 lb flour	4 cups
1 lb granulated or castor sugar	2 cups
1 lb icing sugar	3 cups
8 oz rice	1 cup

Liquid measures

IMPERIAL	AMERICAN
$\frac{1}{4}$ pint liquid	$\frac{2}{3}$ cup liquid
$\frac{1}{2}$ pint	$1\frac{1}{4}$ cups
$\frac{3}{4}$ pint	2 cups
1 pint	$2\frac{1}{2}$ cups
$1\frac{1}{2}$ pints	$3\frac{3}{4}$ cups
2 pints	5 cups ($2\frac{1}{2}$ pints)

American terms

The list below gives some American equivalents for equipment and terms used in this book.

British	American
cling film	saran wrap
confectioners' custard	pastry cream
flan tin	pie pan
frying pan	skillet
greaseproof paper	wax paper
grill	broil/broiler
mince/minced	grind/ground
palette knife	spatula
polythene	plastic
sandwich tin	layer cake pan
Swiss roll tin	jelly roll pan

NOTE: WHEN MAKING ANY OF THE RECIPES IN THIS BOOK, ONLY FOLLOW ONE SET OF MEASURES AS THEY ARE NOT INTERCHANGEABLE.

Introduction

Within the framework of their dietary laws, Jews in every land have adopted and adapted local dishes and from each country added new ones to their now formidable list of 'traditional' dishes. Many of these can be traced very easily to the land of origin. For example, recipes for savoury fish as well as gefillte fish are all common to non-Jewish communities in places situated inland at a great distance from the sea and were originated to give flavour to fresh-water fish. They are eaten very generally in Poland, whereas among Sephardic Jews who lived in maritime countries where salt-water fish was available, gefillte fish was scarcely known.

In Western Europe our Jewish food has tended to mirror that of our countries of origin; mainly it reflects the cooking of Russia, Poland and Austria, but perhaps some of the tastiest food is prepared by the Sephardim. These are Jews who left Spain and settled in the countries of the Mediterranean. Desserts made with nuts, honey and rosewater, confectionery baked with nuts and sesame seeds, each taste a delight and fondly remembered.

Jews in India, the Levant and North Africa all have special local dishes which they claim as traditional, while such combinations as Brussels sprouts cooked with chestnuts, which are very popular throughout Holland and Belgium, have come to be included among Jewish traditional dishes.

Similarly today a new list of 'traditional' foods is being evolved among the settlers in Israel. Here people from such widely spaced countries as Russia, America and the Yemen are adapting their family dishes to suit climate and the local available foods.

Added to the list of our grandmothers' recipes are those which contain the export produce of Israel, the avocado, aubergine (eggplant), melon and citrus fruits, as well as green peppers and other salad vegetables.

These fruits and vegetables, together with the variety of daily foods one is introduced to on visits to Israel, complement our modern approach to a lighter, fresher diet.

However, it was not just the local cooking that contributed to the development of Jewish dishes. Perhaps more important was the need to adhere to the Jewish dietary laws. Observant Jews eat meat and poultry only of animals and birds listed as 'pure' in the Bible and which have been ritually killed in the prescribed fashion. Of particular interest to housewives is the law that states that meat and milk may not be used together in cooking, and that food containing milk may not be eaten after a meat meal until at least three hours have elapsed. From this law grew the need to adapt fish and dairy recipes to form main course dishes and milkless desserts that could be eaten after meat meals.

The Jewish housewife who keeps a kosher kitchen will only buy kosher meat and poultry and will also take care not to use any food product which may have a non-kosher animal ingredient. It is the practice for observant Jews also to use only kosher wines.

Passover, the festival that commemorates the Exodus of the Jews from Egypt, is celebrated in April. At this time no artificial leavening may be used in cooking so instead of wheat flour, matzo meal and potato flour are used. The cake and confectionery made for Passover are a tribute to the ingenuity and imagination of the Jewish housewife – carrot candy, beetroot jam and matzo pudding are delicious.

The dietary laws also control the way in which the housewife prepares her food, and for this reason the layout of kitchen working areas and the storage and cleaning of utensils are all affected. The fact that milk and meat may not be used together in cooking means that separate areas should be planned – one for cooking meat foods, the other for those foods containing dairy products. If there is enough space the easiest and most effective way to do this is to decide what equipment and utensils are needed and then duplicate everything, so that each area has its own sink unit, preparation area and storage space for cutlery and crockery. This plan avoids the possibility of confusion. If the kitchen has one long working area perhaps the most effective plan is to have a double drainer in the centre with workspace and storage to one side being designated for milk and the other for meat. The observant Jewish housewife would not cook in the same oven at the same time both milk and meat dishes, nor use the same dishwasher.

Today some of our more traditional foods can be bought ready made. Kosher packaged foods have become widely available as a result of the growth of the Israeli food industry and the increase in supervision of foods in this country, often made possible by the mechanisation processes introduced into modern food factories.

From Israel are imported convenience foods including quick meals, milk shakes, instant puddings and savoury snacks, as well as latkes, canned gefillte fish and packets of quick cooking kneidel mix. From Israel too come Eastern Mediterranean foods which are being integrated into kosher cooking – we can now buy ready prepared techina and hummus to mix with salads, and halva to serve with our after-dinner coffee.

In this country an increasing variety of prepared foods are available in kosher packs: puff pastry, cheese spreads, mayonnaise and salad cream, ice cream, custard powder and chewing gum. Also the kosher butchers sell meat ready koshered and ready wrapped to be stored in the freezer. It is also possible to buy packs of fish ready minced to make gefillte fish, to buy frozen cheesecake, frozen blintzes and cans of goulash. All these items enable the Jewish housewife to supplement her home cooking when necessary yet still provide the family with the familiar well-loved dishes.

For those who still kosher meat at home the laws of Kashrut are well defined and simple to follow:

Soaking before Salting

1 A special vessel is set aside for the sole purpose of soaking meat, bones or kosher fat, prior to the salting. The meat, bones or fat placed in this vessel should be completely immersed in cold water and left soaking for 30 minutes.

2 The water should not be excessively cold nor should pieces of ice be allowed to float in it.

3 Likewise, meat may not be put into soaking whilst it is in a frozen state. It should be allowed to thaw first. On no account should it be placed in front of the fire to induce thawing, or be put in hot water.

Salting the Meat

1 The meat, having been kept in water for 30 minutes, is then taken out and put on the 'salting board' and left for a few minutes so as to drain off some of its water. It should not be left draining long enough to get dry.

2 The 'salting board' consists of a plastic draining rack, or a perforated or grooved board placed in a slanting position, to allow free draining. This is an essential condition. The blood drawn out by the salt must be allowed to drain away freely from the meat.

3 The salt should be neither too coarse nor too fine.

4 The salt should be sprinkled on all sides, in all cuts and folds, freely yet not too thickly; the right amount to be used is best described as resembling the hoar-frost one sees on the roof on a winter morning.

5 Eggs found in the fowl, whether partly or completely formed, with or without shell, must be salted after soaking, like the fowl. (They should be salted separately, not together with the meat, but are regarded as meat food, i.e., not to be eaten with milk or butter.)

6 Great care should be taken that no piece of salted meat drops back again into the drained liquid, nor should any of the liquid be allowed to fall into any vessel or on to food.

7 After 1 hour all the salted meat is freely rinsed of its bloodstained salt and washed two or three times in a vessel filled with water. The water should always be put in first, so that no chance blood-stain may cling to the sides of the vessel. The meat is then kosher, i.e., fit for food, and may be prepared in any way. The gravy of underdone meat may be eaten without the least scruple.

Kashering of Liver

Liver is not koshered in the same way as meat. It cannot be cooked or fried in an enclosed vessel unless it is first well roasted on an open fire. Before roasting, it should be cut open with a knife kept specially for this purpose. Rinse well with cold water and sprinkle with salt on all sides. Place in a wire basket or on the grid of a grill pan kept specially for this purpose, so that the blood can run away freely. Soon after sprinkling with salt, cook on top of a gas flame until cooked on all sides and rinse well. Strictly speaking, observant housewives will only kasher liver if it catches the flame, and will not therefore use an electric cooker. A wire basket on a portable gas burner should be used instead.

Note Housewives should remember that meat or liver must be kashered before being placed in a deep freezer.

Glossary

Cookery Methods

✡

To bake blind To bake the pastry case (pie shell) before adding the filling.

To baste To spoon fat (or other liquid) over food during cooking to keep it moist.

To blanch To plunge food into boiling water to loosen the skin. To bring food to the boil to whiten it, to reduce saltiness or with vegetables to prepare for freezing.

To braise To brown meat in hot fat, then cook slowly covered with vegetables and a little stock – a combination of roasting and stewing.

To clarify fat Melt the fat and strain into a large bowl. Then pour over double the quantity of boiling water. Stir well and leave until cold and set. Remove the layer of fat from the top of the water, scrape off any sediment from the bottom of the cake, then melt the fat and pour into a basin.

To cream To beat fat with a wooden spoon until light and fluffy.

To dredge To coat lightly with flour or sugar.

To egg and crumb To coat fish cutlets, rissoles, croquettes, etc., before frying. The food is dipped into beaten egg then coated with fine breadcrumbs – fresh or dried.

To fold in A process of combining beaten mixtures with other ingredients so that they retain their lightness.

To glaze To give food a glossy finish by brushing it with beaten egg, milk, sugar syrup or jelly.

To marinate To stand meat or fish in a mixture of vinegar, oil, herbs, and spices for a short time before cooking, to improve the flavour.

To poach To cook just below boiling point in hot liquid in an open pan.

To prove To leave yeast dough in a warm place to rise after it has been shaped into a loaf, rolls, etc.

To purée To rub cooked fruit or vegetables through a sieve or to blend in a liquidiser.

To render fat To melt down fat from meat trimmings, cut into small pieces and bake in a cool oven until all the fat is extracted and only crisp brown pieces remain.

To rub in A method of mixing flour and fat used in cakes and pastry.

To sauté To brown lightly in shallow fat.

To sift To sieve dry ingredients.

To simmer To cook at a temperature below boiling point. Used for soups, stews and sauces.

To skim To remove the fat from the surface of stews or scum from jam.

To steam To cook over boiling water.

To stew To cook slowly in a small quantity of liquid.

Cookery Terms

✡

Au gratin Any dish covered with sauce and topped with breadcrumbs or cheese and then browned under a grill or in the upper part of a hot oven.

Batter A mixture of flour, egg and liquid used for pancakes and coating food.

Bouquet garni A bunch of herbs used for flavouring stocks, soups or stews. Usually a mixture of parsley, bay leaf and thyme, tied together with thread; or a prepared mixture of herbs in a muslin bag.

Consistency The thickness or texture of a mixture such as cake or pudding.

Dropping consistency Uncooked cake or pudding mixture soft enough to drop from a spoon.

Egg wash Used to brush pastry before cooking to produce a glaze. Most usual mixture is equal quantities of beaten egg and milk or water.

Garnish Improving the appearance of a savoury dish with decorations such as parsley or lemon.

Stock Liquid made from meat, vegetables or fish, used as a foundation for soups, stews or sauces.

Kitchen Equipment and Appliances

The purchase of kitchen equipment and appliances will depend mainly on how much money can be allocated for the purpose and also on how much room is available. Many kitchens have only a limited space to store equipment. After these basic considerations priorities will depend on how each individual prefers to work and which of the various food preparation tasks are most liked or disliked.

There may also be the additional problem of having to supplement existing equipment rather than having the ideal situation of planning entirely from scratch. Few people are able to do this. Even the newly married housewife tends to start from the basis of wedding presents and then adds to these according to necessity.

The Cooker

This is the basic requirement and obvious first choice. Identical features can be found on either free-standing or split level cookers. Features worth considering are:

An automatic rotisserie for roasting chicken and meat using the minimum of fat. The meat bastes itself and is moister than when cooked by the conventional roasting method. The rotisserie can also be used for making kebabs. As well as being incorporated into a conventional cooker, a rotisserie can also be bought as a separate unit which can either be wall-mounted or kept on a work surface.

A fan oven holds the same temperature throughout the oven cavity and will cook food evenly on each shelf. This means the oven can be filled to capacity and is ideal for batch cooking for the freezer or for baking for a party or buffet.

An automatic timer to control the oven is a great advantage for working cooks. It is lovely to come home to a hot meal on a winter's evening or to be able to invite guests for dinner and know the food will be ready early in the evening.

A Slow Cooker

The type of separate unit which is an independently heated casserole container is also useful for working cooks. Stews, soups, pot roasts and some desserts can be prepared and left to cook slowly during the day. This method of cooking gives a good flavour to the food especially with the cheaper cuts of meat. It is very economical to use and can be left on all day without the danger of running up large fuel bills.

A Microwave Oven

The purchase of a microwave oven can be justified equally for large families or for single people living alone because its use is so variable. But however the microwave oven is used its effectiveness can be doubled when used in conjunction with a freezer. It can be used to defrost frozen food and is excellent for reheating prepared frozen meals, both home-made and commercially prepared packs.

Prepared, canned and packaged foods can be reconstituted in the oven – and with these items the advantage is the saving of time and extra washing up. Food can be placed in the serving dish, heated in the microwave oven and then taken straight to the table.

When cooking raw foods a good flavour is preserved. Food cooks in its own juices, and vegetables, fruits and fish are particularly tasty and fresh. Chicken and veal are among the other prime foods which lend themselves to this method of cooking.

Increased flavour and a saving of time are two reasons for buying a microwave oven but convenience comes a close third. If a member of the family doesn't appear on time for a meal the portion can be served on to the plate and heated through in the oven when needed. Second helpings for a dinner party are heated when needed instead of having to be kept warm and drying out in the meantime.

Yet it is the saving of time that is the most impressive aspect of a microwave oven. A portion of casserole can be reheated in 45 seconds and a slice of steamed pudding in 10 seconds. An average weight chicken cooked from raw takes less than 15 minutes.

These ovens are particularly easy to use. The interior does not get hot so food does not burn and cleaning is a simple matter of wiping with a damp cloth to remove condensation. As cooking times are short there are virtually no cooking smells.

After the cooker the most popular appliances to spring to mind are those which can be described as food preparation machines. These include table and hand mixers, liquidisers and the whole range of independent specialist machines – the food processor, juice extractors, juice separators, coffee mills and slicers and shredders.

A Hand Mixer

This can be bought as a separate portable appliance or with a bowl and stand as optional extras. There are also hand mixers available which are run on batteries and can therefore be used independently of an electricity supply. A hand mixer is ideal used for creaming fat and sugar, whisking egg whites, whisking cream and reconstituting convenience desserts.

Because a hand mixer is portable and doesn't necessarily need to be used over a work surface, it is a great help in preparing foods that have been cooked but need further attention in the pan, such as creaming potatoes and thickening sauces. Some hand mixers are supplied with plastic beaters which make them particularly suitable for mixing ingredients in non-stick pans or plastic bowls.

A Table Mixer

This is designed to be kept on a work surface and this is much more desirable, if there is sufficient space, than keeping it in a cupboard where the prospect of lifting and assembling it prevents frequent use. Most of the large table mixers are available with a wide range of attachments which could include a liquidiser, can opener, coffee mill, coffee grinder, dough hook, juice extractor, bean slicer and cream maker.

The particular advantage of the large table mixer is that it can be left unattended which considerably reduces the time taken to prepare most dishes. While the mixer is working, other jobs like weighing out ingredients or preparing the baking tins can be finished.

The table mixer can deal with large quantities and heavy mixtures and many people find that once they have one it is possible to make recipes that wouldn't be attempted otherwise. These include heavy fruit cakes where the mixer can be used throughout all the stages of preparation. Breadmaking is another task which becomes much simpler when carried out in a table mixer. Most machines process up to 675 g/ 1½ lb flour, each kneading takes less than 2 minutes, and there is no mess as all the mixture stays in the bowl until it is shaped to be placed in the tin. Other dough mixtures such as cholla and kuchen are equally simple to make.

Pastry can be mixed to the crumb stage in the bowl and the results often give a very short pastry. For those who find pastry difficult to make by hand the mixer may be the answer.

The capacity and versatility of the table mixer make it a natural choice for the preparation of bulk food for freezing – make one cake to eat and one to keep. Extra soup can be prepared in the liquidiser and pastry and bread can be made every other week or each month instead of on a weekly basis.

A Liquidiser (Blender)

This appliance can be attached to a table mixer or can be bought as an independent appliance with its own motor. The preparation tasks that make a liquidiser popular include making mayonnaise, where all the oil is added to the egg and vinegar slowly until the mixture thickens, making soup and fruit purées, making drinks, chopping nuts and making breadcrumbs. However, a liquidiser is more versatile than many people believe and some food preparation previously thought to 'belong' to a mixer can easily be completed by a liquidiser. For example, batters can be made by putting the milk, egg and half the flour in the goblet, blending and then adding the rest of the flour gradually until the mixture is smooth. For whipping cream good results can be obtained by just pouring the double cream (heavy cream) into the goblet and blending for 30 seconds. Cakes using the soft fat all-in-one method can be made in the liquidiser, but it is not suitable for making cakes by the creaming method. French dressing can be made in large quantities by blending the oil, vinegar, mustard, sugar and garlic cloves for about 10 seconds: as a variation add an egg for a thicker mayonnaise-type dressing. Large quantities can be made up and kept in the refrigerator to be used as needed. Most sauces and soft spreading mixtures can be prepared in the liquidiser.

Baby foods can also be prepared at home. Daily family meals – the meat, vegetables, fruit and desserts – can be individually blended for baby foods. As only small quantities are needed portions can be wrapped and frozen to be used another time.

The Food Processor

The latest addition to the family of food preparation machines is the food processor which does many of the chopping and slicing jobs previously carried out by hand or in the mincer. Gefillte fish, chopped herring and chopped liver are three of the most popular time-consuming dishes which can be prepared in this machine. But it will also tackle a host of other jobs such as preparing chopped meat dishes, a whole variety of salad dishes and the complete range of soups. In fact this machine combines the processes carried out by the mincer, liquidiser and slicer and shredder, as well as doing most of the simpler baking tasks.

The Refrigerator

The ideal place to keep fresh food or cooked food that isn't eaten immediately is the refrigerator. Many kitchens are quite warm – about 20°C/68°F – but the inside of a refrigerator is much cooler, usually between 5–7°C/40–43°F. Fresh food stored in the refrigerator keeps crisp and tasty and cooked foods such as casserole dishes and roast meats, can be kept for 2–3 days before eating.

The size of the refrigerator needed will depend on: how often fresh food is bought, how many people there are in the family, how much batch cooking there is, and if there is also a freezer in the house. It is usually the case that where there is a freezer the need for refrigerator space is reduced and the frozen food storage compartment is not used so often.

Most refrigerators have frozen food compartments in which small amounts of frozen food can be stored. These compartments are coded with star markings:

✳   means the compartment is capable of storing frozen food for 1 week

✳✳   for 1 month

✳✳✳   for 3 months

But these compartments cannot be used for freezing down fresh food unless the symbol ✳✳✳ is shown. This is called the freezer symbol.

Double door refrigerators are upright cabinets where the refrigerator and frozen food storage compartments are separated. Access is through two separate doors but there is only one motor and cooling system and both compartments work from a single control. The frozen food storage compartment offers more space than that in the normal refrigerator and some compartments may carry the ✳✳✳ freezer symbol which means small quantities of fresh food may be frozen.

A fridge freezer is also a single unit with two separate doors but in this appliance both compartments are roughly the same size. The top half is usually a refrigerator, the bottom section a food freezer. Both compartments can be controlled separately and the freezer unit will normally carry the ✳✳✳ freezer symbol.

If the main concern is just to store prepacked food – vegetables and standbys like frozen pastry or pre-frozen meals – a double door refrigerator, a small capacity freezer (some manufacturers produce a 1.5–2 cu ft model) or a fridge freezer is the answer.

However, if you are serious about freezing down fresh food and home-cooked food then choose either a large capacity fridge freezer or a separate food freezer.

The Freezer

There are many types of freezer cabinets to choose from. There are independent upright or chest models, or the freezer space may be combined with the refrigerator. The fridge freezer model takes up little space and supplies ample storage space for the majority of family requirements.

Freezing is the simplest and most convenient way of keeping food at home and the only method of preservation which doesn't change the way the food looks or tastes. Owning a freezer has been compared to having a supermarket at home – a good description of a well stocked cabinet.

Most foods freeze successfully if they are fresh when stored and adequately packed. Almost all vegetables which are normally cooked may be frozen with good results, the exceptions being those vegetables which contain a high percentage of water, such as onions, marrows, celery, tomatoes and green peppers. These vegetables lose their crispness when frozen and are best used in soups and cooked dishes. Alternatively, they can be cooked first and stored as purées or mixed vegetable casseroles. Salad vegetables – lettuce, watercress, cucumber, radishes and chicory – cannot be frozen but most herbs freeze well. They should be quite fresh and can be placed whole in polythene bags. When needed for flavouring a few stalks can be crumbled and used in cooking.

Most fruits are suitable for freezing if their quality is good. If fruit is from the garden it should be picked when fully ripe but still firm. During a glut fruit can be bought at reasonable prices from market gardens, local markets and supermarkets. Unfortunately when fruit is at its best for freezing – that is just firm and ripe – it is at its most expensive to buy.

Soft fruit bought more cheaply at the end of the season will give poor results when frozen whole but is ideal to freeze as part of a cooked dish or as a purée.

All fruits, except pineapple, pears and citrus fruit, can be successfully frozen as purées. Fruit bought at the end of the season can also be frozen whole to be used in jam when defrosted. It is useful to freeze the skin of citrus fruit whole in polythene bags; it can then be grated when frozen hard for flavouring.

Many butchers sell meat for the freezer which has already been koshered and is ready to be packed. Other butchers sell ready koshered frozen packs to be stored at home. If you are preparing meat for the freezer at home it should be stored in cuts or joints which are suitable quantities for a family meal. Where possible bone meat to save space in the freezer and trim surplus fat from all the pieces. Chill the meat in the refrigerator for a short time before putting it in the freezer. Separate chops with pieces of cellophane so that they can be removed singly for cooking. Minced (ground) meat can be stored in convenient quantities in small containers, but meatballs should be shaped and placed uncovered on trays in the freezer until they are hard. Once frozen they can then be transferred to polythene bags, sealed and used individually as needed.

Baked foods will probably be the largest part of the freezer store. Breads, cakes, pastries, biscuits and pies all freeze very well.

Before preparing the food for the freezer decide how it will be served. For example, pies and puddings to be eaten cold can be baked before storage, otherwise prepare as for the oven but freeze before baking. Then transfer the pudding or pie from the freezer to the oven and it will thaw and heat as though just baked, though the cooking time should be increased a little.

It may also be more convenient to prepare the components of a finished dish rather than complete the preparation before freezing. Store each component separately, that is dry fruit packs or fruit in syrup, choux pastry cases, flan and pastry cases, ice cream, whipped cream, savoury fillings. On defrosting different combinations can be chosen: fruit and cream, fruit flan and ice cream, sweet or savoury choux pastry. An added advantage to this scheme is that each item individually has a longer storage life than the made-up dish. It also allows greater flexibility in the use of the freezer stock. Shortcrust pastry can be shaped into pie cases, flan cases or pie lids before storing, baked or unbaked.

When storing unbaked pastry, store pie lids and pastry cases in flat rounds, separated by foil, then the rounds can be used a layer at a time.

Pies Pies should be made in foil dishes or plates, and frozen uncovered without making a steam vent. When frozen the large pies can be left in the foil dish and over-wrapped in foil and the small pies removed from the patty tins and packed loose in polythene bags. To thaw, the pies should be unwrapped and placed in a preheated oven, allowing extra time for thawing. Cut a vent in the pie when the pastry begins to thaw.

To freeze baked pies they should be prepared in foil dishes, cooked quickly and wrapped in heavy duty foil. Allow 2–4 hours for the pie to defrost at room temperature depending on its size.

Sandwiches All white or brown sandwiches and all varieties – closed, rolled or open sandwiches – freeze well. Unsuitable fillings are hard-boiled eggs and all salad vegetables. Use seasoning sparingly as the flavour increases during storage.

Cakes All types of cakes, plain or rich, freeze well especially Swiss rolls and sponge cakes which normally do not keep long after baking. Cakes can be frozen decorated or plain. Scones and undecorated cakes can be simply wrapped in polythene bags. Decorated cakes should be frozen overnight unpacked on a tray. Next morning the decoration will be hard and the cake can be foil wrapped. Remove the wrapping again before the cake defrosts or it will stick to the melting icing. Decorated cakes should be stored in boxes for extra protection.

Pancakes Pancakes can be frozen already filled, providing the filling contains food which is suitable for freezing. Avoid fillings which contain hard-boiled eggs, and be careful not to over-season savoury fillings. Freeze in an overwrapped foil dish and thaw direct from the freezer in a moderate oven for 30 minutes. Alternatively, freeze pancakes and fillings separately.

Most made-up dishes normally served at home can be frozen. The few foods which are not satisfactory and should be left out of made-up dishes are: hard-boiled eggs which go rubbery, boiled potatoes which go floury, and spaghetti. Add these items when the dish has been defrosted. When preparing cooked dishes for the freezer, consider how the food will be served. This will affect the type of pack used, the quantity of food in each pack and the method of freezing each item.

After cooking, pack the food in quantities of one, two, three or four portions depending on the number in the family. It is easy to add an extra portion but difficult to thaw half a casserole. If the dish needs to go straight into the oven from the freezer, pack in foil dishes or lined casseroles.

A few spices, mint and thyme tend to become stronger during storage, and as a general rule it is best to under-season cooked dishes such as casseroles, soups and sauces, and adjust the flavour before serving.

As with the baked foods, thought should be given to the possible alternatives. If a complete made-up dish is stored such as curry or goulash, then no other choice is possible on defrosting. If the freezer con-

tains chicken joints, minced (ground) beef, chuck steak, curry sauce, goulash sauce, stock, tomato purée, parsley, chives, green peppers and mixed vegetable packs, all these foods can be used in different combinations, or used separately with fresh food.

A final word of caution. A freezer is such a boon to cooking that it is possible to get carried away. Freeze only food which the family enjoys. This may seem common sense but it is not always followed. If the family does not normally eat the food, then don't freeze it.

The Dishwasher

It makes sense to talk about a dishwasher as the final appliance to use in the kitchen. It is not directly associated with cooking but will be used during the day as part of every task carried out in connection with food preparation. There is no doubt that people who own a dishwasher feel its main advantage is in keeping the kitchen tidier. Dishes can be cleared into the machine as they are used and at all times during the day the work surface is clear – clear of dirty dishes waiting to be washed and of rinsed dishes left to drain.

A dishwasher also saves time. Washing up is normally done either after food preparation, cooking or baking, and after each meal. If dishes are merely cleared into the dishwasher then the time normally spent washing up by hand (up to 11 hours a week) can be channelled in other directions.

Washing up with a dishwasher is more hygienic. One of the major differences of washing dishes in a machine is the water temperature which in the dishwasher can be heated to between 55 and 65°C/130 and 150°F on a standard wash.

A further attractive point is that having a dishwasher considerably reduces family arguments, especially in homes where there are teenage children who create more of their 'own' mess by eating continually and leaving dishes strewn everywhere. Packing them in the dishwasher is usually an acceptable alternative.

Gefillte fish (see page 38); Cherry soup (see page 33); Bagel dough (see page 150)

Starters and Soups

The first course is always important as it sets the scene for the rest of the meal, so soups and starters should be tasty and very welcoming.

This chapter includes many of the traditional recipes and in most homes it is these foods that both the family and guests find most pleasure in eating. However, it is also true that traditional starters can be very time-consuming to prepare and date back to the time when many more hours were given to shopping and cooking than is possible now. So it is sensible to take advantage of the much wider range of kosher-prepared foods such as vacuum-packed frozen smoked salmon and frozen melon balls, as well as home-frozen herbs – parsley, mint and chives for seasoning and garnishing dishes.

Chopped liver (see page 23)

Mixed Hors d'Oeuvres

Special divided dishes are made for serving mixed hors d'oeuvres, but if one of these is not available, use a set of small dishes, placing them on a large plate or on a tray; or, if preferred, put the individual hors d'oeuvres directly on to a large dish, separating them with a small garnish of cress or watercress.

Having the hors d'oeuvres all together simplifies serving and makes the choice easier for the guests. It is usual to serve about six varieties and here are some suggestions for various combinations.

> herring salad
> sliced sausage
> radishes
> gherkins (sweet dill pickles)
> potato salad
> egg and onion

> pickled herring
> Russian salad
> red cabbage
> sweet corn with mayonnaise
> fresh cucumber
> mushrooms in oil

> egg mayonnaise
> olives
> sardines
> sliced tomato
> asparagus tips (canned)
> fresh cucumber

> smoked salmon
> black (ripe) olives
> potato salad
> sliced tomato
> celery and cream cheese
> gherkins (sweet dill pickles)

Egg Mayonnaise

Allow 1 hard-boiled egg per person. Cut the hard-boiled eggs in half and place them flat side down on a plate or lettuce leaf. Season with salt and freshly ground black pepper. Coat with home-made mayonnaise (see page 99) and garnish with finely chopped parsley, sliced tomatoes and black olives.

Chopped Herring

SERVES 4

METRIC/IMPERIAL	AMERICAN
2 salt herrings	2 salt herrings
1 thick slice white bread	1 thick slice white bread
2 tablespoons vinegar	3 tablespoons vinegar
1 egg, hard-boiled	1 egg, hard-cooked
1 large sour apple	1 large sour apple
1 small onion, finely grated	1 small onion, finely grated
2 tablespoons vegetable oil	3 tablespoons vegetable oil
white pepper	white pepper
lettuce leaves	lettuce leaves

Soak the herrings in cold water for 24 hours, changing the water two or three times. Then wash them thoroughly, dry and remove the heads, tails and all the bones. Place on a chopping board kept specially for the purpose and cut into pieces.

Cut the crust from the bread and soak it in vinegar. When all the liquid has been absorbed break up the bread with a fork.

Separate the egg yolk and the white, sieve the egg yolk and set aside for the garnish. Peel and core the apple and cut into quarters.

Place the apple and the egg white with the herring and bread and chop very finely. Mix in the grated onion, vegetable oil and a little pepper to taste.

Serve on lettuce leaves, sprinkled with the sieved egg yolk. *(Illustrated on page 29)*

Herring Salad

SERVES 4

METRIC/IMPERIAL	AMERICAN
2 salt herring fillets	2 salt herring fillets
1 large cooked potato	1 large cooked potato
1 dessert apple	1 dessert apple
1 small pickled cucumber	1 small dill cucumber
1 small onion	1 small onion
1 egg, hard-boiled	1 egg, hard-cooked
mayonnaise (see page 99)	mayonnaise (see page 99)
1 small cooked beetroot	1 small cooked beet
chopped fresh dill or parsley to garnish	chopped fresh dill or parsley to garnish

Cut the herring fillets into strips about 2.5 cm/1 inch long. Peel and dice the potato and apple, dice the cucumber and peel and finely chop the onion.

Separate the yolk and white of the egg and chop both. Set aside the white for garnish.

Mix together all the prepared ingredients and add enough mayonnaise to bind to a fairly soft mixture.

Arrange on a serving dish and garnish with strips of the cooked beetroot, chopped egg white and chopped dill or parsley. *(Illustrated on page 29)*

Smoked Salmon

Allow about 50 g/2 oz smoked salmon per person. Place thin freshly cut slices on individual dishes either flat or rolled up. Sprinkle with a little fresh lemon juice and season with freshly ground black pepper. Serve with thinly sliced brown bread.

If served as part of a mixed hors d'oeuvres, serve the slices overlapping each other and garnish with lemon wedges and sprigs of parsley. *(Illustrated on page 29)*

Chopped Liver

SERVES 4

METRIC/IMPERIAL	AMERICAN
50 g/2 oz chicken fat	4 tablespoons chicken fat
225 g/8 oz chicken livers (see note)	½ lb chicken livers (see note)
1 small onion, peeled	1 small onion, peeled
2 eggs, hard-boiled	2 eggs, hard-cooked
1 tablespoon fine fresh white bread-crumbs	1 tablespoon fine fresh white bread crumbs
salt and freshly ground black pepper	salt and freshly ground black pepper

Melt the chicken fat in a frying pan and fry the livers for a few minutes until tender. Drain and cool and reserve any left-over chicken fat.

Separate the yolks and whites of the eggs and sieve one yolk or one egg white for garnish.

Finely mince together the remaining egg yolk and whites, the livers and onion. Add the breadcrumbs and seasoning to taste. Mix to a firm paste, adding the reserved chicken fat if necessary.

Serve garnished with sieved egg yolk or egg white. *(Illustrated on page 20)*

Note Calf's or ox liver may be used in place of chicken livers. In this case fry the onion in the chicken fat, slice the liver and cook it slowly with the onions for about 10 minutes. Then mince all the ingredients as in the main recipe.

Egg and Onion

SERVES 4–6

METRIC/IMPERIAL	AMERICAN
5 eggs, hard-boiled	5 eggs, hard-cooked
1 large onion	1 large onion
65 g/2½ oz chicken fat (see note)	5 tablespoons chicken fat (see note)
salt and freshly ground black pepper	salt and freshly ground black pepper
black olives to garnish	ripe olives to garnish

Shell and chop the eggs and peel and finely chop the onion. Mix together and add the chicken fat to bind. Season to taste. Serve garnished with black olives. *(Illustrated on page 29)*

Note For milk meals, use vegetable fat instead of chicken fat and when in season spring onions (scallions) can be used.

Aubergine Salad

SERVES 4

METRIC/IMPERIAL	AMERICAN
1 aubergine, about 450 g/1 lb	1 eggplant, about 1 lb
vegetable oil for shallow frying	vegetable oil for shallow frying
2 cloves garlic, peeled	2 cloves garlic, peeled
1 tablespoon lemon juice	1 tablespoon lemon juice
freshly ground black pepper	freshly ground black pepper

Peel and slice the aubergine, sprinkle with salt and leave on a plate, covered, for 30 minutes. Drain off the water and dry on absorbent kitchen paper. Shallow fry in hot oil until brown on both sides. Drain well.

Put the aubergine, garlic, lemon juice and black pepper in a liquidiser and blend until smooth. Adjust the seasoning if necessary.

Pour into ramekin dishes and chill well before serving.

Avocado Dip

SERVES 4

METRIC/IMPERIAL	AMERICAN
1 ripe avocado (see method)	1 ripe avocado (see method)
1 egg, hard-boiled	1 egg, hard-cooked
1 small onion	1 small onion
2 tomatoes	2 tomatoes
1 clove garlic	1 clove garlic
1 teaspoon lemon juice	1 teaspoon lemon juice
salt and freshly ground black pepper	salt and freshly ground black pepper
paprika	paprika pepper
mayonnaise (see page 99)	mayonnaise (see page 99)

Avocados tend to discolour quickly when cut; for this reason the dip should be prepared as near to serving time as possible and without the use of metal implements. The avocado should be ripe and ready to eat.

Cut the avocado in half, remove the stone and skin. Shell and chop the hard-boiled egg, peel and finely chop the onion and tomatoes, peel and crush the garlic.

Place the avocado, egg, onion, tomato and garlic in a mixing bowl and mash with a wooden spoon until the ingredients blend together. Add the lemon juice and season with salt, pepper and a pinch of paprika. Stir in enough mayonnaise to make a soft consistency.

Chill slightly and serve in individual portions on lettuce, accompanied by fresh white bread or crisp crackers.

Quick Melon Cocktail

METRIC/IMPERIAL	AMERICAN
1 (454-g/1-lb) pack frozen melon balls	1 (16-oz) package frozen melon balls
castor sugar	superfine sugar
ground ginger	ground ginger
chopped fresh mint (optional)	chopped fresh mint (optional)

Place the melon balls – while not quite fully defrosted and still firm – in shallow glass dishes, allowing 6 per serving.

Serve with sugar and ground ginger or sugar and chopped fresh mint.

Globe Artichokes

Strip off the larger outside leaves from each artichoke, cut off the stalk and trim the base. With a pair of kitchen scissors snip off the point of each leaf. Carefully open the leaves in the centre and with a small spoon scoop out and discard the choke. Wash thoroughly and soak for 30 minutes in cold water to which a little vinegar has been added. Rinse in fresh water and drain.

Add a teaspoon of lemon juice to a saucepan of lightly salted boiling water and put in the artichokes heads downwards. Boil rapidly for 5 minutes then simmer gently, partly covered with a lid, for 30–45 minutes until the bottoms are quite tender.

Drain and serve hot with melted butter or cold with French dressing (see page 96).

Stock

The basis of a good soup is surely the stock. The one below is made from meat bones and vegetables.

METRIC/IMPERIAL	AMERICAN
1 kg/2 lb beef, mutton or veal bones	2 lb beef, mutton or veal bones
2.25 litres/4 pints water	10 cups water
2 teaspoons salt	2 teaspoons salt
2 medium carrots	2 medium carrots
3 sticks celery	3 stalks celery
2 medium onions	2 medium onions
1 small turnip	1 small turnip
4 peppercorns	4 peppercorns
1 bay leaf	1 bay leaf

Wash and chop the bones and put into a saucepan with the water and salt. Bring slowly to the boil then boil quickly for a minute until the scum has risen. Remove the scum, cover the pan tightly and simmer gently for 3 hours. Meanwhile wash and peel the vegetables and cut into thick slices. Add to the meat stock with the peppercorns and bay leaf and simmer, covered, for a further 1 hour. Strain and store in the refrigerator for up to 4 days.

Stock can also be prepared in a pressure cooker. Place the bones and salted water in the open cooker, bring to the boil and remove the scum. Add the remaining ingredients (making sure the cooker is no more than half full), bring to high (15 lb) pressure and cook for 40 minutes. Allow the pressure to reduce at room temperature, then strain.

It is also useful to make stock and freeze it in containers until needed; and to keep 'general stock', the juice from roasting or braising meat or casseroling chicken, to form the basis of a quick soup.

In addition, kosher Israeli soup cubes and soup packs are good standbys for a first course, either to serve as they are or with the addition of home-prepared vegetables or meat, especially in a small family where the time taken to make stock is hardly justified.

Cabbage Borsht

✡

SERVES 6–8

METRIC/IMPERIAL	AMERICAN
2.25 litres/4 pints stock, preferably from boiled meat	5 pints stock, preferably from boiled meat
2 teaspoons sugar	2 teaspoons sugar
juice of ½ lemon	juice of ½ lemon
pinch of oregano	dash of oregano
salt and freshly ground black pepper	salt and freshly ground black pepper
225 g/8 oz cooked beetroot	½ lb cooked beets
225 g/8 oz potato	½ lb potato
225 g/8 oz sour apples	½ lb sour apples
225 g/8 oz white cabbage	½ lb white cabbage
1 large onion	1 large onion
1 green pepper	1 green pepper
1 tablespoon tomato purée	1 tablespoon tomato concentrate

Pour the stock into a large saucepan and bring to the boil. Remove from the heat and add the sugar, lemon juice, oregano and seasoning to taste.

Meanwhile peel and coarsely grate the beetroot, potato and apples. Finely shred the cabbage. Peel and chop the onion, seed and finely dice the green pepper. Add the prepared vegetables and tomato purée to the hot stock and return to the boil. Lower the heat and simmer for about 1 hour.

The soup should have a sweet and sour flavour, so adjust the seasoning to taste.

Chicken Soup

✡

SERVES 6–8

METRIC/IMPERIAL	AMERICAN
1 boiling fowl	1 stewing chicken
2.25 litres/4 pints cold water	5 pints cold water
2–3 teaspoons salt	2–3 teaspoons salt
1 large onion	1 large onion
1 large carrot	1 large carrot
1 large stick celery	1 large stalk celery
salt and freshly ground black pepper	salt and freshly ground black pepper

Wash the chicken well, cut into joints and break up the carcass. Scald the feet and gizzard by immersing in boiling water, then drain, cool and remove and discard the outer skin. Wash the neck. Place all the chicken in a thick-based saucepan, add the cold water and seasoning and bring slowly to the boil. Reduce the heat and skim well, using a wet metal spoon.

Peel and slice the onion and carrot, wash and slice the celery and add to the chicken. Cover the pan and simmer gently for 2½–3 hours or until the chicken is tender. Strain the stock into a bowl and set aside to cool. Reserve the carrots. (The chicken can be used in other recipes.) Place the soup in the refrigerator and when cold skim the fat from the surface.

Reheat the soup with the reserved carrots and adjust the seasoning. This soup is traditionally served with kneidlech, kreplech, lockshen or mandeln, recipes for which are at the end of this chapter.

Spring Soup

SERVES 4–5

METRIC/IMPERIAL	AMERICAN
175 g/6 oz carrots	6 oz carrots
small bunch spring onions	small bunch scallions
6 lettuce leaves	6 lettuce leaves
1.15 litres/2 pints chicken or meat stock	5 cups chicken or meat stock
salt and freshly ground black pepper	salt and freshly ground black pepper
1 tablespoon chopped chives to garnish	1 tablespoon chopped chives to garnish

Scrape and dice the carrots, trim and thinly slice the spring onions, wash and finely shred the lettuce. Bring the stock to the boil and add the vegetables with a little salt. Cover and simmer gently for about 30 minutes. Season and serve garnished with chopped chives.

Lentil Soup

SERVES 6–8

METRIC/IMPERIAL	AMERICAN
450 g/1 lb lentils	1 lb lentils
2 large onions	2 large onions
2 large carrots	2 large carrots
1 small turnip	1 small turnip
2 sticks celery	2 stalks celery
2.25 litres/4 pints stock or salt beef liquor (see note)	5 pints stock or corned beef liquor (see note)
salt and freshly ground black pepper	salt and freshly ground black pepper
1 bay leaf	1 bay leaf
chopped parsley to garnish	chopped parsley to garnish

Wash the lentils thoroughly. Peel and thickly slice the onions, carrots and turnip. Wash and chop the celery. Place all the ingredients except the parsley in a saucepan over a moderate heat. Bring to the boil then lower the heat and simmer gently for 1½ hours. Remove the bay leaf and blend the mixture in a liquidiser. Return the soup to the saucepan and bring to the boil again. Adjust the seasoning and serve sprinkled with the chopped parsley.

Note This soup is tastier made with the liquor in which salt beef has been cooked but if this is not available, bone or vegetable stock can be used. In this case a small piece of wurst cooked with the soup is an improvement. Add this after the soup has been simmering for 45 minutes.

Split Pea Soup

SERVES 4–6

METRIC/IMPERIAL	AMERICAN
225 g/8 oz split peas	1 cup split peas
1.75 litres/3 pints stock (see method)	7½ cups stock (see method)
2 large sticks celery	2 large stalks celery
1 medium onion	1 medium onion
1 medium carrot	1 medium carrot
1 medium turnip	1 medium turnip
salt and freshly ground black pepper	salt and freshly ground black pepper
chopped mint to garnish	chopped mint to garnish

This soup is best made with the liquor that remains after boiling a piece of smoked beef, a tongue or wurst.

Soak the peas overnight in plenty of cold water. Drain and place in a large saucepan with the stock. Wash and chop the celery, peel and chop the onion, carrot and turnip and add to the stock. Season lightly. Bring to the boil over a moderate heat then lower the heat and simmer for about 2 hours.

Blend in a liquidiser, return to the saucepan and bring to the boil again. Adjust the seasoning, if necessary, and serve sprinkled with chopped mint.

Artichoke Soup

SERVES 4–6

METRIC/IMPERIAL	AMERICAN
1 kg/2 lb Jerusalem artichokes	2 lb Jerusalem artichokes
2 medium onions	2 medium onions
1.15 litres/2 pints water	5 cups water
salt	salt
600 ml/1 pint milk	2½ cups milk
25 g/1 oz margarine	2 tablespoons margarine
25 g/1 oz flour	¼ cup flour
parsley to garnish	parsley to garnish

Wash the artichokes and peel thinly with a potato peeler. To prevent discoloration, drop each one as it is peeled into a bowl of cold water to which a little lemon juice or vinegar has been added. Thickly slice the artichokes, peel and slice the onions and place both in a saucepan with the water and salt. Bring quickly to the boil, then lower the heat and simmer for 25–30 minutes, until the vegetables are tender. Sieve or blend the mixture in a liquidiser and return to the saucepan. Add the milk and bring to the boil.

Melt the margarine in a small saucepan, remove from the heat and stir in the flour to make a roux. Return to the heat and, still stirring, cook for 2 minutes. Gradually blend some of the soup with the roux until it is quite thin, then pour this back into the soup and bring to the boil, stirring continuously until the soup thickens. Lower the heat and simmer for 5 minutes. Adjust the seasoning, if necessary, and serve garnished with chopped parsley.

Summer Borsht

SERVES 4

METRIC/IMPERIAL	AMERICAN
500 g/1 lb raw beetroot	1 lb raw beets
1.15 litres/2 pints water	5 cups water
1 teaspoon sugar	1 teaspoon sugar
juice of ½ lemon	juice of ½ lemon
4 tablespoons soured cream	5 tablespoons dairy sour cream
2 spring onions, finely chopped	2 scallions, finely chopped

Scrub the beetroot and peel with a potato peeler, then cut into thin strips. Place in a saucepan with cold water and bring to the boil, then reduce the heat and simmer for 30 minutes until the beetroot is tender. Add the salt, sugar and lemon juice. Taste and adjust the seasoning, if necessary, to give a sweet and sour flavour. (At this stage the liquid can be refrigerated and will keep for 2–3 days.)

The soup should be served chilled with a tablespoon of soured cream spooned on top of each plate, and sprinkled with finely chopped spring onions.

Egg and onion (see page 24); Smoked salmon (see page 23); Chopped herring (see page 22); Herring salad (see page 23)
Overleaf: Green salad (see page 91); Halibut with egg and lemon sauce (see page 36); Gefillte fish (see page 38); Beetroot horseradish sauce (see page 83); Fried plaice fillets (see page 40)

Cherry Soup

✡

SERVES 4–6

METRIC/IMPERIAL	AMERICAN
675 g/1½ lb fresh or canned sour Morello cherries	1½ lb fresh or canned sour Morello cherries
900 ml/1½ pints water	3¾ cups water
stick of cinnamon	stick of cinnamon
salt	salt
100 g/4 oz sugar	½ cup sugar
1 teaspoon cornflour	1 teaspoon cornstarch
fresh or soured cream for serving	fresh or dairy sour cream for serving

Wash and stone fresh cherries; drain, rinse and stone canned cherries. Place in a saucepan with the water, cinnamon, salt and sugar. Bring to the boil and simmer for about 10 minutes or until the cherries are soft. Pour into a liquidiser, add the cornflour and blend until smooth. Return to the saucepan and simmer for 5 minutes.

Chill well and serve with fresh or soured cream. *(Illustrated on page 19)*

Einlauf

✡

METRIC/IMPERIAL	AMERICAN
3 tablespoons flour	scant ¼ cup flour
pinch of salt	dash of salt
1 egg	1 egg
3 tablespoons water	scant ¼ cup water

Sift the flour and salt into a bowl. Add the egg and water and beat until smooth. Pour very slowly from the end of a spoon into boiling soup. Cover and boil for 3 minutes before serving.

Baked carp (see page 44)

Lockshen (Noodles)

✡

METRIC/IMPERIAL	AMERICAN
2 eggs	2 eggs
salt and freshly ground black pepper	salt and freshly ground black pepper
ground ginger	ground ginger
flour	flour

Beat the eggs with a little salt and pepper and a little ground ginger. Add sufficient flour to make a stiff paste. Knead thoroughly, then roll out very thinly on a floured board. Set aside for 2 hours to dry.

Cut the dough into strips about 7.5 cm/ 3 inches by 3.5 cm/1½ inches. Place the strips on top of one another and cut across into match-like strips. Toss lightly to separate them and spread on the board to dry. If not required for immediate use, dry completely and store in an airtight container.

To serve, add to boiling soup and boil for 10 minutes.

Kneidlech (Matzo Meal Dumplings)

✡

METRIC/IMPERIAL	AMERICAN
40 g/1½ oz margarine	3 tablespoons margarine
2 tablespoons hot water	3 tablespoons hot water
1 large egg, beaten	1 large egg, beaten
¼ teaspoon salt	¼ teaspoon salt
2 teaspoons chopped parsley	2 teaspoons chopped parsley
50 g/2 oz matzo meal	½ cup matzo meal

Put the margarine into a bowl and add the remaining ingredients. Mix to a stiff batter. Chill the mixture for at least 1 hour.

With wet hands, roll the mixture into small balls and drop a few at a time into boiling soup. When all the balls have been added and the soup has returned to the boil, cover the pan and continue boiling for 20 minutes. Serve immediately.

Kreplech
(Stuffed Dumplings)

✡

METRIC/IMPERIAL	AMERICAN
For the dough	*For the dough*
lockshen dough (see page 33)	lockshen dough (see page 33)
For the filling	*For the filling*
100 g/4 oz cooked meat, finely minced (see method)	½ cup cooked meat, finely ground (see method)
2 teaspoons grated onion	2 teaspoons grated onion
2 teaspoons chopped parsley	2 teaspoons chopped parsley
chicken fat	chicken fat
salt and freshly ground black pepper	salt and freshly ground black pepper
ground ginger	ground ginger

Make up the lockshen dough and cut into 5-cm/2-inch squares.

For the filling, use any left-over cold meat, minced finely. Mix with the onion and parsley, season with salt, pepper and a pinch of ginger. Bind with chicken fat. Place a little filling in each square, dampen the edges with water and fold diagonally to form a triangle, pressing the edges together firmly. firmly. Leave on a floured board for 1 hour to dry.

Drop a few at a time into boiling soup and cook for 15 minutes.

Mandeln (Soup Nuts)

✡

METRIC/IMPERIAL	AMERICAN
2 eggs	2 eggs
175 g/6 oz flour	1½ cups flour
1 teaspoon salt	1 teaspoon salt
2 tablespoons cooking oil	3 tablespoons cooking oil

Beat the eggs lightly. Sift the flour and salt into a mixing bowl and make a well in the centre. Pour the egg and oil into it. Mix all the ingredients to a soft dough by working flour into the egg and oil a little at a time.

Cover the dough and refrigerate for 30 minutes.

With floured hands form into pencil-thin rolls and cut into 1-cm/½-inch pieces. Place on well-greased baking sheets and bake in a moderate oven (180°C, 350°F, Gas Mark 4) for 20 minutes until golden brown. Shake the baking sheets occasionally to brown the mandeln evenly. Serve hot in a separate dish and spoon into the soup at the table.

When made in advance, reheat for 10 minutes in a moderate oven.

Liver Balls

✡

SERVES 3–4

METRIC/IMPERIAL	AMERICAN
100 g/4 oz calf's or chicken liver	¼ lb calf or chicken liver
25 g/1 oz fine fresh white breadcrumbs	½ cup fine fresh white bread crumbs
6 tablespoons stock	½ cup stock
¼ teaspoon grated onion	¼ teaspoon grated onion
½ beaten egg	½ beaten egg
salt and freshly ground black pepper	salt and freshly ground black pepper

Mince the liver finely. Put the breadcrumbs and stock into a small saucepan and stir over a gentle heat until it forms a paste. Remove from the heat and add the liver, onion and beaten egg. Season and mix thoroughly. Roll into tiny balls and drop into boiling soup. Cover and simmer for 10 minutes. Serve hot.

Fish

A fish meal is always easy on the palate and a delight to eat. Many of the fish dishes in this section are served cold and therefore can be prepared ahead of time and refrigerated to be eaten on Shabbat evening or to save some of the last-minute rush when giving a dinner party.

The fish used in these recipes can be either fresh or frozen. In fact, having frozen fish available at home means that there is always a delicious recipe to make without too much pre-planning. If you do not have a freezer, frozen fish can be stored in a 3-star frozen food compartment for up to 3 months. When using frozen fish, it is best to completely defrost the fish before use; slow thawing at room temperature will give the best results.

In many areas fish can be bought prepared and minced for use in making gefillte fish.

It is worth asking the fishmonger to help as much as possible in preparing the fish; he will be happy to fillet it when asked. A flat fish is filleted into four half fillets, a round fish into two, and herrings usually split into two, boned and left in a piece.

Skinning is a job which often has to be done at home. If the recipe allows, it is easier to skin cooked fish.

To skin raw fish, place the fish skin downwards on a board, make a small slit at the tail end between the skin and the flesh, dip your fingers in salt to afford a better grip and then, firmly holding the tip end of the skin with the left hand, work the knife along to the other end of the fillet until it is entirely separated from the skin.

When boiling or poaching fresh fish, try any of the following to give added flavour: bay leaves, chives, dill, juniper berries, oregano or sweet fennel.

Poached Salmon

SERVES 4

A whole small salmon or any cut of a large salmon may be cooked in this way. It is an ideal way of cooking salmon which is to be frozen.

METRIC/IMPERIAL	AMERICAN
1.5-kg/3-lb piece of salmon	3-lb piece of salmon
juice of 1 lemon	juice of 1 lemon
1 teaspoon salt	1 teaspoon salt
6 crushed white peppercorns	6 crushed white peppercorns

Clean and wash the fish and place on a large piece of well-buttered foil or parchment paper. Sprinkle with the lemon juice, salt and peppercorns and wrap loosely. Place in a fish kettle and add enough water to partly cover the wrapped fish. Poach gently for about 30–40 minutes (to calculate the time required, allow 10 minutes for every 450 g/1 lb and 10 minutes extra).

To test if the fish is cooked, pull the fins gently: if they come away easily the fish is cooked.

Leave the fish unwrapped until cold, then remove the skin and serve with melted butter or Hollandaise sauce (see page 83).

Halibut with Egg and Lemon Sauce

SERVES 4

METRIC/IMPERIAL	AMERICAN
4 halibut steaks, about 225 g/8 oz each	4 halibut steaks, about ½ lb each
1 medium onion	1 medium onion
salt and freshly ground white pepper	salt and freshly ground white pepper
3 tablespoons lemon juice	¼ cup lemon juice
For the sauce	*For the sauce*
2 teaspoons cornflour	2 teaspoons cornstarch
3 tablespoons lemon juice	¼ cup lemon juice
1 tablespoon sugar	1 tablespoon sugar
450 ml/¾ pint fish stock (see method)	2 cups fish stock (see method)
2 eggs	2 eggs

Wash and dry the halibut and place in a buttered flameproof dish. Peel and thinly slice the onion and add to the fish together with the lemon juice, salt, pepper and enough water to cover. Place over a moderate heat and cook the fish very gently for about 30 minutes or until just cooked but still firm and moist.

Drain, remove the skin and bone the fish. Arrange in a clean serving dish. Reserve the stock and make up to the required amount with water, if necessary.

To make the sauce Mix the cornflour with the lemon juice and sugar in a small saucepan. Add the reserved fish stock and bring to the boil over a moderate heat, stirring continuously until the sauce thickens. Simmer for 3 minutes. Remove from the heat and when slightly cool pour on to the lightly beaten eggs in the top of a double saucepan. Stir continuously until it thickens – do not re-boil or the sauce will curdle.

When the sauce has cooled slightly, pour over the prepared halibut and leave to cool.

This dish may be covered and stored in a refrigerator, and should be served cold.
(Illustrated on pages 30–31)

Baked Fish with Oranges

SERVES 4

METRIC/IMPERIAL	AMERICAN
4 cod or haddock cutlets	4 cod or haddock cutlets
¼ teaspoon ground allspice or cinnamon	¼ teaspoon ground allspice or cinnamon
grated rind and juice of 2 oranges	grated rind and juice of 2 oranges
salt and freshly ground black pepper	salt and freshly ground black pepper
1 tablespoon grated onion	1 tablespoon grated onion
2 tablespoons grated cheese	3 tablespoons grated cheese
2 tablespoons fresh brown breadcrumbs	3 tablespoons fresh brown bread crumbs
25 g/1 oz margarine	2 tablespoons margarine

Clean the fish and place in a greased oven-proof dish. Sprinkle with the allspice or cinnamon, the orange rind and juice, salt and pepper, onion, grated cheese and bread-crumbs, dot with margarine and bake in a moderate oven (180°C, 350°F, Gas Mark 4) for 35–40 minutes. Serve hot.

Fish Florentine

SERVES 4

METRIC/IMPERIAL	AMERICAN
6 plaice or lemon sole fillets	6 plaice or lemon sole fillets
salt and freshly ground black pepper	salt and freshly ground black pepper
lemon juice	lemon juice
1 (227-g/8-oz) packet frozen chopped spinach	1 (8-oz) package frozen chopped spinach
½ teaspoon dry mustard	½ teaspoon dry mustard
generous pinch of ground nutmeg	generous dash of ground nutmeg
50 g/2 oz cheese, grated	½ cup grated cheese
300 ml/½ pint coating white sauce (see page 82)	1¼ cups coating white sauce (see page 82)

Skin the fish, season with salt and pepper and sprinkle over a few drops of lemon juice. Roll up and place on a greased baking dish, cover with foil and bake in a moderate oven (160°C, 325°F, Gas Mark 3) for 10 minutes.

Cook the spinach as directed on the packet and season with ground black pepper, the mustard powder and nutmeg.

Heat the sauce gently with any liquor from cooking the fish. Add most of the cheese and stir until melted.

Spread the spinach on a greased shallow ovenproof dish. Arrange the fish rolls on top and coat with the sauce. Sprinkle with the remaining cheese and return to a moder-ately hot oven (200°C, 400°F, Gas Mark 6) for 10 minutes or until hot and golden brown.

Gefillte Fish

✡

SERVES 4–6

METRIC/IMPERIAL	AMERICAN
For the stock	*For the stock*
head, skin and bones of fish	head, skin and bones of fish
900 ml/1½ pints water	3¾ cups water
1 onion	1 onion
1 large carrot	1 large carrot
1 stick celery	1 stalk celery
salt and freshly ground white pepper	salt and freshly ground white pepper
For the fish mixture	*For the fish mixture*
1 kg/2 lb white fish (see note)	2 lb white fish (see note)
1 large onion	1 large onion
1 tablespoon ground almonds (optional)	1 tablespoon ground almonds (optional)
1 tablespoon chopped parsley	1 tablespoon chopped parsley
2 large eggs, beaten	2 large eggs, beaten
salt and freshly ground white pepper	salt and freshly ground white pepper
medium matzo meal	medium matzo meal

Put the fish head, skin and bones in a saucepan with the water. Peel and slice the onion and half of the carrot, wash and slice the celery. Add to the saucepan with salt and pepper. Bring to the boil over a high heat, then lower the heat and simmer for 30 minutes. Strain and reserve.

Meanwhile, to prepare the fish mixture, cut the fish into small pieces. Peel and slice the onion. Coarsely mince both and place in a bowl with the ground almonds, if used, the chopped parsley and the beaten eggs. Season and, working the mixture by hand, add sufficient medium matzo meal to bind to a fairly stiff consistency. With wet hands, roll the mixture into balls about 3.5 cm/ 1½ inches in diameter.

Peel and thinly slice the remaining half carrot, add to the fish stock, bring to the boil and simmer for 10 minutes. Add the fish balls to the stock. Cover the saucepan and cook gently for 1 hour. Carefully lift out the balls and place on a serving dish with a slice of carrot on each. Spoon a little of the fish stock over the balls; this will set to a jelly when cold.

Serve cold with beetroot horseradish sauce (see page 83) or hot with egg and lemon sauce (see page 87). *(Illustrated on pages 30–31)*

Note This recipe should be prepared with thick fish such as hake, haddock, cod or a mixture of all three. If possible, buy the fish filleted but ask the fishmonger for the skin, bones and head for the stock. Otherwise, prepare the fish at home.

Baked Herring with Apple

✡

SERVES 4

METRIC/IMPERIAL	AMERICAN
4 herrings, with heads removed	4 herrings, with heads removed
3 large potatoes	3 large potatoes
2 sour apples	2 sour apples
25 g/1 oz margarine	¼ cup margarine
salt and freshly ground black pepper	salt and freshly ground black pepper

Clean and bone the herrings and cut each one into 2 fillets. Rinse under cold running water and drain well. Peel and thinly slice the potatoes, peel and chop the apples.

Grease a deep casserole dish and arrange half of the sliced potatoes standing up round the sides. Place half of the fillets in the bottom of the dish, season and sprinkle with half of the chopped apple. Repeat the layers. Cover the top with sliced potato, sprinkle with salt and dot with the margarine.

Cover the dish with a lid or aluminium foil and bake in a moderate oven (180°C, 350°F, Gas Mark 4) for about 45 minutes, removing the lid for the last 15 minutes. Serve hot.

Soused Herring

SERVES 4

METRIC/IMPERIAL	AMERICAN
4 herrings, with heads removed	4 herrings, with heads removed
salt and freshly ground black pepper	salt and freshly ground black pepper
1 large onion	1 large onion
2 tomatoes	2 tomatoes
1½ teaspoons pickling spice	1½ teaspoons pickling spice
2 small bay leaves	2 small bay leaves
150 ml/¼ pint water	⅔ cup water
150 ml/¼ pint vinegar	⅔ cup vinegar
chopped gherkins to garnish	chopped sweet dill pickles to garnish

Clean and bone the herrings. Rinse well under cold running water then drain and season. Peel and very thinly slice the onion, thinly slice the tomato. Place the onion and tomato in the centre of each herring and roll it up, beginning at the tail end. Secure with a cocktail stick and place close together in a deep ovenproof dish. Add the pickling spice, preferably tied in a small piece of muslin so that it can be easily removed, and the bay leaves.

Pour over the water and vinegar, adding a little extra of each, if necessary, to completely cover the herrings. Cover the dish with a lid or foil and bake the herrings in a moderate oven (180°C, 350°F, Gas Mark 4) for 1 hour. Remove from the oven, uncover and set aside until cold.

Serve cold, garnished with chopped gherkins and accompanied by potato salad (see page 91).

Trout with Almonds and Fruit

SERVES 4

METRIC/IMPERIAL	AMERICAN
4 whole rainbow trout (see method)	4 whole rainbow trout (see method)
seasoned flour	seasoned flour
vegetable oil and butter for shallow frying	vegetable oil and butter for shallow frying
150 g/6 oz flaked almonds	1½ cups flaked almonds
100 g/4 oz butter, melted	1 cup melted butter
2 dessert apples	2 dessert apples
2 teaspoons lemon juice	2 teaspoons lemon juice
2 teaspoons chopped parsley	2 teaspoons chopped parsley

Buy the fish whole but cleaned and with the head removed. Wash the fish well under cold running water and dry on absorbent kitchen paper. Coat lightly with seasoned flour. Shallow fry in a mixture of half butter and half vegetable oil until the fish is crisp and brown. Place in a shallow casserole dish and keep hot.

Fry the flaked almonds in the butter until golden brown. Peel and dice the apples and add to the almonds together with the lemon juice and chopped parsley. Pour this sauce on to the fish and bake in a moderately hot oven (200°C, 400°F, Gas Mark 6) for 10 minutes. Serve hot.

Gefillte Fish Fried

✡

SERVES 4–6

Use the basic gefillte fish mixture recipe (see page 38) and make into balls in the same way. The fish balls may be either deep or shallow fried. Deep frying will give round balls of fish while shallow frying lends itself to a fishcake shape.

For deep frying Heat the oil. Drop the balls in a few at a time, making sure that the oil keeps bubbling. Fry until they are golden brown, then lift out and drain well on absorbent kitchen paper.

For shallow frying Flatten the balls slightly until they are more the shape of a fishcake. Fry in oil about 2.5 cm/1 inch deep until the fish is golden brown on both sides. Lift out and drain well.

Serve cold with beetroot horseradish sauce (see page 83).

Fried Fish

✡

Most white fish is suitable for frying. Small fish can be fried whole, flat fish like sole and plaice in fillets, and large fish such as cod, hake, haddock and halibut cut into steaks or cutlets.

When frying fish, do not let the pieces touch each other or put in too many pieces at a time; this cools the oil which will then soak into the fish and make it soggy and greasy.

To fry fish for serving cold Use a frying pan with sufficient oil to just cover the fish. The oil should be heated to 190°C (375°F). Put on one plate plain flour seasoned with salt and on another beat up one or more eggs, according to the quantity of fish to be fried. Wash the fish in cold water and dry on absorbent kitchen paper.

Dip each piece of fish in seasoned flour then coat with egg and, when the oil has reached the correct heat, fry each piece until golden brown on each side, turning carefully with a fish slice. Always put the skin side of fillets downwards first to prevent them from curling. When cooked, drain on absorbent kitchen paper.

To fry fish for serving hot Prepare the fish as above but after dipping in flour and coating with egg the pieces of fish should be well coated with dried breadcrumbs or medium matzo meal. The oil should be heated to 190°C (375°F).

Serve fried fish with lemon wedges or beetroot horseradish sauce (see page 83). *(Illustrated on pages 30–31)*

Haricot stew (see page 51); Potato latkes (see page 75)

Salmon Cutlets

SERVES 6

METRIC/IMPERIAL	AMERICAN
1 (212-g/7½-oz) can pink salmon or tuna fish	1 (7½-oz) can pink salmon or tuna fish
1 small onion	1 small onion
salt and freshly ground black pepper	salt and freshly ground black pepper
1 egg, beaten	1 egg, beaten
3 tablespoons medium matzo meal	¼ cup medium matzo meal
vegetable oil for shallow frying	vegetable oil for shallow frying

Place the salmon and its juices in a mixing bowl. Peel and finely grate the onion and add to the salmon, together with the salt, pepper and beaten egg. Mix well with a fork, then add the matzo meal to bind the mixture to a fairly soft consistency. Set aside for 15 minutes.

On a lightly floured surface, shape the salmon mixture into 6 flat rounds. Shallow fry in vegetable oil until golden brown on both sides. Drain well. Serve hot or cold.

Note This recipe can also be made with canned mackerel – but in this case drain off most of the oil from the fish before using.

Fish Soufflé

SERVES 2–3

METRIC/IMPERIAL	AMERICAN
350 g/12 oz white fish	¾ lb white fish
½ small onion	½ small onion
25 g/1 oz butter	2 tablespoons butter
25 g/1 oz flour	¼ cup flour
200 ml/7 fl oz warm milk	¾ cup warm milk
50 g/2 oz Cheddar cheese, grated	½ cup grated Cheddar cheese
1 tablespoon chopped parsley	1 tablespoon chopped parsley
salt and freshly ground black pepper	salt and freshly ground black pepper
1 teaspoon lemon juice	1 teaspoon lemon juice
2 eggs, separated	2 eggs, separated

Lightly poach the fish. Drain well, discard the skin and bones and flake with a fork. Peel and chop the onion.

Melt the butter in a small saucepan. Stir in the flour and cook gently for 1 minute to make a roux. Remove from the heat and stir in the milk gradually, mixing well between each addition. Bring to the boil, stirring continuously until the mixture thickens. Simmer for 3 minutes, then remove from the heat and cool slightly.

Add the fish, cheese, onion, parsley, salt, pepper and lemon juice and mix well. Beat in the egg yolks one at a time.

Whisk the egg whites until stiff and fold into the fish mixture with a spoon. Turn the mixture into a greased 1-litre/1½-pint (U.S. 2-pint) soufflé dish and bake in a moderately hot oven (200°C, 400°F, Gas Mark 6) for 30 minutes.

Serve at once directly from the dish.

Note For smoked haddock soufflé, use about 225 g/8 oz cooked smoked haddock in place of the white fish and omit the cheese and parsley.

Holishkes (stuffed cabbage leaves) (see page 54); Carrot tzimmas (see page 50); Tomato salad (see page 93); Minced meat with kasha (see page 51); Meatballs in a casserole (see page 53)

Haddock in a Crust

SERVES 4–6

METRIC/IMPERIAL	AMERICAN
450 g/1 lb smoked haddock fillet	1 lb smoked haddock fillet
300 ml/½ pint milk	1¼ cups milk
300 ml/½ pint water	1¼ cups water
1 bay leaf	1 bay leaf
1 medium onion	1 medium onion
2 tomatoes	2 tomatoes
2 gherkins	2 sweet dill pickles
15 g/½ oz butter	1 tablespoon butter
oregano	oregano
50 g/2 oz cooked long-grain rice	½ cup cooked long-grain rice
2 tablespoons top of the milk	3 tablespoons top of the milk
salt and freshly ground black pepper	salt and freshly ground black pepper
225 g/8 oz puff pastry	½ lb puff paste
milk for glazing	milk for glazing

Clean the fish and place in a pan with the milk and water. Add the bay leaf and poach the fish over a low heat for about 10 minutes. Drain, discard the skin and bones and flake with a fork.

Peel and finely chop the onion and tomatoes and finely chop the gherkins. Melt the butter in a frying pan and gently fry the onion and tomato with the oregano until soft. Remove from the heat.

Mix the cooked rice with the top of the milk, season and add the finely chopped gherkins.

Roll the pastry into a square about 25–30 cm/10–12 inches and place on a baking sheet. Put layers of the rice, fish and onion mixtures down the centre. Dampen the pastry on each side, then starting 2.5 cm/1 inch from the filling on each side cut the pastry into 2.5-cm/1-inch thick slanting strips on each side. Plait the strips over the filling, pressing the ends together firmly. Glaze with milk and bake in a hot oven (220°C, 425°F, Gas Mark 7) for 20 minutes until the pastry is golden brown.

Serve hot or cold with salad.

Baked Carp

SERVES 6

METRIC/IMPERIAL	AMERICAN
1 whole carp, about 1.5 kg/3 lb	1 whole carp, about 3 lb
salt and freshly ground black pepper	salt and freshly ground black pepper
3 medium onions	3 medium onions
1 clove garlic	1 clove garlic
5 tablespoons oil	6 tablespoons oil
6 sprigs fresh parsley	6 sprigs fresh parsley
4 tomatoes	4 tomatoes
juice of ½ lemon	juice of ½ lemon
pinch of powdered saffron or safflower	dash of powdered saffron or safflower
2 tablespoons pine nut kernels	3 tablespoons pine nut kernels
white wine (see method)	white wine (see method)

Gut the fish, wash and pat dry and place in a greased casserole. Season with salt and pepper to taste. Peel and finely chop the onions and garlic and sauté lightly in half the oil in a frying pan. Chop the parsley. Remove the onion and garlic from the pan and mix with the parsley.

Chop the tomatoes and cook lightly in the remaining oil. Mix the lemon juice with the powdered saffron or safflower.

Cover the fish with the onion, garlic, tomato and parsley, and sprinkle with the lemon juice mixture and the pine nut kernels. Add sufficient water to reach halfway up the fish. Bake in a moderately hot oven (190°C, 375°F, Gas Mark 5) for 35–40 minutes. If desired, pour a little white wine over the fish and bake for a further 5 minutes. Serve hot. *(Illustrated on page 32)*

Note Bass makes an excellent substitute.

Meat

Cuts of Meat and Their Uses

✡

Note Nowadays it is not always possible to obtain clod, sticking, suet and kidneys from a kosher butcher.

Beef

Bola	Roast. When boned it can be sliced or grilled and fried.
Wing rib	Roast
Top rib	Roast
Back rib	Braise
Brisket	Slow roast, braise, boil or pickle.
Salted brisket	Boil
Neck Clod Sticking Chuck Shin	Use in stews, pies, puddings, casserole dishes and soups.

Lamb

Best end of neck	Roast – slow roast or braise. When cut into cutlets fry or grill.
Shoulder	Roast
Middle neck and Scrag	Stew or braise
Breast	Stew. If boned it can be stuffed, and boiled or roasted.

Veal

Best end of neck	Roast, braise or pot roast. When cut into cutlets, fry or grill.
Shoulder	Roast
Scrag	Stew
Breast	Stew or braise. If boned, stuffed and rolled, slow roast or braise.

Many kosher butchers sell their meat ready koshered so that it can be cooked without additional attention at home. If the meat is to be koshered at home an outline of the dietary laws will be found on page 10.

The chief methods of cooking meat are baking (usually called roasting), boiling, braising, frying, grilling, pot roasting and stewing.

Roasting

Unless the joint is the best cut and quality and weighs at least 1.25 kg/2½ lb, it is usually better to slow roast, pot roast or braise.

Season the meat with salt and freshly ground pepper, place in a roasting tin with a little dripping and cook by one of the following methods:

Method 1 Start cooking the meat in a very hot oven (240°C, 475°F, Gas Mark 9) and cook at this heat for 10 minutes; then reduce the heat to moderately hot (200°C, 400°F, Gas Mark 6) and cook according to the timetable.

Method 2 Start cooking the meat in a moderately hot oven (190°C, 375°F, Gas Mark 5) and cook at this temperature until the last 15 minutes; then turn the oven to very hot (240°C, 475°F, Gas Mark 9).

Method 3 Slow roasting – an excellent way of roasting cheaper cuts. The meat is cooked the whole time in a moderate oven (180°C, 350°F, Gas Mark 4).

Approximate Time for Roasting

Methods 1 and 2

Beef	Thick cut 30 minutes per 450 g/per lb.
	Thin cut 25 minutes per 450 g/per lb.
Lamb	30 minutes per 450 g/per lb.
Veal	35 minutes per 450 g/per lb.

Method 3

Beef	Thick cut 45 minutes per 450 g/per lb.
	Thin cut 40 minutes per 450 g/per lb.
Lamb	40 minutes per 450 g/per lb.
Veal	45 minutes per 450 g/per lb.

Frying

Shallow frying should be used to cook chops, steaks, kidneys and sausages, and deep frying for fritters, rissoles, croquettes and other made-up dishes.

When frying the fat must be absolutely still with a faint blue smoke just beginning to rise. A thick smoke means the fat is burning.

When the fat bubbles it does not mean that it is boiling, but that it contains moisture which must evaporate before the right degree of heat can be obtained. Put the foods to be fried into the fat immediately the right degree of heat is reached so that the hot fat forms a coating. If the fat is not hot enough, it soaks into the food and a greasy taste will be the result. Reheat the fat between each batch of food being fried, and drain the food on soft absorbent kitchen paper after removing from the pan.

Grilling

Grilling is a simple and quick method of cooking used to cook small portions of food such as chops, steaks, kidneys and sausages.

Grilling times

Steak	12–15 minutes
Chops and cutlets	8–10 minutes
Kidneys	6 minutes
Sausages	8–10 minutes

Pot Roasting

This is an excellent way of cooking a small and not very tender piece of meat on top of the cooker.

Melt 50–75 g/2–3 oz dripping in a pan and when hot, put in the joint. Brown quickly all over, put the lid on and cook very gently until tender (about 2 hours for a boned joint weighing 1–1.25 kg/2–2½ lb), turning gently from time to time. Potatoes or other root vegetables can be cooked around the meat, adding them to the pan in the last hour.

Special recipes will be found in this section for boiling, braising and stewing.

Boiled Salt Beef

To serve hot Prepare, cook and serve with vegetables as for fresh boiled beef (see page 50) but put into tepid water instead of boiling salted water. For a piece weighing 1.75 kg/4 lb allow about 2½ hours cooking.

For cold pressed salt beef Place the meat in tepid water, bring to the boil and add a peeled and chopped carrot, turnip and onion, a few peppercorns and a bouquet garni (parsley, thyme and bay leaf). Cover and simmer gently until the meat is tender. For a piece of meat weighing about 1.75 kg/4 lb this will take 2–2½ hours.

Remove the meat, drain and place between 2 boards or dishes with a heavy weight on top. When cold, slice and serve.

Boiled Ox Tongue

METRIC/IMPERIAL	AMERICAN
1 ox tongue, smoked, salted or fresh	1 beef tongue, smoked, salted or fresh
6 peppercorns	6 peppercorns
2 bay leaves	2 bay leaves
4 cloves	4 cloves

A smoked tongue, if very hard, should be soaked in cold water overnight.

A salted tongue, fresh from the pickle, need only be soaked for 1 hour.

For cooking, put a smoked tongue into cold water, a salted one in tepid water, and a fresh tongue into boiling salted water. The saucepan should be sufficiently large for the tongue to be completely covered with water. Add the peppercorns, bay leaves and cloves and bring to the boil very slowly. Lower the heat, cover the saucepan with a lid and simmer the tongue very gently until tender. This will take about 3 hours for a large fresh or salt tongue and about 4 hours for a large smoked one. Test with a fork at the root end – if it goes in easily the tongue is sufficiently cooked.

Remove the tongue and plunge into cold water, then place on a board and while still warm remove the skin, any small bones and excess fat from the root end. Roll up the tongue and press into a round cake tin just big enough to hold it in shape. Cover the meat with a plate or foil and put a weight on top. Leave the tongue overnight to cool and set in shape.

Boiled Ox Tongue with Sweet and Sour Sauce

SERVES 4–6

METRIC/IMPERIAL	AMERICAN
1 cooked fresh ox tongue (see page 47)	1 cooked fresh beef tongue (see page 47)
For the sauce	*For the sauce*
1 small onion	1 small onion
40 g/1½ oz margarine or chicken fat	3 tablespoons margarine or chicken fat
25 g/1 oz flour	¼ cup flour
450 ml/¾ pint cooking liquor from the tongue	2 cups cooking liquor from the tongue
1 tablespoon golden syrup or sugar	1 tablespoon corn syrup or sugar
2 tablespoons vinegar	3 tablespoons vinegar
25 g/1 oz stoned raisins or sultanas	¼ cup seeded raisins or seedless white raisins
¼ teaspoon ground cinnamon	¼ teaspoon ground cinnamon

Skin the tongue while still warm. Cut enough slices to serve 4–6 and place in a shallow flameproof serving dish.

To make the sauce Peel and finely chop the onion and fry gently in the fat until golden brown. Stir in the flour with a wooden spoon to make a roux and cook very gently until golden brown. Remove from the heat and gradually stir in the cooking liquor, mixing well between each addition. Return to a moderate heat and bring to the boil, stirring continuously until the mixture thickens. Add the syrup, stoned raisins or sultanas, vinegar and cinnamon and simmer gently for 10 minutes. Adjust the sweet and sour flavour of the sauce by adding more syrup or vinegar to taste.

Pour the sauce over the tongue slices and simmer for 10 minutes to heat the tongue through. Serve hot.

To Pickle Tongue or Beef

METRIC/IMPERIAL	AMERICAN
3.5 litres/6 pints water	7½ pints water
450 g/1 lb cooking salt	1 lb coarse salt
150 g/6 oz soft brown sugar	¾ cup soft brown sugar
15 g/½ oz saltpetre	2 tablespoons saltpeter
2 bay leaves	2 bay leaves
3–4 cloves garlic, peeled (optional)	3–4 cloves garlic, peeled (optional)
3 teaspoons mixed pickling spice (optional)	1 tablespoon mixed pickling spice (optional)
1 fresh trimmed ox tongue or 2.75 kg/6 lb boned and rolled brisket of beef	1 fresh trimmed beef tongue or 6 lb boned and rolled brisket of beef

Put the water, salt, sugar, saltpetre and bay leaves in a large saucepan. Add the garlic and pickling spice, if wished, for a more highly spiced pickle. Bring to the boil then lower the heat and simmer gently for 10 minutes, skimming frequently.

Strain the liquid into a large earthenware bowl and leave until completely cold. Place the meat in the cold pickling solution with a heavy plate on top to keep the meat submerged. Cover and refrigerate for 10 days, turning the meat once or twice during this time.

Cholent

SERVES 4–6

This is a traditional dish served on the Sabbath in orthodox homes when a hot meal is required. It is prepared on Friday and cooked in a cool oven until midday the following day.

METRIC/IMPERIAL	AMERICAN
225 g/8 oz haricot or butter beans	1 generous cup navy or butter beans
1 kg/2 lb medium potatoes	2 lb medium potatoes
1 onion	1 onion
1 kg/2 lb boned brisket of beef or unrolled rib of beef	2 lb boned brisket of beef or short ribs of beef
salt and freshly ground black pepper	salt and freshly ground black pepper
paprika	paprika pepper
1 tablespoon sugar	1 tablespoon sugar

Soak the beans in water overnight, then drain. Peel the potatoes and leave them whole. Peel and chop the onion. Put the beans into a saucepan or casserole which has a very tightly fitting lid. Add the onion and half of the potatoes. Place the meat in the centre and fill up with the remaining potatoes. Season each layer with salt, pepper and paprika. Sprinkle over the sugar and cover with boiling water. Place foil over the top before putting on the lid.

Put the casserole in the centre of a moderately hot oven (190°C, 375°F, Gas Mark 5) until it comes to the boil, then turn down the oven to very cool (120°C, 250°F, Gas Mark ½) and leave until required the following day.

Variation

A large dumpling can be added to the cholent.

METRIC/IMPERIAL	AMERICAN
100 g/4 oz self-raising flour	1 cup all-purpose flour sifted with 1 teaspoon baking powder
25 g/1 oz raw chicken fat	2 tablespoons raw chicken fat
1 tablespoon grated onion	1 tablespoon grated onion
2 teaspoons chopped parsley	2 teaspoons chopped parsley
1 large potato, grated	1 large potato, grated
salt and freshly ground black pepper	salt and freshly ground black pepper

Mix all the ingredients together, season and form into a roll. Place the dumpling with the meat in the centre of the cholent.

Boiled Beef and Dumplings

SERVES 6–8

METRIC/IMPERIAL	AMERICAN
1.5–1.75 kg/3–4 lb boned and rolled brisket of beef	3–4 lb boned and rolled brisket of beef
1 head celery	1 head celery
3 carrots	3 carrots
6 onions	6 onions
2 turnips	2 turnips
1 parsnip	1 parsnip
3 cloves	3 cloves
2 peppercorns	2 peppercorns
salt	salt

Make sure the meat is securely tied into shape. Place in a large saucepan and cover with boiling salted water. Bring to the boil and boil for 5 minutes. Skim, then reduce the heat, cover and simmer slowly for 1 hour.

Meanwhile wash the celery and peel the remaining vegetables. Cut into pieces of about equal size. Add the prepared vegetables, cloves and peppercorns to the meat and continue simmering for 1 hour. The meat should always be covered with water and if the level drops too much, add a little boiling water.

To Prepare the Dumplings
Sift 175 g/6 oz plain flour (U.S. 1½ cups all-purpose flour) into a bowl with 1 teaspoon baking powder and 1 teaspoon salt. Grate 50 g/2 oz (U.S. ¼ cup) firm margarine into the flour and add 2 teaspoons chopped parsley, black pepper and a pinch of dried mixed herbs. Add enough cold water to form a fairly slack dough. With floured hands, shape into balls and roll in flour. Add the dumplings to the boiled beef for the last 30 minutes of cooking.

To serve the boiled beef and dumplings, lift the meat on to a hot dish and remove the string. Place the vegetables and dumplings around the meat and pour over a little of the cooking liquor. The remaining liquor makes good soup.

Carrot Tzimmas

SERVES 4–6

METRIC/IMPERIAL	AMERICAN
1.25 kg/2½ lb boned brisket of beef	2½ lb boned brisket of beef
1 large onion	1 large onion
salt and freshly ground black pepper	salt and freshly ground black pepper
450 g/1 lb carrots	1 lb carrots
1 kg/2 lb potatoes	2 lb potatoes
50 g/2 oz chicken fat	¼ cup chicken fat
50 g/2 oz flour	½ cup flour
50 g/2 oz sugar	¼ cup sugar
¼ teaspoon citric acid	¼ teaspoon citric acid

Trim the meat and place in a large saucepan. Peel and thickly slice the onion and add to the meat, together with enough boiling water to cover the meat completely; add salt and pepper to season. Bring to the boil then lower the heat, cover and simmer very gently for 1½ hours.

Meanwhile peel the carrots and cut into thick rings. Peel the potatoes and if they are small leave them whole, otherwise cut into halves.

Add the carrots and potatoes to the meat and simmer gently for a further 40–45 minutes or until the vegetables are just tender.

Transfer the meat and vegetables to a large casserole and reserve the cooking liquor. Melt the fat in the saucepan, remove from the heat and stir in the flour to make a roux. Return the pan to the heat and cook the roux for 2 minutes, stirring continuously with a wooden spoon. Gradually add 600 ml/1 pint (U.S. 2½ cups) of the reserved cooking liquor, mixing well between each addition until the liquid boils and thickens. Stir in the sugar and citric acid and pour over the contents of the casserole. Place uncovered towards the top of a moderate oven (160°C, 325°F, Gas Mark 3) and cook for 30 minutes.
(Illustrated on page 42)

Variation

To make a Prune tzimmas, soak 100 g/4 oz prunes overnight and add to the meat and onions at the beginning of the preparation. Omit the carrots and replace the citric acid with lemon juice.

Meat Loaf

✡

SERVES 4–6

METRIC/IMPERIAL	AMERICAN
50 g/2 oz fine fresh breadcrumbs	½ cup fine fresh bread crumbs
450 g/1 lb minced beef	1 lb ground beef
1 medium onion	1 medium onion
1 small clove garlic, peeled (optional)	1 small clove garlic, peeled (optional)
1 tablespoon tomato purée	1 tablespoon tomato paste
3 sprigs parsley	3 sprigs parsley
1 egg	1 egg
salt and freshly ground black pepper	salt and freshly ground black pepper
pinch of nutmeg	dash of nutmeg

Place the breadcrumbs and minced beef in a mixing bowl. Peel and roughly chop the onion and blend in a liquidiser with the remaining ingredients for a minute until reduced to a purée. Add to the meat and breadcrumbs and mix thoroughly with a wooden spoon.

Turn the mixture into a greased 0.5-kg/1-lb loaf tin and press down lightly. Cover with greased paper or foil and bake in a moderately hot oven (190°C, 375°F, Gas Mark 5) for about 1 hour.

Serve hot with a thick gravy or tomato sauce (see page 85). Alternatively, serve cold with salads and pickles.

Variations

Flavour with curry powder and serve with boiled rice and chutney.

Add a little sausagemeat or minced smoked beef to the mixture before cooking.

Minced Meat with Kasha (Buckwheat)

SERVES 6

METRIC/IMPERIAL	AMERICAN
50 g/2 oz kasha	½ cup kasha
boiling water (see method)	boiling water (see method)
1 medium onion	1 medium onion
3 tablespoons oil	¼ cup oil
450 g/1 lb minced beef	1 lb ground beef
1 tablespoon flour	1 tablespoon flour
1 beef stock cube	1 beef bouillon cube
salt and freshly ground black pepper	salt and freshly ground black pepper
1 clove garlic, crushed	1 clove garlic, crushed
575 g/1¼ lb flaky pastry	1¼ lb puff paste
beaten egg for glazing	beaten egg for glazing
sesame seeds	sesame seeds

Place the kasha in a thick-based saucepan and cook over a low heat for 1 minute to dry the grains, shaking or stirring continuously. Pour over boiling water to cover and cook for 5–10 minutes until all the water has been absorbed and the kasha is swollen and tender. Set aside until required.

Peel and finely chop the onion and fry in the oil until soft. Add the minced beef and cook until all the redness has disappeared. Stir in the flour. Dissolve the stock cube in 150 ml/¼ pint (U.S. ⅔ cup) boiling water, pour over the meat and continue cooking, stirring all the time until the water has been absorbed. Add the cooked kasha, garlic and seasoning to taste and mix well. Remove from the heat and set aside to cool.

Roll the pastry into two 28 × 23-cm/11 × 9-inch oblongs. Spread the meat mixture down the centre of each piece of pastry, dampen the edges and fold the sides over the centre. Seal the fold and the ends well. Brush with beaten egg and sprinkle with sesame seeds. Bake in a moderately hot oven (200°C, 400°F, Gas Mark 6) for 20–25 minutes until the pastry rolls are golden brown. Serve cut into slices. *(Illustrated on page 42)*

Hungarian Goulash

SERVES 4–6

METRIC/IMPERIAL	AMERICAN
675 g/1½ lb stewing beef (or a mixture of beef and veal)	1½ lb chuck beef (or a mixture of beef and veal)
25 g/1 oz seasoned flour	¼ cup seasoned flour
1 large onion	1 large onion
1 clove garlic	1 clove garlic
½ green pepper	½ green pepper
50 g/2 oz dripping	¼ cup meat drippings
1 (396-g/14-oz) can tomatoes	1 (14-oz) can tomatoes
1 tablespoon paprika	1 tablespoon paprika pepper
salt and freshly ground black pepper	salt and freshly ground black pepper
stock or water (see method)	stock or water (see method)
450 g/1 lb small potatoes	1 lb small potatoes
chopped parsley to garnish	chopped parsley to garnish

Cut the meat into 2.5-cm/1-inch cubes and roll in the seasoned flour. Peel and chop the onion. Peel and crush the garlic. Chop the pepper. Melt the dripping in a frying pan over a moderate heat and fry the meat and onion until lightly browned. Transfer to a casserole.

Sieve or liquidise the tomatoes with their juice and add to the meat together with the garlic, green pepper, paprika, seasoning and enough stock or water to cover the meat. Put the lid on the casserole and cook in a cool oven (150°C, 300°F, Gas Mark 2) for about 1½ hours.

Peel the potatoes and cut into small pieces if necessary. Add to the goulash and continue cooking for a further 40 minutes. Serve sprinkled with parsley.

Oriental Stew

SERVES 4–6

METRIC/IMPERIAL	AMERICAN
50 g/2 oz chick peas	⅓ cup chick peas
450 g/1 lb stewing beef	1 lb chuck beef
2 large onions	2 large onions
1 large clove garlic	1 large clove garlic
dripping or olive oil for frying	meat drippings or olive oil for frying
2 tablespoons tomato purée	3 tablespoons tomato paste
900 ml/1½ pints water	3¾ cups water
salt and freshly ground black pepper	salt and freshly ground black pepper
450 g/1 lb courgettes	1 lb zucchini

Soak the chick peas in water overnight, then drain. Cut the meat into 2.5-cm/1-inch cubes. Peel and chop the onions and garlic.

Heat the dripping or oil in a large saucepan and fry the onion until golden brown; stir in the garlic. Add the meat and fry until lightly browned. Stir in the tomato purée, add the chick peas, water and seasoning and bring to the boil. Lower the heat, cover the pan with a lid and simmer the meat very gently for 1½ hours.

Trim the courgettes and cut into 1-cm/½-inch thick slices. Add to the meat and simmer for a further 20–30 minutes or until the courgettes are just tender and all the liquid has been absorbed. Take care towards the end of cooking that the mixture does not become too dry.

Meatballs in a Casserole

SERVES 4

METRIC/IMPERIAL	AMERICAN
450 g/1 lb minced beef	1 lb ground beef
50 g/2 oz fine fresh breadcrumbs	½ cup fine fresh bread crumbs
3 small onions	3 small onions
3 sprigs parsley	3 sprigs parsley
1 egg	1 egg
salt and freshly ground black pepper	salt and freshly ground black pepper
seasoned flour for coating	seasoned flour for coating
2 carrots	2 carrots
2 sticks celery	2 stalks celery
50 g/2 oz dripping	¼ cup meat drippings
1 tablespoon flour	1 tablespoon flour
600 ml/1 pint stock	2½ cups stock

Place the meat and breadcrumbs in a mixing bowl. Peel and coarsely chop one onion and put into a liquidiser with the parsley, egg and seasoning. Alternatively, finely mince the onion and parsley and mix with the egg and seasoning. Add to the meat and breadcrumbs and mix well. Shape the mixture into small balls and coat with seasoned flour.

Peel and slice the remaining onions and the carrots; wash and slice the celery.

Heat the dripping in a frying pan and lightly brown the onions and the meatballs. Remove with a draining spoon and transfer to a casserole. Add the sliced carrots and celery.

Stir the tablespoon of flour into the remaining fat in the pan to make a roux. Cook over a gentle heat, stirring frequently with a wooden spoon until the roux browns. Gradually stir in the stock and heat until it boils and thickens. Pour over the meatballs and vegetables. Cover and cook in a cool oven (150°C, 300°F, Gas Mark 2) for 2 hours. *(Illustrated on page 42)*

Haricot Stew

SERVES 4–6

METRIC/IMPERIAL	AMERICAN
175 g/6 oz haricot beans	1 cup navy beans
450 g/1 lb shin of beef or stewing steak	1 lb beef shank or chuck steak
2 tablespoons vinegar	3 tablespoons vinegar
225 g/8 oz carrots	½ lb carrots
2 leeks	2 leeks
½ green pepper	½ green pepper
50 g/2 oz dripping	¼ cup meat drippings
40 g/1½ oz flour	6 tablespoons flour
900 ml/1½ pints stock or stock made from a beef stock cube	3¾ cups stock or stock made from a beef bouillon cube
salt and freshly ground black pepper	salt and freshly ground black pepper
pinch of paprika	dash of paprika pepper
1 bay leaf	1 bay leaf

Soak the haricot beans in water overnight, then drain. Cut the meat into 2.5-cm/1-inch cubes and trim off the excess fat. Place in a bowl with the vinegar and marinate for 15 minutes, turning occasionally.

Peel the carrots, wash the leeks and green pepper and cut the vegetables into thick slices. Melt the dripping in a saucepan and fry the vegetables until golden brown. Take out the vegetables and reserve. Stir the flour into the remaining fat to make a roux and cook over a moderate heat until browned. Gradually add the stock and stir continuously until it boils and thickens.

Place the meat, haricot beans and browned vegetables in a casserole dish and season with salt, black pepper and paprika. Add the bay leaf and the thickened stock. Cook in a cool oven (150°C, 300°F, Gas Mark 2) for 2½–3 hours until the meat is very tender. *(Illustrated on page 41)*

Cooking Steak

✡

Fried Steak

Heat 50 g/2 oz (U.S. ¼ cup) of chicken fat or dripping or oil in a frying pan until it is really hot. Put in the steak, quickly brown on both sides, then lower the heat. Turn frequently using a spatula or spoon. Take care not to pierce the meat and lose any juice. An average steak will take 10–15 minutes to cook depending on the thickness.

Season with salt and pepper, put on a preheated dish and keep hot while the gravy is being prepared. Alternatively, serve with tomato sauce (see page 85) or wine sauce (see page 86).

Grilled Steak

Use only good quality meat and heat the grill until red hot.

Have the steaks cut 2.5–3.5 cm/1–1½ inches thick, if possible, and brush both sides with melted fat. Grease the grid thoroughly. Place the meat under the grill and cook for 1 minute each side. Reduce the heat slightly and continue cooking, turning the steak about every 2 minutes. Never use a fork or sharp knife to turn the meat in case the surface is pierced and the juice escapes.

Steak will take between 12–15 minutes to cook. Transfer the meat to a preheated dish, pour over any juices from the grill pan and sprinkle with salt and freshly ground pepper.

Variations

For a stronger flavour rub the meat with a little garlic before grilling or sprinkle with a mixture of paprika and garlic salt.

The steak can also be marinated before it is grilled or fried. This gives added flavour and also helps to make the steak tender.

For each 450 g/1 lb of steak allow 2 table-spoons (U.S. 3 tablespoons) olive oil, 1 tablespoon vinegar, a small sliced onion, a piece of bay leaf and a few peppercorns. Mix together and leave the steak in the marinade for 24 hours at least, turning occasionally. Then drain and grill or fry.

Holishkes (Stuffed Cabbage Leaves)

✡

SERVES 4–6

METRIC/IMPERIAL	AMERICAN
12 large cabbage leaves (see note)	12 large cabbage leaves (see note)
100 g/4 oz cooked rice	½ cup cooked rice
450 g/1 lb minced meat	1 lb ground meat
1 tablespoon grated onion	1 tablespoon grated onion
2 tablespoons tomato purée	3 tablespoons tomato paste
salt and freshly ground black pepper	salt and freshly ground black pepper
450 ml/¾ pint stock or water	2 cups stock or water
25 g/1 oz soft brown sugar	2 tablespoons soft brown sugar
juice of 1 large lemon	juice of 1 large lemon

Place the cabbage leaves in a mixing bowl, cover with boiling water and set aside for 5 minutes. Drain, dry and cut away the tough stalk end of the leaves.

Wash and drain the rice and mix with the minced meat, grated onion, 1 tablespoon of the tomato purée, salt and pepper.

Spread each cabbage leaf on a flat surface and place a spoonful of the meat mixture in the centre. Fold over the sides and roll up the leaf like a parcel. Place in a casserole just large enough to take the stuffed leaves. Place the ends of each parcel to the bottom to keep the cabbage leaf folded.

In a small saucepan, combine the stock, remaining tomato purée, sugar and lemon juice. Heat gently until the sugar dissolves, making a thin sweet and sour sauce. Add more sugar or lemon juice to taste if wished. Pour enough of the sauce over the cabbage leaves until they are just covered. Cook in a cool oven (150°C, 300°F, Gas Mark 2) for about 3 hours. Serve hot or cold. *(Illustrated on page 42)*

Note Do not use the tough outer leaves of the cabbage.

Variation

Add 50 g/2 oz sultanas (U.S. ⅓ cup seedless white raisins) to the sauce.

Stuffed Vine Leaves Buy a 425-g/15-oz can of vine leaves and soak the leaves overnight in cold water. Drain. The leaves are quite fragile and should be handled carefully.

Make up the meat mixture and the sauce as for stuffed cabbage leaves. Choose the large vine leaves and stuff them, folding over the leaves to form a parcel in the same way.

Line the casserole dish with half the small leaves which are unsuitable for stuffing. Lay the stuffed leaves on top, pour over the sauce and finish with a layer of the remaining small leaves.

Cook as for the stuffed cabbage leaves.

Baked Lamb with Tomatoes
✡

SERVES 6–8

METRIC/IMPERIAL	AMERICAN
1 large shoulder of lamb, 2.25–2.75 kg/ 5–6 lb	1 large shoulder of lamb, 5–6 lb
2 cloves garlic, crushed	2 cloves garlic, crushed
salt and freshly ground black pepper	salt and freshly ground black pepper
1 (453-g/1-lb) packet frozen French beans	1 (16-oz) package frozen green beans
1 (396-g/14-oz) can tomatoes	1 (14-oz) can tomatoes

Place the lamb in a roasting tin and rub all over with the crushed garlic, pushing a little of the garlic between the flesh and the bone. Season well and surround the meat with the beans taken straight from the packet and the canned tomatoes. Sealing the edges securely, cover the meat and the tin with foil.

Cook in a cool oven (140°C, 275°F, Gas Mark 1) for 4–5 hours, keeping the meat well covered. At the end of this time the meat will have fallen away from the bone.

Stuffed Breast of Lamb
✡

SERVES 4

METRIC/IMPERIAL	AMERICAN
1 boned breast of lamb, 1–1.5 kg/ 2–3 lb	1 boned breast of lamb, 2–3 lb
1 clove garlic, peeled	1 clove garlic, peeled
salt and freshly ground black pepper	salt and freshly ground black pepper
For the stuffing	*For the stuffing*
75 g/3 oz cooked rice	⅓ cup cooked rice
50 g/2 oz sultanas	⅓ cup seedless white raisins
grated rind and juice of ½ lemon	grated rind and juice of ½ lemon
1 small onion, grated	1 small onion, grated
½ teaspoon chopped rosemary	½ teaspoon chopped rosemary
pinch of mixed spice	dash of mixed spice
1 small egg	1 small egg
For roasting	*For roasting*
675 g/1½ lb potatoes	1½ lb potatoes
1 tablespoon dripping	1 tablespoon meat drippings

Rub the meat all over with the garlic and season well. Place on a flat surface, skin downwards.

To prepare the stuffing Place all the ingredients in a bowl and mix well. Spread the meat with the stuffing then roll it up and secure with string or sew into place.

To roast the meat Peel and thickly slice the potatoes and place in a greased roasting tin. Sprinkle with salt and pepper and pour over about 250 ml/8 fl oz (U.S. 1 cup) water.

Put the prepared meat on top, dot with dripping and cover tightly with foil. Place in a hot oven (230°C, 450°F, Gas Mark 8) for 10 minutes then lower the heat to moderately hot (190°C, 375°F, Gas Mark 5) until the meat is cooked. (Allow 30 minutes for each 450 g/1 lb.) Remove the foil for the last 30 minutes.

Lamb Stewed with Rice and Sultanas

SERVES 3–4

METRIC/IMPERIAL	AMERICAN
675 g/1½ lb middle neck of lamb	1½ lb lamb neck slices
salt and freshly ground black pepper	salt and freshly ground black pepper
150 g/6 oz long-grain rice	¾ cup long-grain rice
75 g/3 oz sultanas	⅓ cup seedless white raisins
¼ teaspoon cinnamon	¼ teaspoon cinnamon
900 ml/1½ pints boiling stock	3¾ cups boiling stock

Cut the meat into neat pieces and trim off any excess fat. Season and place in a casserole. Add the rice, sultanas and cinnamon and pour over the boiling stock. Cover with a lid and cook in a moderate oven (160°C, 325°F, Gas Mark 3) for 1½ hours.

Fried Liver

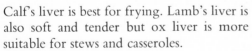

Calf's liver is best for frying. Lamb's liver is also soft and tender but ox liver is more suitable for stews and casseroles.

Cut the liver into thin slices, allowing about 100 g/4 oz per person. Dip in seasoned flour. Melt a little dripping in a frying pan and when hot add the liver and brown on both sides. Then reduce the heat and fry very gently until tender.

Place the liver in a hot dish and pour all but 2 tablespoons (U.S. 3 tablespoons) of the fat from the frying pan. Using a wooden spoon, stir 1 tablespoon of flour into the fat remaining in the frying pan to make a roux. Cook gently until lightly browned. Add 300 ml/½ pint (U.S. 1¼ cups) stock and bring to the boil, stirring continuously. Season to taste and strain over the liver.

Serve with fried onions, or mushrooms and mashed potato.

Liver Kugel

SERVES 4

METRIC/IMPERIAL	AMERICAN
225 g/8 oz ribbon noodles	½ lb ribbon noodles
225 g/8 oz cooked lamb's or calf's liver	½ lb cooked lamb or calf liver
1 medium onion	1 medium onion
2 tablespoons chicken fat	3 tablespoons chicken fat
2 eggs, beaten	2 eggs, beaten
salt and freshly ground black pepper	salt and freshly ground black pepper

Cook the noodles in boiling salted water until tender; then rinse under cold running water and drain well. Mince the liver. Peel and chop the onion and fry in the chicken fat until golden brown. Put all the ingredients into a bowl and mix well.

Turn the mixture into a greased oven-proof dish and bake in a moderate oven (180°C, 350°F, Gas Mark 4) for 45–50 minutes until set and golden brown.

Liver Casserole

SERVES 4

METRIC/IMPERIAL	AMERICAN
450 g/1 lb lamb's or calf's liver	1 lb lamb or calf liver
50 g/2 oz seasoned flour	½ cup seasoned flour
2 medium onions	2 medium onions
50 g/2 oz dripping	¼ cup meat drippings
600 ml/1 pint stock or water	2½ cups stock or water
salt and freshly ground black pepper	salt and freshly ground black pepper
225 g/8 oz potatoes	½ lb potatoes
225 g/8 oz cooking apples	½ lb baking apples

Cut the liver into small pieces and roll in the seasoned flour. Peel and slice the onions.

Melt the dripping in a frying pan, put in

the liver and onions, and fry until both are lightly browned. Lift out with a draining spoon and place in a casserole.

Stir the remaining flour into the fat left in the frying pan to make a roux. Cook gently over a low heat until lightly browned. Gradually add the stock or water and bring to the boil, stirring continuously until it boils and thickens. Season with salt and pepper.

Peel and slice the potatoes and apples and add to the liver and onions, together with the thickened stock. Cover the casserole and place in a moderate oven (180°C, 350°F, Gas Mark 4) for 1½ hours.

Wiener Schnitzel

SERVES 4

METRIC/IMPERIAL	AMERICAN
4 veal escalopes	4 veal scallops
seasoned flour for coating	seasoned flour for coating
1 egg, beaten	1 egg, beaten
fresh white breadcrumbs for coating	fresh white bread crumbs for coating
chicken fat or dripping for frying	chiken fat or meat drippings for frying
To garnish	*To garnish*
lemon slices	lemon slices
sliced stuffed olives	sliced stuffed olives

Ask the butcher to flatten the veal; otherwise snip the edge a little with kitchen scissors to prevent it curling and flatten with a meat mallet or wooden rolling pin so that it is really thin. Dip in seasoned flour, then in beaten egg and coat with fresh breadcrumbs; shake to remove any surplus crumbs. Fry in hot chicken fat or dripping, one at a time, until golden brown. Drain on absorbent kitchen paper and serve.

Traditionally wiener schnitzel is garnished with a slice of lemon with a slice of stuffed olive in the centre. To make a more substantial dish a fried or poached egg can be served on each schnitzel.

Veal Casserole with Mushrooms

SERVES 4

METRIC/IMPERIAL	AMEICAN
450 g/1 lb boned breast of veal	1 lb boned breast of veal
1 large onion	1 large onion
50 g/2 oz smoked beef dripping for frying	1 slice smoked beef meat drippings for frying
1 tablespoon flour	1 tablespoon flour
600 ml/1 pint stock or water	2½ cups stock or water
salt and freshly ground black pepper	salt and freshly ground black pepper
juice of ½ lemon	juice of ½ lemon
100 g/4 oz mushrooms	¼ lb mushrooms
3 tablespoons sherry	¼ cup sherry
1 tablespoon chopped parsley	1 tablespoon chopped parsley
6 stoned green olives	6 pitted green olives

Cut the veal into cubes and place in a casserole.

Peel and thickly slice the onion and chop the smoked beef. Heat the dripping in a saucepan and fry the onion and smoked beef until golden brown. Add the flour and stir with a wooden spoon until it browns. Gradually add the stock or water, stirring continuously until it boils and thickens. Season with salt and pepper, add the lemon juice and pour into the casserole.

Cover and place in a cool oven (150°C, 300°F, Gas Mark 2) for 1 hour. Slice the mushrooms, add to the casserole and cook for a further hour. Stir in the sherry, chopped parsley and olives just before serving.

Poultry

Poultry is extremely versatile and it would be a pity to restrict one's cooking to chicken soup and boiled chicken, even for the traditional Sabbath dish.

The whole bird can be roasted but chicken is best jointed or at least halved to make casseroles and stews. This way it is easier to prepare and serve and the bones, pieces and giblets can be used to make stock or soup. When jointing a fresh chicken the pieces which are not being used can be frozen until they are needed. The butcher will usually cut or joint a chicken for you if you give him instructions when it is ordered.

When buying a chicken allow at least 275 g/10 oz of chicken per person; a 1.5-kg/3-lb chicken will serve 4 people.

If you have bought poultry frozen or have frozen your own, it is best thawed at room temperature, and is not safe to cook until it has completely defrosted.

To Truss Poultry for Roasting

After stuffing, poultry is trussed if it is to be roasted.

Fold the loose neck skin over the back of the bird.

Run a trussing needle through the centre of the two leg joints, then turn the bird on its breast, carry the string in a slanting direction between the two centre bones of the wing, and catching the underneath part of the pinion. Then draw the string over the bird through the pinion and wing at the other side, where it will meet the other end of the string. Tie the ends together.

Place the bird breast downwards and holding it with the left hand, run the needle and string through the back beside the thigh bones. Pull the leg straight out, turn the bird on its back and carry the string over the leg then through the breast, over the other leg, and tie the legs together.

Israeli salad (see page 91); Savoury chicken (see page 63)

Roast Chicken

Clean and season the chicken. If it is to be stuffed, fill the crop end. If two kinds of stuffing are to be used, fill both the crop and body cavities.

Place the chicken in a roasting tin containing hot fat. Allow 20 minutes cooking time for each 450 g/1 lb plus an additional 20 minutes. Cook the chicken in a moderately hot oven (200°C, 400°F, Gas Mark 6). Cover the breast with greased greaseproof paper, baste once or twice during the cooking time and remove the paper for the last 20 minutes of the cooking time to brown the chicken. Alternatively, roast the chicken covered in foil and use the following times:
up to 1.75 kg/4 lb, 30–35 minutes per 450 g/per lb.
between 1.75 kg/4 lb and 3.5 kg/8 lb, 25 minutes per 450 g/per lb.
Fold back the foil for the last 15–20 minutes of the cooking time to brown the chicken.

Note When roasting a stuffed chicken, weigh the bird to calculate the cooking time after it has been stuffed.

Slow Roasting

Brush the chicken with melted margarine and put a small bunch of parsley and 25 g/ 1 oz (U.S. 2 tablespoons) margarine inside the bird. Pour about 2.5 cm/1 inch of chicken stock into a casserole and put in the chicken. Add any giblets, a squeeze of lemon juice and a bouquet garni.

Cover the dish with foil and place in a cool oven (150°C, 300°F, Gas Mark 2) for double the normal roasting time. Baste about every 30 minutes.

To Render Chicken Fat

Remove all the fat and fatty skin from the chicken and cut into pieces about 1 cm/ ½ inch in size. Place in a bowl and cook in a slow oven or in a saucepan over a low heat.

When the pieces turn golden brown and start to crisp, stir in a little sliced onion. Remove when the onion begins to brown. Strain through a sieve, pressing well to extract all the fat. The skin, which should be crisp, can be salted and eaten on its own or crumbled over chopped liver.

Raisin and Walnut Stuffing

METRIC/IMPERIAL	AMERICAN
50 g/2 oz raisins	⅓ cup raisins
50 g/2 oz margarine or chicken fat	½ cup margarine or chicken fat
1 egg, beaten	1 egg, beaten
50 g/2 oz chopped walnuts	½ cup chopped walnuts
2 teaspoons chopped parsley	2 teaspoons chopped parsley
100 g/4 oz fresh breadcrumbs	2 cups fresh soft bread crumbs
salt and freshly ground black pepper	salt and freshly ground black pepper
½ teaspoon cinnamon	½ teaspoon cinnamon

Put the raisins in a small saucepan and cover with water. Bring to the boil, then lower the heat and simmer for 5 minutes. Drain well. Melt the fat and add to the raisins, together with all the remaining ingredients. Mix well.

Use for chicken or turkey.

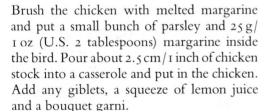

Savoury goose pie (see page 73); Cabbage salad (see page 92); Potato salad (see page 91)

Corn Stuffing

✡

METRIC/IMPERIAL	AMERICAN
1 (326-g/11½-oz) can sweet corn kernels	1 (11½-oz) can corn kernels
1 medium onion	1 medium onion
50 g/2 oz margarine or chicken fat	¼ cup margarine or chicken fat
50 g/2 oz fresh breadcrumbs	1 cup fresh soft bread crumbs
salt and freshly ground black pepper	salt and freshly ground black pepper
1 egg	1 egg

Drain the sweet corn. Peel and finely chop the onion and fry in the fat until golden brown. Remove from the heat and add the breadcrumbs, sweet corn, seasoning and egg and mix well.

Use for chicken or turkey.

Helzel (Stuffed Neck)

✡

METRIC/IMPERIAL	AMERICAN
skin from the neck of the bird	skin from the neck of the bird
1 onion	1 onion
For the stuffing	*For the stuffing*
heart and liver of the bird	heart and liver of the bird
50 g/2 oz margarine	¼ cup margarine
grated rind and juice of ½ lemon	grated rind and juice of ½ lemon
1 egg	1 egg
100 g/4 oz fresh breadcrumbs	2 cups fresh soft bread crumbs
2 teaspoons chopped parsley	2 teaspoons chopped parsley
2 teaspoons grated onion	2 teaspoons grated onion
salt and freshly ground black pepper	salt and freshly ground black pepper

Remove the skin from the neck in one piece. If torn, sew it together. Wash and clean the skin thoroughly. Peel and slice the onion.

To make the stuffing Finely chop the heart and liver. Grate the margarine or use soft margarine. Mix all the ingredients together and if the mixture is too dry add another egg or a little water.

Fill the neck with the stuffing and sew both ends securely. Place in a small oven-proof dish with the sliced onion and a little water. Cook in a moderate oven (180°C, 350°F, Gas Mark 4) for 45 minutes–1 hour until crisp and brown, basting occasionally.

Alternatively, cook the helzel while roasting a chicken.

Alternative filling

Finely chop a little of the raw fat from the bird. To each tablespoon of fat add 3 table-spoons (U.S. ¼ cup) flour and 1 teaspoon finely grated onion. Season with salt and pepper and mix well.

Honeyed Chicken

✡

SERVES 4

METRIC/IMPERIAL	AMERICAN
4 chicken joints	4 chicken joints
seasoned flour	seasoned flour
1 egg	1 egg
1 tablespoon lemon juice	1 tablespoon lemon juice
50 g/2 oz margarine	¼ cup margarine
1 (200-g/7-oz) jar honey	1 (7-oz) jar honey

Rinse the chicken; dry on absorbent kitchen paper and coat in seasoned flour. Beat together the egg and lemon juice and dip each piece of chicken into the egg mixture. Fry in the margarine until golden brown.

Transfer the chicken to a casserole and pour over the honey. Cook in a moderately hot oven (190°C, 375°F, Gas Mark 5) for 1–1½ hours until the chicken is darkly coloured. Serve the juice separately. *(Illustrated on page 155)*

Fried Chicken

Joint a small young chicken and coat with seasoned flour. Heat some chicken fat in a frying pan and brown the chicken joints quickly all over. Lower the heat, cover the pan with a lid or plate and cook the chicken for about 20 minutes until tender, turning occasionally.

Variation

Add garlic salt or powdered ginger to the seasoned flour for a stronger flavour.

Savoury Chicken

SERVES 4

METRIC/IMPERIAL	AMERICAN
4 chicken joints	4 chicken joints
50 g/2 oz soft margarine	¼ cup soft margarine
225 g/8 oz small onions, peeled	½ lb small onions, peeled
2 cloves garlic, crushed	2 cloves garlic, crushed
1 bay leaf	1 bay leaf
grated rind and juice of 1 small lemon	grated rind and juice of 1 small lemon
25 g/1 oz long-grain rice	2 tablespoons long-grain rice
salt and freshly ground black pepper	salt and freshly ground black pepper
250 ml/8 fl oz white wine	1 cup white wine
1 teaspoon chopped parsley	1 teaspoon chopped parsley

Coat the chicken pieces with the margarine and place in a casserole with the onions, garlic, bay leaf, lemon rind and juice and rice. Season well and pour over the wine.

Cover the casserole with foil, sealing the edges well, and put on the lid. Cook in a cool oven (150°C, 300°F, Gas Mark 2) for 2–2½ hours. Sprinkle with chopped parsley before serving. *(Illustrated on page 59)*

Chicken Croquettes

MAKES 4–6

METRIC/IMPERIAL	AMERICAN
225 g/8 oz cooked chicken	½ lb cooked chicken
25 g/1 oz chicken fat	2 tablespoons chicken fat
25 g/1 oz flour	¼ cup flour
150 ml/¼ pint chicken stock	⅔ cup chicken stock
1 teaspoon lemon juice	1 teaspoon lemon juice
1 egg, separated	1 egg, separated
salt and freshly ground black pepper	salt and freshly ground black pepper
fine white breadcrumbs	fine white bread crumbs
fat for deep frying	fat for deep frying

Finely mince the chicken. Melt the fat in a small saucepan and stir in the flour. Gradually add the chicken stock and bring to the boil over a gentle heat until thickened. Remove from the heat, add the chicken, lemon juice, egg yolk and seasoning and mix thoroughly. Spread on a dish and leave to cool.

With floured hands, form into croquettes. Brush with beaten egg white and coat with fine white breadcrumbs. Fry in a frying basket in deep hot fat until golden brown. Drain well and serve with mashed potatoes and peas.

Chicken Risotto

SERVES 3–4

METRIC/IMPERIAL	AMERICAN
remains of a cold chicken	remains of a cold chicken
1 onion	1 onion
1 small green pepper	1 small green pepper
25–50 g/1–2 oz mushrooms	½ cup mushrooms
50 g/2 oz chicken fat	¼ cup chicken fat
900 ml/1½ pint chicken stock (may be made from a cube)	3¾ cups chicken stock (may be made from a cube)
salt and freshly ground black pepper	salt and freshly ground black pepper
¼ teaspoon mace	¼ teaspoon mace
175 g/6 oz long-grain rice	¾ cup long-grain rice
150 ml/¼ pint tomato purée	⅔ cup tomato paste
4–5 sprigs fresh parsley	4–5 sprigs fresh parsley

Remove any skin and bones from the chicken and dice the flesh.

Peel and slice the onion, dice the green pepper, wash and roughly chop the mushrooms. Heat the chicken fat in a medium-sized saucepan and fry the vegetables for 5 minutes. Add the chicken stock and bring to the boil. Season with salt, pepper and mace and add the washed rice.

Cover the saucepan and cook gently for 15–20 minutes until the rice is tender and has absorbed the stock. Do not stir the rice while cooking but shake the saucepan occasionally and fork it gently once or twice. Add the heated tomato purée, the chicken and the chopped parsley and stir for a few minutes until the chicken is heated through.

Chicken Casserole

SERVES 4–6

METRIC/IMPERIAL	AMERICAN
1 chicken or 4–6 chicken joints	1 chicken or 4–6 chicken joints
seasoned flour for coating	seasoned flour for coating
100 g/4 oz fat smoked beef (raw)	¼ lb fat smoked beef (raw)
chicken fat for frying	chicken fat for frying
1 onion	1 onion
40 g/1½ oz flour	6 tablespoons flour
600 ml/1 pint stock	2½ cups stock
100 g/4 oz chopped mushrooms	1 cup chopped mushrooms
salt and freshly ground black pepper	salt and freshly ground black pepper
1 bouquet garni	1 bouquet garni

Joint the chicken if necessary and coat in seasoned flour. Cut the smoked beef into dice.

Melt the fat in a frying pan and quickly brown the chicken joints and smoked beef. Transfer both to a casserole and cover with the mushrooms. Peel and slice the onion and fry in the fat remaining in the pan until golden brown. Stir in the flour and cook until lightly browned. Gradually pour in the stock and bring to the boil, stirring continuously until the mixture thickens. Pour over the chicken and add the seasoning and bouquet garni.

Cover and cook in a cool oven (150°C, 300°F, Gas Mark 2) for about 1½ hours until the chicken is tender. Remove the bouquet garni before serving.

Boiled Chicken from the Soup

✡

Boiled chicken is very tasty and can be eaten cold: it is especially good when mixed with cold smoked tongue. If the chicken is kept in the soup until it is cold, it will remain quite moist. If served hot it can be heated in:

    Curry sauce (see page 86)
    Wine sauce (see page 86)
    Tomato sauce (see page 85) or
    Egg and lemon sauce (see page 87)

Cut the chicken into neat pieces and warm it gently in the sauce.

Alternatively it can be used as the basis of:

    Risotto (see page 64) or
    Croquettes (see page 63).

Roast Turkey

✡

Prepare the turkey as the chicken. Both the breast and the body can be stuffed.

If the turkey is frozen, allow plenty of time to defrost. Usually between 36 hours (for a 4-kg/9-lb bird) and 48 hours in the refrigerator. A 6-kg/13-lb turkey will serve about 10 people. Fill the crop end with stuffing (about 675 g/1½ lb for a 5.5-kg/12-lb bird), draw the flap over and secure firmly. Fill the body with an alternative stuffing and brush the bird over with melted fat. Wrap the bird in two layers of greaseproof paper or one layer of foil and place on a rack in a roasting tin. Start cooking in a hot oven (220°C, 425°F, Gas Mark 7) and after 10 minutes reduce to moderate (180°C, 350°F, Gas Mark 4). Allow 15 minutes per 450 g/per lb for a bird under 5.5 kg/12 lb and 12 minutes per 450 g/per lb for a bird over 5.5 kg/12 lb.

About 30 minutes before the cooking time is complete, open the wrapping so that the skin becomes brown and crisp.

Turkey not used for the first meal can be made into risotto, croquettes or used in the orange casserole. Or it can be frozen. To freeze, cut it off the bone, cut away any fat and freeze in slices in gravy, stock or sauce to prevent the flesh becoming too dry. Any extra stuffing should be packed and frozen separately.

Chestnut Stuffing

✡

MAKES 675 G/1½ LB

METRIC/IMPERIAL	AMERICAN
450 g/1 lb chestnuts	1 lb chestnuts
stock (see method)	stock (see method)
50 g/2 oz margarine, melted	¼ cup melted margarine
75 g/3 oz fresh breadcrumbs	1½ cups fresh soft bread crumbs
225 g/8 oz sausage-meat	½ lb sausage meat
salt and freshly ground black pepper	salt and freshly ground black pepper

Make a small slit in each of the chestnuts, place in a saucepan with water to cover and bring to the boil. Boil for 15 minutes. Take out a few at a time and, while still warm, remove the outer shell and inner skin with a sharp knife.

Place the skinned chestnuts in a saucepan with sufficient stock to cover and boil until quite soft. Drain and rub through a sieve or potato ricer. Add the melted margarine, breadcrumbs, sausagemeat and seasoning and mix thoroughly.

Alternatively, omit the sausagemeat and add an egg to bind the mixture.

Celery Stuffing

✡

MAKES ABOUT 450 G / 1 LB

METRIC/IMPERIAL	AMERICAN
4 large sticks celery	4 large stalks celery
grated rind and juice of $\frac{1}{2}$ lemon	grated rind and juice of $\frac{1}{2}$ lemon
175 g/6 oz fresh breadcrumbs	3 cups fresh soft bread crumbs
salt and freshly ground black pepper	salt and freshly ground black pepper
1 egg	1 egg
50 g/2 oz margarine, melted	$\frac{1}{4}$ cup melted margarine
2 teaspoons chopped parsley	2 teaspoons chopped parsley
2 teaspoons grated onion	2 teaspoons grated onion

Wash the celery and cook until tender. Drain and chop finely. Mix all the ingredients together using a little celery stock to moisten if necessary. Use for turkey.

Apricot Stuffing

✡

MAKES ABOUT 575 G / 1$\frac{1}{4}$ LB

METRIC/IMPERIAL	AMERICAN
225 g/8 oz dried apricots	1$\frac{1}{4}$ cups dried apricots
4 pieces stem ginger	4 pieces preserved ginger
100 g/4 oz fresh breadcrumbs	2 cups fresh soft bread crumbs
50 g/2 oz margarine	$\frac{1}{4}$ cup margarine
1 large egg	1 large egg
salt and freshly ground black pepper	salt and freshly ground black pepper

Soak the apricots overnight in water, then drain and chop into small pieces. Finely chop the ginger. Put the breadcrumbs in a bowl, grate the margarine over them and then add the apricots, ginger, beaten egg and seasoning. Mix well.

Use for roast turkey.

Cranberry Sauce

✡

MAKES ABOUT 600 ML / 1 PINT U.S. 2$\frac{1}{2}$ CUPS)

METRIC/IMPERIAL	AMERICAN
450 g/1 lb fresh or frozen cranberries	1 lb fresh or frozen cranberries
150 ml/$\frac{1}{4}$ pint water	$\frac{2}{3}$ cup water
75 g/3 oz soft brown sugar	6 tablespoons soft brown sugar

If using fresh fruit, pick over and wash the berries carefully. Put the fruit in a saucepan, crush well with the back of a wooden spoon and add the water. Stew gently until soft.

Place in a liquidiser and blend for 30 seconds until the fruit is puréed. Add the sugar and reheat.

Serve with turkey.

Chestnut Sauce

MAKES ABOUT 450 ML / $\frac{3}{4}$ PINT (U.S. 2 CUPS)

METRIC/IMPERIAL	AMERICAN
22–24 chestnuts	22–24 chestnuts
300 ml/$\frac{1}{2}$ pint brown gravy (see method)	1$\frac{1}{4}$ cups brown gravy (see method)
2 tablespoons sherry	3 tablespoons sherry

Make a small slit in each of the chestnuts then boil in water to cover until soft. Drain and, while still warm, remove the outer shell and inner skin with a sharp knife. Press the chestnuts through a sieve or potato ricer. Make the gravy from the turkey juices, add the chestnuts and reheat. Remove from the heat, add the sherry and serve with turkey.

Roast Duck

Have the duck trussed for roasting and fill the body with stuffing. Ducks are never stuffed on the crop end.

Season with salt and pepper, put in a roasting tin and pour over 150 ml/¼ pint (U.S. ⅔ cup) melted dripping. Cover the breast with greaseproof paper. Roast in a hot oven (220°C, 425°F, Gas Mark 7) for the first 15 minutes then reduce to moderately hot (200°C, 400°F, Gas Mark 6).

Allow 20 minutes per 450 g/per lb and 20 minutes over. Alternatively, wrap the duck in foil and allow 30–35 minutes per 450 g/per lb, turning the foil back for the last 15 minutes of cooking time to allow the skin to brown.

Orange Sauce

MAKES ABOUT 300 ML/½ PINT (U.S. 1¼ CUPS)

METRIC/IMPERIAL	AMERICAN
freshly shredded rind and juice of 1 orange	freshly shredded rind and juice of 1 orange
25 g/1 oz fat	2 tablespoons fat
25 g/1 oz flour	¼ cup flour
300 ml/½ pint stock (made from the duck giblets)	1¼ cups stock (made from the duck giblets)
1 teaspoon lemon juice	1 teaspoon lemon juice
1 teaspoon redcurrant jelly	1 teaspoon red currant jelly
salt and freshly ground black pepper	salt and freshly ground black pepper

Put the orange rind into a small saucepan, cover with water and simmer gently for 5 minutes; then drain.

Melt the fat in a small saucepan and stir in the flour. Cook over gentle heat until brown. Gradually add the stock and bring to the boil, stirring continuously until thickened. Add the orange rind and juice and seasoning and stir until boiling. Serve with roast duck.

Apple Sauce

MAKES ABOUT 300 ML/½ PINT (U.S. 1¼ CUPS)

METRIC/IMPERIAL	AMERICAN
450 g/1 lb cooking apples	1 lb baking apples
40 g/1½ oz sugar	3 tablespoons sugar
3 tablespoons water	¼ cup water
15 g/½ oz margarine	1 tablespoon margarine

Peel, core and slice the apples and cook with the sugar and water until tender. The quantity of water and sugar will vary according to the kind of apple used but the sauce should be a little tart.

While the apples are still hot, add the margarine and beat until the apples are reduced to a pulp. Or rub through a sieve and then add the margarine.

Serve with duck or goose.

Sage and Onion Stuffing

MAKES ABOUT 450 G/1 LB

METRIC/IMPERIAL	AMERICAN
450 g/1 lb large onions	1 lb large onions
10 fresh sage leaves or 1–1½ teaspoons dried sage	10 fresh sage leaves or 1–1½ teaspoons dried sage
liver from the bird (if available)	liver from the bird (if available)
salt and freshly ground black pepper	salt and freshly ground black pepper

Peel and quarter the onions and boil gently until just tender. Drain well and chop finely.

Meanwhile remove the stalks from the sage leaves and soak the leaves in boiling water for 5 minutes. Dry well and chop finely. If dried sage leaves are used, chop finely. Simmer a small portion of the liver and mince finely. Mix together all the ingredients and season with salt and pepper.

Use for duck or goose.

Orange Salad

✡

SERVES 3–4

Remove the rind and pith from 3–4 oranges. This is easily done if, before peeling, the oranges are soaked in boiling water for 2–3 minutes. Cut the oranges into very thin slices, remove any pips and place in a glass bowl. Sprinkle lightly with a little castor (superfine) sugar, oil and lemon juice. Season with salt and pepper.

Serve with roast duck.

Pineapple Salad

✡

SERVES 4

METRIC/IMPERIAL	AMERICAN
175 g/6 oz cooked potatoes, peeled and diced	1 cup peeled and diced cooked potatoes
3 tablespoons small pineapple cubes	$\frac{1}{4}$ cup small pineapple cubes
3 tablespoons diced cucumber	$\frac{1}{4}$ cup diced cucumber
1 tablespoon chopped nuts	1 tablespoon chopped nuts
salt and freshly ground black pepper	salt and freshly ground black pepper
mayonnaise (see page 99)	mayonnaise (see page 99)
1 teaspoon chopped parsley	1 teaspoon chopped parsley
4 large lettuce leaves	4 large lettuce leaves
watercress	watercress

Mix together the potato, pineapple, cucumber and nuts. Season with salt and pepper and moisten with mayonnaise. Place in the centre of a bowl with chopped parsley and surround with shredded lettuce and sprigs of watercress.

Serve with roast poultry.

Roast Goose

✡

Prepare and stuff as for duck.

Season with salt and pepper. Place pieces of fat from the inside of the bird over the breast, then cover with greaseproof paper. Put in a roasting tin and pour in 150 ml/$\frac{1}{4}$ pint (U.S. $\frac{2}{3}$ cup) melted dripping. Roast in a hot oven (220°C, 425°F, Gas Mark 7) for 15 minutes then lower the heat to moderate (180°C, 350°F, Gas Mark 4).

Allow 15 minutes per 450 g/per lb and 15 minutes over.

The bird can be garnished with apple rings. Choose good-sized cooking apples; peel, core and slice them thickly. Using some of the fat from the goose, fry them on both sides until lightly browned.

Apple Stuffing

✡

MAKES 575–675 G/$1\frac{1}{4}$–$1\frac{1}{2}$ LB

METRIC/IMPERIAL	AMERICAN
100 g/4 oz long-grain rice	$\frac{1}{2}$ cup long-grain rice
675 g/$1\frac{1}{2}$ lb cooking apples	$1\frac{1}{2}$ lb baking apples
25 g/1 oz margarine	2 tablespoons margarine
4–5 tablespoons water	5–6 tablespoons water
25 g/1 oz sugar	2 tablespoons sugar
1 egg yolk	1 egg yolk
salt and freshly ground black pepper	salt and freshly ground black pepper

Cook the rice following the instructions on page 109. Drain well.

Peel, core and slice the apples and place in a saucepan with the margarine and water. Cover and cook over a low heat until soft. Drain off any excess water then add all the ingredients and mix well.

Use for roast goose.

Stuffed aubergines (see page 79)

68

Gooseberry Sauce

✡

MAKES 300–450 ML/½–¾ PINT (U.S. 1¼–2 CUPS)

METRIC/IMPERIAL	AMERICAN
225 g/8 oz green gooseberries	½ lb green gooseberries
150 ml/¼ pint water	⅔ cup water
25 g/1 oz sugar	2 tablespoons sugar
25 g/1 oz margarine	2 tablespoons margarine

Cook the gooseberries with the water until soft. Blend in a liquidiser for 30 seconds or rub through a sieve to make a purée. Return the purée to the saucepan, add the sugar and margarine and reheat.

Serve with goose or duck.

Savoury Goose Pie

✡

SERVES 3–4

METRIC/IMPERIAL	AMERICAN
left-over cold goose and stuffing	left-over cold goose and stuffing
left-over apple sauce	left-over apple sauce
salt and freshly ground black pepper	salt and freshly ground black pepper
4 tablespoons thick gravy or red wine	⅓ cup thick gravy or red wine
225 g/8 oz vegetarian puff pastry	½ lb vegetarian puff paste
1 egg, beaten	1 egg, beaten

Put a layer of sliced cold goose in a pie dish, spread with apple sauce and cover with a second layer of goose and a layer of stuffing. Season with salt and pepper and pour over the gravy or wine. Roll out the pastry and cover the top. Brush with beaten egg.

Preceding pages: *Fried courgettes (see page 77);*
Sauerkraut (see page 76); Sesame potato patties (see
page 75); Carrots with parsnips (see page 79);
Aubergine bake (see page 78)

Baked spinach turnovers (see page 80)

Bake in a hot oven (230°C, 450°F, Gas Mark 8) until the pastry is lightly browned, then reduce the temperature to moderate (180°C, 350°F, Gas Mark 4) for about 30 minutes in total until the pastry is crisp. *(Illustrated on page 60)*

Vegetarian Puff Pastry

✡

METRIC/IMPERIAL	AMERICAN
225 g/8 oz plain flour	2 cups all-purpose flour
½ teaspoon salt	½ teaspoon salt
225 g/8 oz kosher margarine	½ lb kosher margarine
2 teaspoons lemon juice	2 teaspoons lemon juice
6–8 tablespoons cold water	½–⅔ cup cold water

Sift the flour and salt into a mixing bowl and rub in 15 g/½ oz (U.S. 1 tablespoon) of the margarine, until the mixture resembles fine breadcrumbs. Add the lemon juice and water and mix to form a soft dough with a palette knife. Knead until smooth. Place in a polythene bag and chill in the refrigerator for 20 minutes.

Roll out into a rectangle 38 × 13 cm/ 15 × 5 inches. Shape the remaining margarine into a rectangle 13 × 10 cm/5 × 4 inches and place in the centre of the dough. Fold the bottom third up to cover the fat and the top third down over the folded dough. Seal the edges with a rolling pin, turn the dough so the right hand edge faces you. Repeat as for first rolling, seal edges, cover with polythene and leave to rest in the refrigerator for 20 minutes.

Repeat the second rolling and folding four times, allowing the dough to rest if it becomes too soft. After the final rolling the pastry should be left to rest for 20 minutes. Roll out and use as required.

Vegetables

Many of the daily vegetables we use now are frozen. They provide us with very nearly the equivalent of fresh vegetables in food value without the accompanying time needed for preparation or the problem of disposing of the waste. Daily or even weekly shopping can be bypassed, providing there is a good store of vegetables in the freezer. It is worth carefully following the manufacturers' instructions for preparing frozen vegetables, especially the cooking times given on the pack.

Vegetables are at their best when they are just cooked and, as part of the freezing process includes blanching, a small part of the cooking has been done in advance. Getting each dish ready for serving at the same time poses problems sometimes and the vegetables tend to be left boiling until all the dishes are ready to be served. If you have a microwave oven prepare the vegetables in advance, cooking them exactly to time. Drain and place in a serving dish, then reheat in the microwave oven and take the vegetables straight to the table when needed. It is important to remember that dishes made of stainless steel or decorated with a metallic paint are not suitable for use in a microwave oven.

Fresh vegetables should be cooked in a covered saucepan in a minimum amount of water and, as with frozen vegetables, should not be overcooked. This is important, not only to keep the flavour of the vegetables but also to help conserve the vitamins and minerals. As many of the vitamins in vegetables are water soluble, steaming helps vegetables to keep their food value.

Collapsible stainless steel steamers are inexpensive and because their size is adjustable they can be slipped into most everyday saucepans.

A pressure cooker which has its own trivet at the base of the pan has obvious advantages – the vegetables are virtually steamed and the cooking time is very brief.

Potatoes with Soured Cream

SERVES 4

METRIC/IMPERIAL	AMERICAN
675 g/1½ lb potatoes	1½ lb potatoes
½ small onion	½ small onion
salt and freshly ground black pepper	salt and freshly ground black pepper
200 ml/7 fl oz soured cream	¾ cup dairy sour cream
25 g/1 oz butter	2 tablespoons butter
chopped parsley to garnish	chopped parsley to garnish

Peel the potatoes and boil in salted water until just cooked. Peel and finely chop the onion. Drain and slice the potatoes and arrange in layers with the chopped onion in a greased casserole. Season the soured cream and pour over the potatoes. Cut the butter into small slivers and dot over the cream. Bake in a moderately hot oven (200°C, 400°F, Gas Mark 6) for about 20 minutes until the top is brown. Sprinkle with chopped parsley before serving.

Sesame Potato Patties

SERVES 4–6

METRIC/IMPERIAL	AMERICAN
450 g/1 lb potatoes, boiled in their skins	1 lb potatoes, boiled in their skins
8 black olives	8 ripe olives
½ clove garlic, crushed	½ clove garlic, crushed
1 teaspoon salt	1 teaspoon salt
15 g/½ oz margarine	1 tablespoon margarine
2 tablespoons medium matzo meal	3 tablespoons medium matzo meal
sesame seeds for coating	sesame seeds for coating
vegetable oil for frying	vegetable oil for frying

Peel the potatoes, place in a large mixing bowl and mash until free of lumps. Stone and chop the olives and add to the potatoes, together with the garlic, salt, margarine and matzo meal. Mix well and shape into patties.

Shake some sesame seeds on to a flat plate and press each side of the patties into the seeds. Fry the patties in shallow oil or on a lightly oiled griddle until they are golden brown on each side. *(Illustrated on pages 70–71)*

Potato Latkes

METRIC/IMPERIAL	AMERICAN
575 g/1¼ lb potatoes	1¼ lb potatoes
25 g/1 oz flour	¼ cup flour
1 egg, well beaten	1 egg, well beaten
salt and freshly ground black pepper	salt and freshly ground black pepper
vegetable oil for frying	vegetable oil for frying

Peel the potatoes and soak in cold water for 30 minutes. Dry well then grate on a fine grater into a colander or sieve. Press gently to drain off as much liquid as possible. Transfer the grated potatoes to a mixing bowl, add the flour and egg and season well with salt and a little pepper.

Heat a little vegetable oil in a frying pan. When hot, drop in tablespoons of the mixture and fry until brown on the underside. Turn and brown on the other side. Drain well on absorbent kitchen paper and serve hot. *(Illustrated on page 41)*

Variation

Add grated onion to the mixture.

Serve sprinkled with castor sugar.

Potato Kugel (Pudding)

✡

SERVES 4

METRIC/IMPERIAL	AMERICAN
675 g/1½ lb potatoes	1½ lb potatoes
1 small onion	1 small onion
1 tablespoon chicken fat or margarine	1 tablespoon chicken fat or margarine
1 egg, beaten	1 egg, beaten
salt and freshly ground black pepper	salt and freshly ground black pepper

Peel the potatoes and cook in boiling salted water. Drain well and mash until smooth. Peel and finely grate the onion and add to the potato together with the chicken fat or margarine, the beaten egg, salt and pepper. Mix very well. Transfer the mixture to a greased, shallow ovenproof dish and bake in a cool oven (150°C, 300°F, Gas Mark 2) for 2 hours.

Stuffed Baked Potatoes

✡

Choose large potatoes of uniform size if possible, scrub them clean, prick with a fork and bake in a moderate oven (160°C, 325°F, Gas Mark 3) until they are soft. This takes about 1 hour but the time will vary according to the size of the potato. When cooked, cut each potato in half and remove the pulp carefully, keeping the skin intact. Place the pulp in a mixing bowl and mash until it is free of lumps. Add 1 teaspoon margarine or butter for each potato and season with salt and freshly ground black pepper.

Add any of the following ingredients, fill the case with the mixture and smooth over with a wet knife. Put a small knob of butter or margarine on the top and return to the oven for 8–10 minutes until the filling is hot.

Suggested stuffings

Grated cheese Use 1 tablespoon for each ½ potato, and sprinkle with grated cheese and a little paprika before reheating.

Fish Use flaked smoked haddock, canned salmon or tuna. Allow 1 tablespoon fish for each ½ potato.

Meat Use minced, salt or smoked beef or tongue. Allow 1 tablespoon meat to each ½ potato and add ½ teaspoon lightly fried onion and ½ teaspoon margarine to each tablespoon of meat.

Cottage cheese For each ½ potato add 1 tablespoon cottage cheese mixed with chopped spring onions (scallions), a little lemon juice and chopped parsley. This cottage cheese filling should not be returned to the oven but the filled potato should be served immediately.

Sauerkraut

SERVES 6–8

METRIC/IMPERIAL	AMERICAN
1 onion	1 onion
2 large cooking apples	2 large baking apples
50 g/2 oz margarine	¼ cup margarine
450 g/1 lb sauerkraut	1 lb sauerkraut
150 ml/¼ pint boiling water	⅔ cup boiling water
1 potato	1 potato
1 teaspoon sugar	1 teaspoon sugar
caraway seeds	caraway seeds

Peel and thinly slice the onion. Peel, core and dice the apples.

Melt the margarine in a large saucepan. Add the sauerkraut, apples and onion and stir well. Pour over the boiling water. Put the lid on the pan and cook over a moderate heat for 30 minutes. Peel and finely grate the potato and add to the sauerkraut together with the sugar and a few caraway seeds. Continue cooking for a further 15 minutes until the sauerkraut is tender. An alternative method is to cook the sauerkraut in a casserole in the oven. Serve hot. *(Illustrated on pages 70–71)*

Fried Courgettes

SERVES 4–6

METRIC/IMPERIAL	AMERICAN
450 g/1 lb courgettes	1 lb zucchini
seasoned flour for coating	seasoned flour for coating
salt and freshly ground black pepper	salt and freshly ground black pepper
vegetable oil for frying	vegetable oil for frying

Wash the courgettes and dry thoroughly. Slice into 1-cm/½-inch rings and put on a plate. Sprinkle with salt and set aside for 30 minutes. Rinse under cold running water and dry well on absorbent kitchen paper. Coat the courgettes in seasoned flour and black pepper. Shallow fry in hot oil until golden brown on both sides. Serve hot. *(Illustrated on pages 70–71)*

Baked Onions

SERVES 4

METRIC/IMPERIAL	AMERICAN
450 g/1 lb small onions	1 lb small onions
1 tablespoon soft brown sugar	1 tablespoon soft brown sugar
salt and freshly ground black pepper	salt and freshly ground black pepper
freshly grated nutmeg	freshly grated nutmeg
50 g/2 oz margarine	¼ cup margarine
300 ml/½ pint stock, made with a chicken stock cube	1¼ cups stock, made with a chicken bouillon cube

Peel the onions and cook in boiling salted water for 5–10 minutes. Drain well and transfer to a greased, shallow ovenproof dish. Sprinkle with brown sugar, salt, pepper and nutmeg and dot with the margarine. Pour over the stock, cover and bake in a moderate oven (180°C, 350°F, Gas Mark 4) for 1 hour, keeping the onions well basted with the stock.

Red Cabbage with Apple

SERVES 6–8

METRIC/IMPERIAL	AMERICAN
675 g/1½ lb red cabbage	1½ lb head red cabbage
2 large cooking apples	2 large baking apples
1 large onion	1 large onion
50 g/2 oz margarine	¼ cup margarine
1 teaspoon salt	1 teaspoon salt
450 ml/¾ pint stock or water	2 cups stock or water
1 teaspoon sugar	1 teaspoon sugar
2 tablespoons vinegar or lemon juice	3 tablespoons vinegar or lemon juice
1 teaspoon cornflour	1 teaspoon cornstarch
½ teaspoon dry mustard	½ teaspoon dry mustard

Remove and discard any withered outer leaves and cut the cabbage into quarters. Cut out the hard centre stalk and shred the cabbage finely. Put in a bowl and cover with boiling water. Set aside for 15 minutes and then drain. Peel, core and slice the apples. Peel and slice the onion.

Melt the margarine in a large saucepan, add the cabbage and stir well with a wooden spoon. Sprinkle with the salt, cover the saucepan and cook gently for 10 minutes, stirring occasionally. Add the stock or water, the apples, onion, sugar and vinegar. Simmer very slowly with the lid on for 50 minutes or until the cabbage is tender.

Strain off the liquid into a small saucepan and add the cornflour and mustard, blended in a little cold water. Bring to the boil, stirring continuously until it thickens, then lower the heat and simmer for 2 minutes. Transfer the cabbage to a hot serving dish and pour the sauce over. Serve hot. Sausages are very good with red cabbage. Lay them on top of the cabbage for the last 30 minutes of cooking.

Chestnuts and Brussels Sprouts

METRIC/IMPERIAL	AMERICAN
450 g/1 lb Brussels sprouts	1 lb Brussels sprouts
225 g/8 oz chestnuts (see note)	½ lb chestnuts (see note)
25 g/1 oz margarine	2 tablespoons margarine
salt and freshly ground black pepper	salt and freshly ground black pepper
freshly grated nutmeg	freshly grated nutmeg

Slit the skins of the chestnuts and cook in boiling water for 15 minutes. Take out a few at a time and remove the outer and inner skins with a sharp knife. Place the skinned chestnuts in salted water and bring to the boil. Cook until tender and then drain (the water can be added to soup or used in stock). Meanwhile prepare and cook the sprouts.

Mix together the hot sprouts and cooked chestnuts, place in a casserole dish, dot with margarine and sprinkle with salt, freshly ground black pepper and a little nutmeg. Place in a moderate oven (160°C, 325°F, Gas Mark 3) for 10 minutes and serve immediately.

Note Dried chestnuts reconstituted can be used if fresh chestnuts are not available.

Meatless Carrot Tzimmas

SERVES 4

METRIC/IMPERIAL	AMERICAN
450 g/1 lb carrots	1 lb carrots
2 tablespoons chicken fat	3 tablespoons chicken fat
75 g/3 oz brown sugar	¼ cup brown sugar
300 ml/½ pint water	1¼ cups water
salt	salt
pinch of ground ginger	dash of ground ginger

Scrape and dice the carrots. Heat the chicken fat in a saucepan, add the carrots and cook over a moderate heat until lightly browned.

Boil the sugar and water together for 5 minutes and add to the carrots. Boil gently for 10–15 minutes or until the carrots are tender and most of the water has evaporated. Stir in a little salt and a pinch of ginger and serve hot.

Aubergine Bake

SERVES 4

METRIC/IMPERIAL	AMERICAN
1 large aubergine, about 450 g/1 lb	1 large eggplant, about 1 lb
2 large tomatoes	2 large tomatoes
olive oil for frying	olive oil for frying
1 small clove garlic, crushed	1 small clove garlic, crushed
salt and freshly ground black pepper	salt and freshly ground black pepper
25 g/1 oz fine fresh breadcrumbs	½ cup fine fresh bread crumbs
1 tablespoon chopped parsley	1 tablespoon chopped parsley
15 g/½ oz hard cheese, grated	2 tablespoons hard cheese, grated
oregano	oregano

Wash the aubergine and cut into rounds about 5 mm/¼ inch thick. Put on a plate, sprinkle with salt and set aside for about 30 minutes. Rinse under cold running water and dry well on absorbent kitchen paper.

Place the tomatoes in boiling water for a minute, drain, remove the skins and cut into thick slices.

Heat the olive oil and fry the aubergine slices until brown on each side. Add the garlic and tomatoes and seasoning. Fry gently for 3–4 minutes. Remove from the frying pan and place in a shallow ovenproof dish.

Mix together the breadcrumbs, parsley, cheese and oregano, sprinkle over the aubergine and tomatoes and bake in a moderately hot oven (200°C, 400°F, Gas Mark 6) for 8–10 minutes or until lightly browned. Serve hot. *(Illustrated on pages 70–71)*

Stuffed Aubergines

SERVES 4

METRIC/IMPERIAL	AMERICAN
4 medium aubergines	4 medium eggplants
2 yellow or red peppers	2 yellow or red peppers
2 small onions	2 small onions
50 g/2 oz butter or margarine	¼ cup butter or margarine
50 g/2 oz fresh breadcrumbs	1 cup fresh soft bread crumbs
50 g/2 oz cheese, grated, (see note)	½ cup grated cheese (see note)
salt and freshly ground black pepper	salt and freshly ground black pepper

Remove the stalks from the aubergines and cook in boiling salted water for 15 minutes.

Meanwhile remove the stalks and seeds from the peppers. Reserve half a pepper and chop the remainder. Peel and chop the onions.

Melt the butter or margarine in a saucepan, add the onions and peppers and cook gently for 5 minutes. Add the breadcrumbs and cheese then season lightly. Drain the aubergines and place in cold water until cool enough to handle.

Halve the aubergines and scoop out the flesh; chop this and add to the pepper and onion mixture. Fill the aubergine shells with the mixture, arrange on a greased ovenproof dish and cook in a moderately hot oven (200°C, 400°F, Gas Mark 6) for 30 minutes. Slice the reserved pepper and arrange on the aubergines 5 minutes before the end of the cooking time. *(Illustrated on page 69)*

Note The cheese may be replaced with chopped cooked meat, if preferred, in which case use margarine for cooking the vegetables.

Fried Leeks

SERVES 4–6

METRIC/IMPERIAL	AMERICAN
675 g/1½ lb leeks	1½ lb leeks
vegetable oil for frying	vegetable oil for frying
salt and freshly ground black pepper	salt and freshly ground black pepper
chopped parsley	chopped parsley

Cut off the root end and the upper green part of the leeks (the green part can be used for soup). Remove any coarse outer layers and cut the leeks in half lengthways. Wash thoroughly, especially between the layers, to remove any grit. Drain and dry well on absorbent kitchen paper. Cut across into rough slices.

Heat a little vegetable oil in a thick-based frying pan and add the leeks. Season, place a lid on the pan and fry for about 5 minutes until they begin to soften. Transfer to a hot serving dish and sprinkle with parsley.

Carrots with Parsnips

SERVES 6–8

METRIC/IMPERIAL	AMERICAN
450 g/1 lb carrots	1 lb carrots
450 g/1 lb parsnips	1 lb parsnips
25 g/1 oz butter or margarine	2 tablespoons butter or margarine
salt and freshly ground black pepper	salt and freshly ground black pepper

Peel and dice the vegetables and boil in salted water until tender. Drain, mash well with the butter or margarine and add seasoning to taste. Serve immediately.

Alternatively this vegetable mixture is very good reheated and will keep in the refrigerator for 2 or 3 days. To reheat, place in a greased casserole, cover and bake in a moderate oven (180°C, 350°F, Gas Mark 4) for 30 minutes. *(Illustrated on pages 70–71)*

Asparagus

✡

METRIC/IMPERIAL	AMERICAN
450 g/1 lb asparagus (see method)	1 lb asparagus (see method)
French dressing (see page 96) or mayonnaise (see page 99) or Hollandaise sauce (see page 83)	French dressing (see page 96) or mayonnaise (see page 99) or Hollandaise sauce (see page 93)

Select freshly cut asparagus if possible, but it will keep for a day or two in a cool place if the ends of the stalks are kept in water.

Wash and scrape the stalks from the base of the green tips downwards. Cut to a convenient length and tie in two or four bundles with tape, keeping the tips together. Soak in cold water for 1 hour. Have ready a saucepan, half-filled with boiling water and large enough to allow the asparagus to lie down flat.

Boil the asparagus gently for about 20 minutes or until the green part is tender. Drain well and serve warm with French dressing, mayonnaise, Hollandaise sauce or melted butter. Alternatively, serve cold with mayonnaise or French dressing.

Marrow with Cheese

✡

SERVES 6–8

METRIC/IMPERIAL	AMERICAN
1 kg/2 lb marrow	2 lb summer squash
1 large onion	1 large onion
25 g/1 oz butter	2 tablespoons butter
3 eggs	3 eggs
225 g/8 oz hard cheese, grated	2 cups hard cheese, grated
1 tablespoon double cream (optional)	1 tablespoon heavy cream (optional)
salt and freshly ground black pepper	salt and freshly ground black pepper
chopped parsley	chopped parsley

Wash and peel the marrow. Take out the seeds and cut the flesh into 2.5-cm/1-inch cubes. Poach in salted water until tender then drain very well and place in a greased casserole dish. Peel and finely chop the onion and sauté in the butter until soft but not brown. Spoon the onion over the marrow. Beat the eggs, add the grated cheese and cream, if used, season with pepper and just a little salt, add the chopped parsley and pour over the marrow. Bake in a moderate oven (180°C, 350°F, Gas Mark 4) for about 20 minutes until a pale, golden colour.

Baked Spinach Turnovers

✡

MAKES 20

METRIC/IMPERIAL	AMERICAN
For the dough	*For the dough*
225 g/8 oz butter	1 cup butter
1 teaspoon salt	1 teaspoon salt
350 g/12 oz self-raising flour	3 cups all-purpose flour sifted with 3 teaspoons baking powder
lukewarm water	lukewarm water
For the filling	*For the filling*
50 g/2 oz cheese, grated	½ cup grated cheese
200 g/7 oz cooked spinach	1 cup cooked spinach
3 egg yolks	3 egg yolks
For the glaze	*For the glaze*
1 egg yolk	1 egg yolk
1 teaspoon water	1 teaspoon water
sesame seeds	sesame seeds

Melt the butter and rub it into the salt and flour. Add enough water to make a manageable dough. Roll out on a lightly floured board and cut out 20 small rounds.

Mix the filling ingredients together and put a generous teaspoon on to each round.

Combine the egg yolk and water, brush the edges of the rounds and pinch together. Brush with the glaze. Sprinkle with sesame seeds and arrange on a greased baking sheet. Bake in a moderately hot oven (190°C, 375°F, Gas Mark 5) for 25 minutes. *(Illustrated on page 72)*

Sauces

Sauces add richness and flavour to the most simple food. But it is true to say that they take up extra time which may be at a premium, especially before the evening meal. A sauce is best made just before serving but if this is not possible make it in advance and keep it warm in a double saucepan over boiling water. Hot sauces should be served really hot so do reheat thoroughly before serving. Chill cold sauces – they should be served really cold.

If you have a microwave oven, sauces can be made up early in the day and reheated in the sauceboat just as the meal is going to the table.

Sauces can be frozen in rigid plastic containers and defrosted overnight in the refrigerator.

Large quantities of basic white sauce can be made up and frozen in 300 ml/$\frac{1}{2}$ pint (U.S. $1\frac{1}{4}$ cups) portions, then defrosted and made up into parsley or cheese sauce as they are needed.

Small portions of unused sauce can be frozen in ice cube trays. Divide into cubes once frozen and store the cubes together in a polythene bag. Select the number of cubes needed and reheat these slowly, preferably in a non-stick pan. Bulk quantities of curry or tomato sauce can be frozen in cubes and used for sauce or in small quantities for flavouring soups and casseroles.

The basis of most hot sauces is butter but chicken fat or margarine can be substituted for meat meals. The liquid can be milk, milk and water, or the stock of fish, meat or vegetables. The sauce can be thickened with arrowroot, cornflour, potato flour or rice flour mixed smoothly with a little cold liquid. Add to the boiling liquid and simmer gently for 5–10 minutes.

For a coating sauce allow

25 g/1 oz (U.S. 2 tablespoons) fat
25 g/1 oz (U.S. ¼ cup) flour to
300 ml/½ pint (U.S. 1¼ cups) liquid

For a pouring sauce allow

25 g/1 oz (U.S. 2 tablespoons) fat
25 g/1 oz (U.S. ¼ cup) flour to
300–450 ml/¾–1 pint (U.S. 2½ cups) liquid

For a thick binding sauce allow

25 g/1 oz (U.S. 2 tablespoons) fat
25 g/1 oz (U.S. ¼ cup) flour
150 ml/¼ pint (U.S. ⅔ cup) liquid

Basic White Sauce

MAKES ABOUT 300 ML/½ PINT (U.S. 1¼ CUPS)

METRIC/IMPERIAL	AMERICAN
25 g/1 oz butter	2 tablespoons butter
25 g/1 oz flour	¼ cup flour
300 ml/½ pint milk or stock	1¼ cups milk or white stock
salt and white pepper	salt and white pepper
lemon juice	lemon juice

Melt the butter in a small thick-based sauce-pan. Add the flour and mix well together. Cook over a very gentle heat for 1–2 minutes without browning. Remove the pan from the heat and pour in the liquid gradually, mixing well between each addition. Then bring to the boil over a gentle heat, stirring continuously until it boils and thickens. Add salt and pepper to taste and simmer for 5 minutes. Remove from the heat and add a squeeze of lemon juice.

Note For a meat meal use chicken fat or margarine instead of butter, and white stock instead of milk.

Variations

Cheese sauce Add 50–100 g/2–4 oz (U.S. ½–1 cup) grated Cheddar cheese and a little made mustard. Stir over a low heat until the cheese melts but do not allow the sauce to boil.

Mustard sauce Add 2 teaspoons dry mustard to the flour before blending with the fat, and stir in 1 tablespoon vinegar before serving.

Parsley sauce Add 1 tablespoon finely chopped parsley.

Piccalilli sauce Add 1 tablespoon finely chopped piccalilli (to serve with herrings or white fish).

Quick White Sauce

MAKES ABOUT 300 ML/½ PINT (U.S. 1¼ CUPS)

METRIC/IMPERIAL	AMERICAN
25 g/1 oz butter or margarine	2 tablespoons butter or margarine
25 g/1 oz flour	¼ cup flour
300 ml/½ pint milk or white stock	1¼ cups milk or white stock
salt and white pepper	salt and white pepper
little lemon juice	little lemon juice

Put all the ingredients into a thick-based saucepan. Place over a moderate heat and bring to the boil, whisking continuously with a hand whisk. Cook for 2–3 minutes until the sauce has thickened and is smooth and glossy.

Gravy

MAKES ABOUT 300 ML/$\frac{1}{2}$ PINT (U.S. 1$\frac{1}{4}$ CUPS)

METRIC/IMPERIAL	AMERICAN
1 tablespoon fat from the meat (see method)	1 tablespoon meat drippings (see method)
meat juices (see method)	meat juices (see method)
1 tablespoon flour	1 tablespoon flour
300 ml/$\frac{1}{2}$ pint stock or water	1$\frac{1}{4}$ cups stock or water
vegetable extract (optional)	vegetable extract (optional)
gravy browning (optional)	gravy coloring (optional)

After removing a joint of meat from a roasting tin, pour off all but 1 tablespoon of the fat and the meat juices. To the fat and meat juices left in the tin add 1 tablespoon of flour and stir over a gentle heat until it browns. Gradually add the stock or water with a little vegetable extract added, if wished. Bring to the boil, stirring continuously, then simmer for 3 minutes. If necessary, add a few drops of gravy browning and then strain into a gravy boat.

Hollandaise Sauce

MAKES ABOUT 300 ML/$\frac{1}{2}$ PINT (U.S. 1$\frac{1}{4}$ CUPS)

METRIC/IMPERIAL	AMERICAN
25 g/1 oz butter or margarine	2 tablespoons butter or margarine
15 g/$\frac{1}{2}$ oz flour	2 tablespoons flour
300 ml/$\frac{1}{2}$ pint vegetable stock	1$\frac{1}{4}$ cups vegetable stock
2 egg yolks	2 egg yolks
1 tablespoon lemon juice	1 tablespoon lemon juice
salt and freshly ground black pepper	salt and freshly ground black pepper

Melt half the butter in a small thick-based saucepan over a low heat. Stir in the flour and cook for 1–2 minutes, stirring frequently.

Gradually add the stock, mixing well between each addition, then bring to the boil, stirring continuously until the mixture boils and thickens slightly. Cook for 2 minutes. Remove from the heat and cool.

Mix the egg yolks with 1 tablespoon cold water and beat into the sauce. Put in a double saucepan and stir over a gentle heat until it thickens. The sauce must not boil or it will curdle. Add the lemon juice and remaining butter little by little. Add seasoning to taste then pour through a fine sieve. Serve warm.

Horseradish Sauce

Scrub and scrape the horseradish root then grate finely. Add sufficient white vinegar to cover and castor sugar to taste.

Variations

Mix horseradish with an equal quantity of grated sour cooking apple, before adding sugar and vinegar.

Add 1 tablespoon grated horseradish to 150 ml/$\frac{1}{4}$ pint (U.S. $\frac{2}{3}$ cup) mayonnaise.

Beetroot horseradish sauce
Peel and grate 1 medium beetroot and mix with 225 g/8 oz finely grated horseradish root. Add $\frac{1}{2}$ teaspoon salt and sufficient white vinegar to cover. Add castor sugar to taste.

As an alternative to horseradish sauce, finely grate some raw swede (rutabaga), then to 75 g/3 oz (U.S. $\frac{1}{2}$ cup) add 2 teaspoons made English mustard and sufficient vinegar to moisten.

Horseradish Sauce (Hot)

MAKES ABOUT 300 ML / ½ PINT (U.S. 1¼ CUPS)

METRIC/IMPERIAL	AMERICAN
1 teaspoon sugar	1 teaspoon sugar
300 ml / ½ pint white sauce (see page 82)	1¼ cups white sauce (see page 82)
1 tablespoon grated horseradish root	1 tablespoon grated horseradish root
1 teaspoon vinegar	1 teaspoon vinegar

Add the sugar to the sauce and bring slowly to the boil, stirring frequently. Mix the horseradish with the vinegar then stir into the hot sauce.

Creamed Horseradish

METRIC/IMPERIAL	AMERICAN
2 tablespoons mayonnaise (see page 99)	3 tablespoons mayonnaise (see page 99)
1 tablespoon grated horseradish root	1 tablespoon grated horseradish root
½ teaspoon finely chopped chives or spring onions	½ teaspoon finely chopped chives or scallions
½ teaspoon finely chopped parsley	½ teaspoon finely chopped parsley
1 tablespoon single or double cream	1 tablespoon light or heavy cream

Beat all the ingredients together lightly and chill well.
Serve with hot or cold fish dishes.

Mint Sauce

METRIC/IMPERIAL	AMERICAN
3 tablespoons chopped fresh mint (see method)	¼ cup chopped fresh mint (see method)
1 tablespoon granulated sugar	1 tablespoon sugar
2 tablespoons boiling water	3 tablespoons boiling water
150 ml / ¼ pint malt vinegar	⅔ cup malt or white wine vinegar

Pick the leaves from the stalks and wash and dry thoroughly. Place on a chopping board, sprinkle with a little of the sugar and chop very finely. It is very much easier to chop the leaves when they are sprinkled with sugar.

Put the chopped leaves and remaining sugar into a bowl, add the boiling water and set aside until cold. Add the vinegar.

Variation

Honey mint sauce Mix together 1 tablespoon each of honey and chopped mint and 4 tablespoons (U.S. ⅓ cup) hot malt vinegar. It is best left to stand until the following day.

Tartare Sauce

MAKES ABOUT 300 ML / ½ PINT (U.S. 1¼ CUPS)

METRIC/IMPERIAL	AMERICAN
300 ml / ½ pint mayonnaise (see page 99)	1¼ cups mayonnaise (see page 99)
2 teaspoons finely chopped chives	2 teaspoons finely chopped chives
2 teaspoons finely chopped gherkins	2 teaspoons finely chopped sweet dill pickles
1 teaspoon chopped parsley	1 teaspoon chopped parsley
2 finely sliced spring onions	2 finely sliced scallions

Mix all the ingredients together and chill well.
Serve with cold fish dishes.

Hot Tartare Sauce

MAKES ABOUT 300 ML/½ PINT (U.S. 1¼ CUPS)

METRIC/IMPERIAL	AMERICAN
300 ml/½ pint white sauce (see page 82 and method)	1¼ cups white sauce (see page 82 and method)
1 tablespoon mayonnaise (see page 99)	1 tablespoon mayonnaise (see page 99)
½ teaspoon vinegar	½ teaspoon vinegar
1 teaspoon finely chopped onion	1 teaspoon finely chopped onion
1 teaspoon chopped capers	1 teaspoon chopped capers
1 teaspoon chopped parsley	1 teaspoon chopped parsley
1 teaspoon chopped chives	1 teaspoon chopped chives

Make the white sauce using half milk and half fish stock. While the sauce is hot, add the mayonnaise, vinegar, chopped onion, capers, parsley and chives, and reheat without boiling.

Serve with boiled, baked or fried fish.

Tomato Sauce

MAKES ABOUT 450 ML/¾ PINT (U.S. 2 CUPS)

METRIC/IMPERIAL	AMERICAN
225 g/8 oz tomatoes (see note)	½ lb tomatoes (see note)
50 g/2 oz margarine	¼ cup margarine
1 tablespoon chopped onion	1 tablespoon chopped onion
300 ml/½ pint stock	1¼ cups stock
1 clove garlic, crushed	1 clove garlic, crushed
½ teaspoon oregano (optional)	½ teaspoon oregano (optional)
25 g/1 oz flour	¼ cup flour
½ teaspoon sugar	½ teaspoon sugar
salt and freshly ground black pepper	salt and freshly ground black pepper

Scald the tomatoes in boiling water for ½ minute, then drain, peel and roughly chop.

Melt half the margarine in a saucepan, add the chopped onion and cook over a gentle heat for 5 minutes. Add the tomatoes, stock, garlic and oregano, cover and cook slowly for 20 minutes. Rub through a sieve or blend for 1 minute in a liquidiser to make a tomato purée.

Melt the remaining margarine in a thick-based saucepan, stir in the flour and gradually add the tomato purée, mixing well between each addition. Bring to the boil, stirring continuously until the sauce thickens. Add the sugar, season to taste and simmer for 5 minutes.

Note Concentrated tomato purée (paste) or drained canned tomatoes can replace fresh tomatoes.

Sweet and Sour Sauce

MAKES ABOUT 300 ML/½ PINT (U.S. 1¼ CUPS)

METRIC/IMPERIAL	AMERICAN
25 g/1 oz margarine	2 tablespoons margarine
25 g/1 oz flour	¼ cup flour
300 ml/½ pint stock	1¼ cups stock
2 tablespoons vinegar	3 tablespoons vinegar
1 tablespoon brown sugar or golden syrup	1 tablespoon brown sugar or corn syrup
salt and freshly ground black pepper	salt and freshly ground black pepper

Melt the margarine in a thick-based saucepan. Stir in the flour and cook over a gentle heat until brown. Gradually add the stock and vinegar, mixing well between each addition. Bring to the boil, stirring continuously until the mixture thickens. Add the sugar or syrup, season to taste and simmer for 5 minutes.

Serve with root vegetables, fish or boiled brisket.

Wine Sauce

MAKES ABOUT 300 ML/½ PINT (U.S. 1¼ CUPS)

METRIC/IMPERIAL	AMERICAN
300 ml/½ pint thickened gravy (see page 83)	1¼ cups thickened gravy (see page 83)
2 tablespoons red wine	3 tablespoons red wine
2 tablespoons redcurrant jelly	3 tablespoons red currant jelly
juice of ½ lemon	juice of ½ lemon
salt and freshly ground black pepper	salt and freshly ground black pepper

Bring the gravy to the boil and stir in the remaining ingredients. Simmer for 1 minute and serve hot with cutlets or roast mutton.

Cumberland Sauce

MAKES ABOUT 300 ML/½ PINT (U.S. 1¼ CUPS)

METRIC/IMPERIAL	AMERICAN
225 g/8 oz redcurrant jelly	½ lb red currant jelly
1 tablespoon made English mustard	1 tablespoon made English mustard
salt and freshly ground black pepper	salt and freshly ground black pepper
2 tablespoons red wine	3 tablespoons red wine
1 teaspoon dark rum	1 teaspoon dark rum
2 teaspoons lemon juice	2 teaspoons lemon juice
2 teaspoons orange juice	2 teaspoons orange juice
¼ teaspoon Worcestershire sauce	¼ teaspoon Worcestershire sauce

Mix all the ingredients together and serve cold with roast lamb or warm with boiled tongue.

Curry Sauce

MAKES ABOUT 300 ML/½ PINT (U.S. 1¼ CUPS)

METRIC/IMPERIAL	AMERICAN
1 small apple	1 small apple
1 onion	1 onion
25 g/1 oz margarine	2 tablespoons margarine
1 tablespoon flour	1 tablespoon flour
1 tablespoon curry powder	1 tablespoon curry powder
1 teaspoon curry paste	1 teaspoon curry paste
300 ml/½ pint stock	1¼ cups stock
1 teaspoon chutney	1 teaspoon chutney
1 teaspoon lemon juice	1 teaspoon lemon juice
salt	salt
25 g/1 oz sultanas (optional)	¼ cup seedless white raisins (optional)
2 teaspoons desiccated coconut (optional)	2 teaspoons shredded coconut (optional)

Peel and roughly chop the apple, peel and finely chop the onion. Fry both in the margarine until the onion is lightly browned. Stir in the flour, curry powder and curry paste and cook for 1–2 minutes. Gradually add the stock and stir continuously until the liquid boils and thickens. Add the chutney, lemon juice and salt, and the sultanas and coconut if used. Cover and simmer gently for 20 minutes.

Egg and Lemon Sauce

MAKES ABOUT 450 ML/$\frac{3}{4}$ PINT (U.S. 2 CUPS)

METRIC/IMPERIAL	AMERICAN
grated rind and juice of 2 lemons	grated rind and juice of 2 lemons
450 ml/$\frac{3}{4}$ pint chicken broth	2 cups chicken bouillon
2 teaspoons cornflour	2 teaspoons corn-starch
2 egg yolks, beaten	2 egg yolks, beaten
salt and freshly ground black pepper	salt and freshly ground black pepper

Add the lemon rind to the chicken broth and bring to the boil. Mix the cornflour with the lemon juice to a smooth paste and stir into the hot broth. Bring to the boil, stirring continuously until the soup boils and thickens slightly. Lower the heat and simmer for 5 minutes. Remove from the heat and cool.

Add the cooled soup to the beaten egg yolks in the top of a double saucepan. Place over a moderate heat and stir until the sauce thickens, being careful not to let it boil. Season to taste and serve with boiled chicken.

Barbecue Sauce

MAKES ABOUT 150 ML/$\frac{1}{4}$ PINT (U.S. $\frac{2}{3}$ CUP)

METRIC/IMPERIAL	AMERICAN
3 tablespoons vinegar	$\frac{1}{4}$ cup vinegar
1 teaspoon made English mustard	1 teaspoon made English mustard
1 teaspoon brown sugar	1 teaspoon brown sugar
1 tablespoon redcurrant jelly	1 tablespoon red currant jelly
$\frac{1}{2}$ teaspoon paprika	$\frac{1}{2}$ teaspoon paprika
3 tablespoons tomato ketchup	$\frac{1}{4}$ cup tomato ketchup
2 tablespoons water	3 tablespoons water

Place all the ingredients together in a small thick-based saucepan and heat gently until well blended. Serve hot with barbecued meat such as lamb chops, chicken and beefburgers.

Jam Sauce

MAKES ABOUT 300 ML/$\frac{1}{2}$ PINT (U.S. 1$\frac{1}{4}$ CUPS)

METRIC/IMPERIAL	AMERICAN
4 tablespoons apricot jam	$\frac{1}{3}$ cup apricot jam
300 ml/$\frac{1}{2}$ pint water	1$\frac{1}{4}$ cups water
juice of $\frac{1}{2}$ lemon	juice of $\frac{1}{2}$ lemon
1 teaspoon cornflour	1 teaspoon corn-starch
1 tablespoon sherry (optional)	1 tablespoon sherry (optional)

Put the jam, water and lemon juice in a saucepan and bring slowly to the boil. Mix the cornflour to a smooth thin paste with a little cold water, stir into the jam and simmer for 5 minutes. Strain if necessary to remove any fruit skin, reheat and add the sherry.

Serve hot with sponge puddings and ice creams.

Custard Sauce

MAKES 300 ML/$\frac{1}{2}$ PINT (U.S. 1$\frac{1}{4}$ CUPS)

METRIC/IMPERIAL	AMERICAN
300 ml/$\frac{1}{2}$ pint milk	1$\frac{1}{4}$ cups milk
2 egg yolks	2 egg yolks
1 tablespoon sugar	1 tablespoon sugar
few drops vanilla essence	few drops vanilla extract

Heat the milk but do not let it boil. Beat the egg yolks with the sugar, pour on the hot milk and strain into a saucepan. Stir over a gentle heat until it thickens. Do not let it boil or it will curdle. Remove from the heat and add the vanilla essence.

Marmalade Sauce

MAKES ABOUT 300 ML/½ PINT (U.S. 1¼ CUPS)

METRIC/IMPERIAL	AMERICAN
1 teaspoon cornflour	1 teaspoon corn-starch
300 ml/½ pint water	1¼ cups water
3 tablespoons orange marmalade	¼ cup orange marmalade
25 g/1 oz sugar	2 tablespoons sugar
juice of ½ lemon	juice of ½ lemon

Mix the cornflour to a smooth thin paste with a little of the water. Pour the remaining water into a small saucepan and add the marmalade, sugar and lemon juice. Heat gently until warm, then stir in the cornflour paste and stir continuously until boiling. Simmer for 5 minutes.

Serve hot with sponge puddings.

Syrup Sauce

MAKES ABOUT 150 ML/¼ PINT (U.S. ⅔ CUP)

METRIC/IMPERIAL	AMERICAN
2 tablespoons golden syrup	3 tablespoons maple syrup
juice of ½ lemon	juice of ½ lemon
150 ml/¼ pint water	⅔ cup water
1 teaspoon cornflour	1 teaspoon corn-starch
¼ teaspoon ground ginger	¼ teaspoon ground ginger

Put the syrup, lemon juice and water in a saucepan and bring to the boil. Mix the cornflour and ginger to a thin smooth paste with a little cold water, add to the syrup mixture and stir continuously until it boils. Simmer gently for 5 minutes.

Serve hot with ginger puddings and ice creams.

Hard Sauce

MAKES ABOUT 100 G/4 OZ (U.S. ½ CUP)

METRIC/IMPERIAL	AMERICAN
50 g/2 oz butter or margarine	¼ cup butter or margarine
50 g/2 oz soft brown sugar	¼ cup soft brown sugar
1 tablespoon brandy or rum	1 tablespoon brandy or rum

Cream the butter or margarine and sugar together until soft and fluffy. Beat in the brandy or rum very gradually.

Chill before serving.

Butterscotch Sauce

MAKES ABOUT 200 ML/7 FL OZ (U.S. ¾ CUP)

METRIC/IMPERIAL	AMERICAN
175 g/6 oz soft brown sugar	¾ cup soft brown sugar
50 g/2 oz butter	¼ cup butter
1 tablespoon golden syrup	1 tablespoon corn or maple syrup
4 tablespoons milk	⅓ cup milk

Heat all the ingredients together in a double saucepan for 30 minutes. Serve warm over vanilla ice cream.

Sherry Sauce

✡

MAKES ABOUT 150 ML/$\frac{1}{4}$ PINT (U.S. $\frac{2}{3}$ CUP)

METRIC/IMPERIAL	AMERICAN
2 egg yolks	2 egg yolks
50 g/2 oz castor sugar	$\frac{1}{4}$ cup sugar
2 tablespoons sherry	3 tablespoons sherry

Put all the ingredients in the top of a double saucepan or in a bowl over a saucepan of hot water and whisk until thick and frothy.

Serve immediately with hot sponge puddings and ice cream.

Fudge Sauce

✡

MAKES ABOUT 200 ML/7 FL OZ (U.S. $\frac{3}{4}$ CUP)

METRIC/IMPERIAL	AMERICAN
5 tablespoons golden syrup	6 tablespoons corn syrup
1 (170-g/6-oz) can evaporated milk	1 (6-oz) can evaporated milk

Place the golden syrup and evaporated milk in a small thick-based saucepan and cook over a gentle heat for 3–4 minutes. Stand the pan in cold water until the sauce is cold.

Serve cold with ice creams, profiteroles and sponge puddings.

Chocolate Sauce

✡

MAKES ABOUT 100 ML/4 FL OZ (U.S. $\frac{1}{2}$ CUP)

METRIC/IMPERIAL	AMERICAN
50 g/2 oz plain chocolate	2 squares semi-sweet chocolate
4 tablespoons golden syrup	$\frac{1}{3}$ cup corn syrup
15 g/$\frac{1}{2}$ oz margarine	1 tablespoon margarine
$\frac{1}{2}$ teaspoon instant coffee powder	$\frac{1}{2}$ teaspoon instant coffee powder

Place the ingredients in a bowl over a saucepan of hot water. When the chocolate and syrup have softened, beat until smooth and glossy.

Serve warm with ice creams, profiteroles and sponge puddings.

Rum Sauce

✡

MAKES A SCANT 300 ML/$\frac{1}{2}$ PINT (U.S. 1$\frac{1}{4}$ CUPS)

METRIC/IMPERIAL	AMERICAN
2 egg yolks	2 egg yolks
1 tablespoon castor sugar	1 tablespoon sugar
150 ml/$\frac{1}{4}$ pint water	$\frac{2}{3}$ cup water
strained juice of 1 lemon	strained juice of 1 lemon
6 tablespoons dark rum	$\frac{1}{2}$ cup dark rum

Beat the egg yolks into the sugar in the top of a double saucepan or in a bowl over a saucepan of hot water. Add the water, lemon juice and rum. Stir over hot but not boiling water until the sauce thickens.

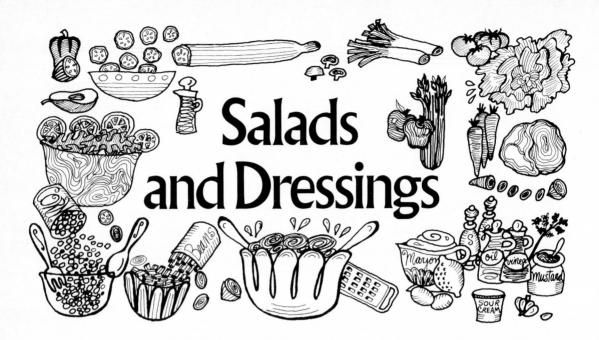

Salads and Dressings

Salads can start a meal, accompany the main course or be the main item on the menu. The ingredients from which salads can be made are almost unlimited. They include cooked and raw vegetables and fruit, beans and peas, nuts, cheese, rice, meat and eggs. A salad may be made from one ingredient only or from a combination of ingredients; unlike the majority of recipes quantities are not critical and ingredients may be left out or added according to availability and personal taste.

For speed and convenience use frozen or canned vegetables: canned sweet corn, asparagus, green beans and artichoke hearts are ideal and frozen peas, beans and mixed vegetables can be included in many winter salads.

Beans provide an economical addition to salad dishes and here the canned varieties are preferable to the dried ones which have to be soaked and cooked for a long time before they are ready for use. Chick peas and bean sprouts are less well known but are inexpensive and tasty additions to many recipes.

Grated cheese and cottage cheese added to or served with a salad makes a full meal while fresh herbs and nuts bring out the flavour of fruit and vegetables.

If you live near a continental greengrocer try the large Mediterranean tomatoes. They are more filling and tasty and are worth using where tomatoes constitute the main ingredient of the dish.

Green Salad

SERVES 4

METRIC/IMPERIAL	AMERICAN
1 lettuce	1 head lettuce
1 bunch watercress	1 bunch watercress
½ large cucumber	1 cucumber
1 green pepper	1 green pepper
6 spring onions	6 scallions
French dressing (see page 96)	French dressing (see page 96)

Wash and dry all the salad vegetables. Slice the unpeeled cucumber finely. Cut the green pepper and the spring onions into thin slices. Place the lettuce leaves and watercress sprigs in a salad bowl, add the prepared vegetables and toss in French dressing. (*Illustrated on pages 30–31*)

Israeli Salad

SERVES 4–6

METRIC/IMPERIAL	AMERICAN
1 lettuce	1 head lettuce
3 large tomatoes	3 large tomatoes
1 green pepper	1 green pepper
½ large cucumber	1 cucumber
few spring onions	few scallions
few radishes	few radishes
3 tablespoons chopped parsley	¼ cup chopped parsley
French dressing (see page 96)	French dressing (see page 96)

Wash and dry all the salad vegetables. Finely shred the lettuce and cut the tomatoes, green pepper and unpeeled cucumber into small dice. Slice the spring onions and radishes quite finely. Place the prepared vegetables with the parsley in a large salad bowl, add French dressing and toss well. (*Illustrated on page 59*)

Potato Salad

SERVES 4

METRIC/IMPERIAL	AMERICAN
450 g/1 lb potatoes (new, if in season)	1 lb potatoes (new, if in season)
2 spring onions, chopped, or 1 tablespoon chopped onion	2 scallions, chopped, or 1 tablespoon chopped orrion
1 tablespoon chopped parsley	1 tablespoon chopped parsley
salt and freshly ground black pepper	salt and freshly ground black pepper
oil and vinegar for the dressing	oil and vinegar for the dressing
½ teaspoon made mustard	½ teaspoon made mustard
150 ml/¼ pint mayonnaise (see page 99)	⅔ cup mayonnaise (see page 99)

Use waxy potatoes in preference to floury ones and of an even size, if possible. When new potatoes are not available choose the smallest of the old ones. Scrub thoroughly and boil slowly in their jackets until soft, taking care not to overcook. When cooked drain and leave in a colander.

When cool enough to handle, remove the skins and cut into dice or slices. Add the finely chopped onion and parsley, season and moisten with oil and vinegar mixed in equal parts. Leave until quite cold.

Mix the made mustard with the mayonnaise and mix into the potato salad. Pile into a salad bowl and serve at room temperature.

Note Potato salad is decidely better if dressed with the oil and vinegar when the potatoes are hot and mixed with the mayonnaise when cold. (*Illustrated on page 60*)

Variations

Add chives or gherkins (sweet dill pickles).

Add chopped raw celery, using as much potato as celery.

Cabbage Salad

Cabbage is always a very popular base for a salad, especially in the winter when many salad vegetables are not available.

Choose a medium-sized firm cabbage, remove the outside leaves, cut into quarters and cut out the hard centre stalk. Wash carefully and if necessary crisp in very cold water for about 15 minutes. Drain and dry well. Put on a board and with a very sharp knife cut across into fine shreds.

Use the cabbage in any (or a mixture) of the following combinations:

1 Serve plain with French dressing.

2 After dressing, sprinkle with caraway seeds.

3 Mix equal quantities of shredded red and white cabbage, and sprinkle with chopped nuts. *(Illustrated on page 60)*

4 Mix with equal quantities of grated raw carrot, thinly sliced green pepper and finely chopped onion.

5 Mix with grated apple and shredded celery.

6 Soak 50 g/2 oz of seedless raisins until they swell, drain then mix with the shredded cabbage.

7 Add a small carton of plain yogurt, thinned with a little lemon juice, instead of the normal dressing.

Dressing for cabbage The vinaigrette dressing (see page 96) with a teaspoon of tomato purée (paste) added is ideal for cabbage salads, but for a blander taste use the French dressing (see page 96).

Coleslaw

SERVES 6–8

METRIC/IMPERIAL	AMERICAN
450 g/1 lb white cabbage	1 lb head white cabbage
For the dressing	*For the dressing*
½ teaspoon mustard	½ teaspoon mustard
2 teaspoons sugar	2 teaspoons sugar
½ teaspoon salt	½ teaspoon salt
4 tablespoons vinegar	⅓ cup vinegar
4 tablespoons water	⅓ cup water
25 g/1 oz chicken fat or margarine	2 tablespoons chicken fat or margarine
1 teaspoon flour	1 teaspoon flour
1 egg	1 egg

Trim and finely shred the cabbage and place in a large salad bowl.

To make the dressing Mix together the mustard, sugar, salt, vinegar and water. Melt the fat in a small saucepan. Add the flour and stir with a wooden spoon until smooth, then gradually add the vinegar mixture and stir until boiling. Simmer for 5 minutes. Lightly beat the egg, pour over the dressing and mix well. Pour the hot dressing over the cabbage, toss and leave until quite cold before serving.

Apple and Celery Salad

SERVES 6–8

METRIC/IMPERIAL	AMERICAN
1 medium head celery	1 medium head celery
3 large dessert apples	3 large dessert apples
6 shelled walnuts	6 shelled walnuts
3 tablespoons mayonnaise (see page 99)	¼ cup mayonnaise (see page 99)
lemon juice	lemon juice

Wash and dice the celery, peel and dice the apples and chop the walnuts into rough pieces. Thin the mayonnaise with a little lemon juice and pour over the salad.

Filling Tomato Salad

SERVES 3–4

METRIC/IMPERIAL	AMERICAN
2 large tomatoes	2 large tomatoes
2 thick slices bread	2 thick slices bread
8 black olives	8 ripe olives
2 tablespoons chopped parsley	3 tablespoons chopped parsley
salt and freshly ground black pepper	salt and freshly ground black pepper
For the dressing	*For the dressing*
2 tablespoons wine vinegar	3 tablespoons wine vinegar
4 tablespoons olive oil	$\frac{1}{3}$ cup olive oil
6 tablespoons lemon juice	$\frac{1}{2}$ cup lemon juice
$\frac{1}{4}$ teaspoon sugar	$\frac{1}{4}$ teaspoon sugar
1 large clove garlic, crushed (optional)	1 large clove garlic, crushed (optional)
2 spring onions, finely chopped, for garnish	2 scallions, finely chopped, for garnish

Peel and finely chop the tomatoes. Use day-old bread about 2.5 cm/1 inch thick and cut into small cubes. Stone and finely chop the olives.

To make the dressing Mix all the ingredients together. Put the bread cubes into a salad bowl and pour the dressing over them. Leave for about 10 minutes for the bread to soak up the liquid.

Add the tomatoes, olives, chopped parsley and seasoning to taste. Mix well with a fork and garnish with chopped spring onions. *(Illustrated on page 42)*

Radish Salad with Soured Cream

SERVES 4

METRIC/IMPERIAL	AMERICAN
2 bunches radishes	2 bunches radishes
salt and freshly ground black pepper	salt and freshly ground black pepper
1 hard-boiled egg	1 hard-cooked egg
soured cream dressing (see page 99)	sour cream dressing (see page 99)
2 spring onions, chopped, for garnish	2 scallions, chopped, for garnish

Wash and trim the radishes and cut into thin slices. Sprinkle with salt and pepper. Separate the egg yolk and white. Sieve the yolk and chop the white. Mix the egg yolk with the soured cream dressing and pour over the radishes. Chill and serve garnished with egg white and chopped spring onions. *(Illustrated on page 97)*

Cucumber Salad with Soured Cream

SERVES 4–6

METRIC/IMPERIAL	AMERICAN
1 cucumber	1 cucumber
salt	salt
soured cream dressing (see page 99)	sour cream dressing (see page 99)
chopped parsley for garnish	chopped parsley for garnish

Peel the cucumber with a potato peeler and cut into very thin slices. Place on a dish, sprinkle with salt and leave for 30 minutes. Drain thoroughly and cover the cucumber with soured cream dressing. Chill and serve garnished with chopped parsley. *(Illustrated on page 97)*

Rice Salad

SERVES 4

METRIC/IMPERIAL	AMERICAN
100 g/4 oz long-grain rice	½ cup long-grain rice
100 g/4 oz cooked tongue	¼ lb cooked tongue
100 g/4 oz cooked peas	¾ cup cooked peas
2 tablespoons currants	3 tablespoons currants
For the dressing	*For the dressing*
4 tablespoons olive oil	⅓ cup olive oil
2 tablespoons lemon juice	3 tablespoons lemon juice
salt and white pepper	salt and white pepper
½ teaspoon sugar	½ teaspoon sugar
2 teaspoons chopped mint for garnish	2 teaspoons chopped mint for garnish

Wash the rice and cook in lightly salted water for about 15 minutes until soft. Drain and rinse under cold running water. Chop the tongue. Mix the rice, tongue, peas and currants in a salad bowl. Mix all the ingredients for the dressing and pour over the rice mixture. Mix well and garnish with the mint. *(Illustrated on page 98)*

Note Cooked chicken can be used instead of the tongue.

Chicory Salad (1)

SERVES 2

METRIC/IMPERIAL	AMERICAN
1 head chicory	1 head Belgian endive
1 small green pepper	1 small green pepper
1 banana	1 banana
For the dressing	*For the dressing*
1 tablespoon olive oil	1 tablespoon olive oil
2 teaspoons lemon juice	2 teaspoons lemon juice
½ teaspoon ground ginger	½ teaspoon ground ginger
salt	salt
pinch of sugar	dash of sugar

Trim the chicory and wash and drain the leaves. Blanch the green pepper in boiling water for 3 minutes, drain and cut into strips. Slice the banana.

Arrange the chicory on a plate with the green pepper and banana on top. Mix together all the ingredients for the dressing and pour over the salad. *(Illustrated on page 98)*

Chicory Salad (2)

SERVES 2

Prepare one head of chicory as for the previous recipe, then finely shred the leaves.

Mix the chicory with a peeled and diced dessert apple, moisten with mayonnaise and garnish with sliced tomato.

Bean and Corn Salad

SERVES 4

METRIC/IMPERIAL	AMERICAN
1 (283-g/10-oz) can red kidney beans	1 (10-oz) can red kidney beans
1 (326-g/11½-oz) can sweet corn	1 (11½-oz) can corn
1 (227-g/8-oz) packet frozen green beans	1 (8-oz) package frozen green beans
vinaigrette dressing (see page 96)	vinaigrette dressing (see page 96)

Drain the canned beans and the corn. Cook the green beans then rinse under cold running water and drain well. Mix all the vegetables together and toss in the vinaigrette dressing before serving. *(Illustrated on page 98)*

Note This is a filling tasty salad which also looks good because of the combination of colours. The size of cans can be varied, depending on individual tastes and the number of people to be served. Cut green beans should be used in preference to sliced beans and canned beans can replace frozen beans.

Avocado Salad

SERVES 4–6

METRIC/IMPERIAL	AMERICAN
225 g/8 oz white cabbage	½ lb white cabbage
50 g/2 oz shelled walnuts	½ cup shelled walnuts
4 large tomatoes	4 large tomatoes
1 large ripe avocado	1 large ripe avocado
For the dressing	*For the dressing*
2 tablespoons olive oil	3 tablespoons olive oil
2 tablespoons vinegar	3 tablespoons vinegar
salt and freshly ground black pepper	salt and freshly ground black pepper
½ onion	½ onion
1 clove garlic	1 clove garlic

Shred the cabbage, chop the walnuts, peel and slice the tomatoes. Peel and stone the avocado and chop into rough pieces. Arrange the cabbage, walnuts and tomatoes in a salad bowl with the avocado on top.

To make the dressing Put the oil and vinegar into a liquidiser, add the salt, pepper, onion and the garlic cut into slices. Blend for 30 seconds then pour over the salad. *(Illustrated on page 97)*

Carrot Salad

SERVES 4

METRIC/IMPERIAL	AMERICAN
450 g/1 lb carrots	1 lb carrots
50 g/2 oz raisins (see note)	⅓ cup raisins (see note)
For the dressing	*For the dressing*
4 tablespoons oil	⅓ cup oil
2 tablespoons lemon juice	3 tablespoons lemon juice
8 sprigs parsley	8 sprigs parsley
½ teaspoon sugar	½ teaspoon sugar
salt and freshly ground black pepper	salt and freshly ground black pepper
2 cloves garlic	2 cloves garlic

Peel and grate the carrots. Place in a salad bowl with the raisins.

To make the dressing Pour the oil and lemon juice into a liquidiser. Add the parsley, sugar, salt, pepper and the garlic cut into slices. Blend for 30 seconds and pour over the carrot. *(Illustrated on page 98)*

Note Sultanas (seedless white raisins) may be used instead of raisins, but these should be soaked first to make them swell.

Cottage Cheese Salad

SERVES 2

METRIC/IMPERIAL	AMERICAN
1 small lettuce	1 small head lettuce
½ bunch radishes	½ bunch radishes
6 spring onions	6 scallions
1 (225-g/8-oz) carton cottage cheese	1 (8-oz) carton cottage cheese
1 (142-ml/5-fl oz) carton natural yogurt	⅔ cup plain yogurt
salt	salt

Wash and dry the lettuce. Shred the leaves finely and place in a salad bowl. Wash and trim the radishes and cut into thin slices. Prepare and clean the spring onions and chop finely. Mix the radishes with the cottage cheese and spoon over the lettuce. Add a little salt to the yogurt and pour over the cheese. Garnish with the chopped spring onion.

Salad Dressings

In this section are listed the basic dressings required for the salads in this chapter. However, the final choice of ingredients is optional.

Oil Olive oil has a distinctive flavour and is specially good with Mediterranean-type salads, including tomatoes and olives. However, many people find the taste heavy and in all cases vegetable or corn oil can be substituted.

Vinegar The herb-flavoured vinegars such as tarragon add interest to salad dressings but are much more expensive than malt vinegar. In most cases lemon juice is an acceptable alternative, with its lighter fresher taste, and it is worth trying to appreciate the difference.

The French and vinaigrette dressings can be made in large quantities and stored in a large screw-top jar in the refrigerator until needed. This is especially useful in the summer when salads are more likely to be eaten regularly.

The soured cream dressing should be eaten the same day and the mayonnaise will keep for 2–3 days in the refrigerator.

French Dressing

MAKES ABOUT 200 ML/7 FL OZ (U.S. $\frac{3}{4}$ CUP)

METRIC/IMPERIAL	AMERICAN
6 tablespoons salad oil	$\frac{1}{2}$ cup salad oil
4 tablespoons vinegar or lemon juice	$\frac{1}{3}$ cup vinegar or lemon juice
salt and freshly ground black pepper	salt and freshly ground black pepper
$\frac{1}{4}$ teaspoon sugar	$\frac{1}{4}$ teaspoon sugar

Lightly whisk all the ingredients together in a bowl or shake well in a screw-top jar.

Vinaigrette Dressing

MAKES ABOUT 200 ML/7 FL OZ (U.S. $\frac{3}{4}$ CUP)

METRIC/IMPERIAL	AMERICAN
6 tablespoons salad oil	$\frac{1}{2}$ cup salad oil
4 tablespoons vinegar or lemon juice	$\frac{1}{3}$ cup vinegar or lemon juice
salt and freshly ground black pepper	salt and freshly ground black pepper
$\frac{1}{2}$ teaspoon sugar	$\frac{1}{2}$ teaspoon sugar
$\frac{1}{2}$ teaspoon dry mustard	$\frac{1}{2}$ teaspoon dry mustard
1 small clove garlic, crushed	1 small clove garlic, crushed
parsley and chives (see note)	parsley and chives (see note)

Lightly whisk all the ingredients together in a bowl or shake well in a screw-top jar.

Note These are optional and depend on the season or the salad to be covered.

Avocado salad (see page 95); Radish salad with soured cream (see page 93); Cucumber salad with soured cream (see page 93)

Mayonnaise

MAKES ABOUT 300 ML/½ PINT (U.S. 1¼ CUPS)

METRIC/IMPERIAL	AMERICAN
2 egg yolks	2 egg yolks
¼ teaspoon made mustard	¼ teaspoon made mustard
¼ teaspoon sugar	¼ teaspoon sugar
salt and white pepper	salt and white pepper
cayenne	cayenne pepper
300 ml/½ pint salad oil	1¼ cups salad oil
2 teaspoons tarragon vinegar	2 teaspoons tarragon vinegar
1 tablespoon distilled vinegar or lemon juice	1 tablespoon distilled vinegar or lemon juice

Put the egg yolks into a bowl with the mustard, sugar, salt, pepper and cayenne. Use a wooden spoon, rotary whisk or wire whisk and add the oil drop by drop, beating continuously until the mixture thickens. Add a few drops of vinegar and then continue with the oil and vinegar alternately until all the ingredients are combined.

Quick Mayonnaise

MAKES ABOUT 300 ML/½ PINT (U.S. 1¼ CUPS)

METRIC/IMPERIAL	AMERICAN
1 teaspoon salt	1 teaspoon salt
1 teaspoon sugar	1 teaspoon sugar
¼ teaspoon dry mustard	¼ teaspoon dry mustard
pinch of cayenne	dash of cayenne pepper
1 tablespoon lemon juice	1 tablespoon lemon juice
1 tablespoon vinegar	1 tablespoon vinegar
1 tablespoon tarragon vinegar	1 tablespoon tarragon vinegar
2 egg yolks	2 egg yolks
250 ml/8 fl oz oil	1 cup oil

Put the salt, sugar, mustard, cayenne, lemon juice and vinegar into a liquidiser and blend for 15 seconds. Add the egg yolks and one-third of the oil and blend until the mixture begins to thicken. Trickle the remaining oil in slowly while the liquidiser is on and, if wished, stir in any of the following:
Chopped chives, spring onions (scallions), creamed horseradish sauce, soured cream, French mustard, chopped capers, sweet pickle, Worcestershire sauce, paprika, curry powder.

Soured Cream Dressing

MAKES ABOUT 150 ML/¼ PINT (U.S. ⅔ CUP)

METRIC/IMPERIAL	AMERICAN
1 (142-ml/5-fl oz) carton soured cream (see note)	⅔ cup dairy sour cream (see note)
1 tablespoon lemon juice	1 tablespoon lemon juice
½ teaspoon sugar	½ teaspoon sugar

Mix all the ingredients together and chill slightly before using.

Note Substitute natural yogurt for the soured cream for an equally refreshing dressing.

Carrot salad (see page 95); Bean and corn salad (see page 94); Rice salad (see page 94); Chicory salad (see page 94)

Lunch and Supper Dishes

Lunch and supper are the meals where the tendency may be not to cook, but to snack. Fresh brown bread and cheese is everybody's idea of a tasty snack, but not every day! The dishes in this chapter are not complicated; many of them take only a few minutes to prepare and the small effort is worth the 'lift' and feeling of relaxation that comes from taking a break.

Most of the ingredients are those that you would normally keep a supply of in the refrigerator or store cupboard. Mixtures of frozen or fresh vegetables, eggs and cheese together make a great variety of nutritious and slimming snacks. Ready prepared vegetarian pastry, or your own taken from the freezer, in addition to the food above can turn a quite ordinary dish into an interesting flan or quiche.

If omelettes are a family favourite a special pan is a good investment. A pan with a 15-cm/6-inch base will accommodate a 2–3 egg omelette, and an 18-cm/7-inch pan will do for up to 4 eggs. A 15- or 18-cm/6 or 7-inch soufflé dish will serve for both sweet and savoury soufflés and an 18- or 20-cm/7 or 8-inch flan tin for most pastry items. These dishes provide a basic 'kit' for the types of recipe most often chosen for lunch and supper dishes.

Ingredients left from a baking session can be kept and used to enrich snack meals. Extra yolks or whites of eggs can be added to omelettes or to soups to thicken them, and grated cheese wrapped in cling film and refrigerated or used straight from the freezer can be sprinkled on as a topping for a vegetable casserole or poached eggs. Milk left over from brushing pastry can be added to meatless soups to make them more filling.

Plain Omelette

METRIC/IMPERIAL	AMERICAN
3 eggs	3 eggs
2 tablespoons water	3 tablespoons water
I teaspoon chopped parsley	I teaspoon chopped parsley
salt and freshly ground black pepper	salt and freshly ground black pepper
15 g/½ oz butter or margarine	I tablespoon butter or margarine

Break the eggs into a bowl and beat them just sufficiently to blend the yolks and whites. Beat in the water and parsley and season with salt and pepper.

Place the omelette pan over a gentle heat. When it is hot put in the butter and as it melts tilt the pan to grease the sides, taking care that the butter does not brown. Pour in the eggs and increase the heat to moderate.

As soon as the omelette begins to set round the edge of the pan, loosen and lift it with a palette knife and tilt the pan to allow the uncooked egg to run underneath. When the egg is cooked underneath and just set on top, slip a palette knife round the side nearest the handle and double the omelette over. Leave in the pan for another moment then loosen underneath with the knife, tilt the pan and turn the omelette out on to a warmed plate.

The omelette should be soft and creamy inside with a smooth, yellow surface.

Variations

Seasoned omelettes Any of the following may be added to the egg before cooking: Chopped chives, grated onion, a pinch of mixed herbs or chopped spring onions (scallions).

Cheese omelette Add a tablespoon of finely grated dry cheese and sprinkle a little more on top before serving.

Asparagus omelette Add a few asparagus tips before cooking and garnish with a few more tips warmed in butter.

Filled Omelettes

When the omelette has been cooked and loosened from the pan, put the hot filling on one half, fold the other half over it and tilt the pan so that the omelette rolls on to the warmed plate.

Savoury filling

METRIC/IMPERIAL	AMERICAN
15 g/½ oz margarine	I tablespoon margarine
I small onion, peeled and finely chopped	I small onion, peeled and finely chopped
2 tomatoes, peeled and diced (drained, canned tomatoes will do)	2 tomatoes, peeled and diced (drained, canned tomatoes will do)
I clove garlic, crushed	I clove garlic, crushed
½ small green pepper, diced	½ small green pepper, diced

Melt the margarine in a frying pan, add the onion and fry until soft. Add the remaining ingredients and cook slowly for 10–15 minutes until the green pepper is soft.

Mushroom filling

Rinse and dry 50 g/2 oz (U.S. ½ cup) mushrooms then cut into thin slices. Sauté in a little butter or margarine in a covered saucepan for 10 minutes then season with salt and pepper.

Spanish Omelette

SERVES 1

METRIC/IMPERIAL	AMERICAN
1 medium potato	1 medium potato
1 shallot or ¼ large onion	1 shallot or ¼ large onion
1 tablespoon olive oil	1 tablespoon olive oil
1 egg	1 egg
salt and freshly ground black pepper	salt and freshly ground black pepper
pinch of paprika	dash of paprika pepper
½ teaspoon chopped parsley	½ teaspoon chopped parsley

Peel and very thinly slice the potato. Peel and finely chop the shallot or onion. Heat the oil in a frying pan and fry the potatoes and onions until golden brown. Beat the egg well, add the seasoning and parsley and pour over the cooked vegetables. Cook over a moderate heat until set and slightly brown on the underside. Fold over, slide on to a warm plate and serve with a salad.

Pancakes

MAKES 8–10

METRIC/IMPERIAL	AMERICAN
100 g/4 oz flour	1 cup flour
pinch of salt	dash of salt
1 egg	1 egg
300 ml/½ pint milk	1¼ cups milk
margarine or butter for frying	margarine or butter for frying
castor sugar	sugar
lemon juice	lemon juice

Sift the flour and salt into a bowl and make a well in the centre. Add the egg and half the milk and, using a wooden spoon or wire whisk, work in the flour so that the batter in the centre is smooth all the time. When all the flour has been absorbed, beat well for 2–3 minutes to make the mixture light and

airy. Then stir in the remaining liquid and pour into a jug ready for use.

To prepare the pan Warm a small frying pan, rub the base with a little salt and wipe clean with a piece of absorbent kitchen paper. This 'tempering' or 'proving' ensures that the pancakes will not stick – it need not be done again during the frying.

Melt the margarine or butter in a small saucepan and pour a little into the prepared frying pan over a moderate heat. When sizzling hot pour the excess back into the saucepan. A film of fat will be left on the surface of the pan which will be sufficient to fry the pancake.

Slowly pour just enough batter to cover the bottom of the pan. When set and lightly browned on one side, turn or toss and cook the other side. Turn out on to sugared paper and sprinkle with castor sugar and lemon juice. Serve immediately or roll up and keep hot on a plate over a saucepan of hot water until all the pancakes are ready.

Savoury pancakes

Cheese Add 50 g/2 oz (U.S. ½ cup) grated cheese to the batter; when fried, roll up and sprinkle with grated cheese.

Onion Add 1 finely grated onion, 1 tablespoon chopped parsley and a pinch of mixed herbs to the batter. Serve with thinly sliced leeks or onions fried a golden brown.

Stuffed pancakes Make pancakes with a plain batter and before rolling up put a spoonful of hot savoury filling (see page 101) in the centre.

Flaked smoked fish Mix cooked smoked haddock or cod with 2 chopped hard-boiled eggs, 2 teaspoons chopped parsley and a few drops of lemon juice. Bind together with white sauce or cheese sauce (see page 82).

Blintzes

MAKES ABOUT 12

METRIC/IMPERIAL	AMERICAN
For the basic batter	*For the basic batter*
110 g/4 oz plain flour	1 cup flour
pinch of salt	dash of salt
2 eggs	2 eggs
300 ml/½ pint water	1¼ cups water
filling (see below)	filling (see below)

To make the batter Sift the flour and salt into a mixing bowl. Mix the egg and water together and pour into the flour a little at a time, whisking continuously until all the liquid has been added and the mixture is smooth. If wished, use an electric mixer on slow speed. Leave the batter to stand for at least 30 minutes while the filling is being prepared.

To fry the blintzes Use an 18-cm/7-inch omelette pan so that the shape of the pancake can be well formed. Heat the pan then lightly grease with oil. Pour in 2 tablespoons of the batter, just sufficient to make a very thin pancake, and tilt the pan so that the batter runs level. Cook over a gentle heat on one side only until the batter will just hold its shape. Turn out on to a wooden board or clean teacloth with the cooked side uppermost. Fry the rest of the batter in the same way.

To fill the blintzes Put a tablespoon of the filling in the centre of each pancake and fold over into a triangle or envelope shape, pressing the edges well together. Fry in hot butter on both sides until golden brown. Serve hot. *(Illustrated on page 128)*

Note Blintzes once filled and fried are best served immediately, but if this is not possible they can be kept hot in the oven. They can be made in advance and refrigerated or frozen at the parcel stage.

Fillings

Cream cheese Use about 350 g/12 oz cream cheese, add a little sugar and grated lemon rind. Season with salt and pepper.

Curd cheese

METRIC/IMPERIAL	AMERICAN
450 g/1 lb curd cheese	1 lb curd cheese
2 egg yolks	2 egg yolks
1 tablespoon sugar	1 tablespoon sugar
¼ teaspoon cinnamon	¼ teaspoon cinnamon
salt to taste	salt to taste

Mix all the ingredients together for the filling and serve the blintzes with cold soured cream.

Apple

METRIC/IMPERIAL	AMERICAN
225 g/8 oz apples, peeled and grated	½ lb apples, peeled and grated
25 g/1 oz ground almonds	¼ cup ground almonds
grated rind and juice of ½ lemon	grated rind and juice of ½ lemon
1 tablespoon castor sugar	1 tablespoon superfine sugar
pinch of cinnamon	dash of cinnamon

Mix together the apple, almonds and lemon rind and juice for the filling and sprinkle the finished pancakes with sugar and cinnamon.

Meat Mince left-over cooked meat, add a little grated onion and chopped parsley, season with salt and pepper and add tomato ketchup to taste. Mix well and bind with beaten egg. Serve the blintzes covered with tomato sauce or thick gravy.

Lockshen and Cheese Kugel

SERVES 4

METRIC/IMPERIAL	AMERICAN
50 g/2 oz butter	$\frac{1}{4}$ cup butter
225 g/8 oz broad noodles	$\frac{1}{2}$ lb broad noodles
3 eggs, well beaten	3 eggs, well beaten
225 g/8 oz curd cheese	$\frac{1}{2}$ lb curd cheese
2 (142-ml/5-fl oz) cartons soured cream	$1\frac{1}{3}$ cups dairy sour cream
100 g/4 oz brown sugar	$\frac{1}{2}$ cup brown sugar
1 teaspoon salt	1 teaspoon salt

Grease a casserole dish very thoroughly. Soften the butter by leaving it at room temperature but don't allow it to oil. Boil the noodles in salted water until cooked but still firm. Drain and, while they are still hot, mix all the ingredients together.

Pour the mixture into a casserole and bake in a moderately hot oven (200°C, 400°F, Gas Mark 6) for 15 minutes, then lower the heat to moderate (180°C, 350°F, Gas Mark 4) for a further 1 hour. Serve hot.

Spinach Soufflé

SERVES 4

METRIC/IMPERIAL	AMERICAN
1 (227-g/8-oz) packet frozen chopped spinach, defrosted	1 (8-oz) package frozen chopped spinach, defrosted
25 g/1 oz butter or margarine	1 tablespoon butter or margarine
25 g/1 oz flour	$\frac{1}{4}$ cup flour
150 ml/$\frac{1}{4}$ pint milk	$\frac{2}{3}$ cup milk
3 eggs, separated	3 eggs, separated
salt and freshly ground black pepper	salt and freshly ground black pepper
pinch of mace	dash of mace
pinch of nutmeg	dash of nutmeg
$\frac{1}{2}$ teaspoon lemon juice	$\frac{1}{2}$ teaspoon lemon juice

Grease a 15-cm/6-inch soufflé dish. Drain the spinach well then toss in a small pan over a low heat to remove the excess moisture.

Melt the butter in a small thick-based saucepan. Stir in the flour and cook gently for 1–2 minutes. Remove from the heat and gradually add the milk, stirring well between each addition. Bring to the boil, stirring continuously until the mixture boils and thickens, then simmer for 2 minutes, still stirring. Remove from the heat. Lightly beat the egg yolks and add with the spinach, seasonings and lemon juice.

Whisk the egg whites until stiff and fold into the spinach mixture. Pour into the soufflé dish and bake in a preheated moderately hot oven (190°C, 375°F, Gas Mark 5) for 25–30 minutes until the soufflé is well risen and firm. Serve immediately.

Cheese Soufflé

SERVES 4

METRIC/IMPERIAL	AMERICAN
25 g/1 oz butter	2 tablespoons butter
20 g/$\frac{3}{4}$ oz flour	3 tablespoons flour
150 ml/$\frac{1}{4}$ pint milk	$\frac{2}{3}$ cup milk
75 g/3 oz cheese, finely grated	$\frac{3}{4}$ cup finely grated cheese
salt and white pepper	salt and white pepper
cayenne	cayenne pepper
pinch of dry mustard	dash of dry mustard
2 eggs, separated, and 1 extra egg white	2 eggs, separated, and 1 extra egg white

Grease a 15-cm/6-inch soufflé dish. Melt the butter in a small thick-based saucepan. Stir in the flour and cook gently for 1–2 minutes, then remove from the heat. Gradually add the milk, mixing well after each addition, then bring to the boil, stirring continuously until the mixture is thick. Remove from the heat, beat in the cheese, seasonings and egg yolks one at a time.

Whisk the egg whites until very stiff and fold into the cheese mixture. Pour into the soufflé dish and bake in a preheated moderately hot oven (190°C, 375°F, Gas Mark 5) for about 30 minutes until well risen and just firm in the centre. Serve immediately.

Cheese and Corn Flan

✡

SERVES 4–6

METRIC/IMPERIAL	AMERICAN
For the pastry case	*For the pie shell*
110 g/4 oz soft margarine	½ cup soft margarine
225 g/8 oz plain flour	2 cups all-purpose flour
1–2 tablespoons water to mix	2–3 tablespoons water to mix
For the filling	*For the filling*
1 (326-g/11½-oz) can sweet corn kernels	1 (11½-oz) can corn kernels
100 g/4 oz cheese, grated	1 cup grated cheese
150 ml/¼ pint milk	⅔ cup milk
2 eggs	2 eggs
salt and freshly ground black pepper	salt and freshly ground black pepper
pinch of dry mustard	dash of dry mustard

To make the pastry Put the margarine in a mixing bowl with 2 tablespoons (U.S. 3 tablespoons) flour and the water. Using a fork, cream the ingredients until well mixed then work in the remaining flour to form a soft dough. Knead lightly on a floured surface until smooth. Chill for 30 minutes then roll out and line a 20-cm/8-inch flan dish or ring.

Drain the sweet corn, mix with the cheese and place in the flan case. Beat the milk and eggs together, add the seasoning and pour over the corn and cheese.

Bake in a moderate oven (180°C, 350°F, Gas Mark 4) for 35–40 minutes until set.

Serve hot or cold.

Asparagus Flan

✡

SERVES 4–6

METRIC/IMPERIAL	AMERICAN
For the pastry case	*For the pie shell*
110 g/4 oz soft margarine	½ cup margarine
225 g/8 oz plain flour	2 cups all-purpose flour
1–2 tablespoons water to mix	2–3 tablespoons water to mix
For the filling	*For the filling*
450 g/1 lb fresh asparagus or 1 (425-g/15-oz) can asparagus	1 lb fresh asparagus or 1 (15-oz) can asparagus
2 eggs	2 eggs
1 (142-ml/5-fl oz) carton single cream	⅔ cup light cream
salt and freshly ground black pepper	salt and freshly ground black pepper

Make up the pastry as for the cheese and corn flan (see left) and line a 20-cm/8-inch flan dish or ring. Bake the pastry case 'blind' in a moderately hot oven (200°C, 400°F, Gas Mark 6) for 10 minutes. To bake 'blind', line the inside of the case with a round of greaseproof paper and fill with baking beans.

Meanwhile, cook and drain the fresh asparagus or, if using canned asparagus, drain well. Reserve 8 even-sized asparagus spears, chop the remainder and place in the pastry case. Whisk together the eggs and cream and season with salt and pepper. Arrange the reserved asparagus spears in the flan case in a cartwheel design and pour over the egg and cream mixture.

Place in the centre of a moderate oven (180°C, 350°F, Gas Mark 4) for 25–30 minutes until set and golden brown.

Serve hot or cold.

Baked Courgettes

SERVES 6

METRIC/IMPERIAL	AMERICAN
1 kg/2 lb courgettes	2 lb zucchini
75 g/3 oz butter	$\frac{1}{3}$ cup butter
1 (142-ml/5-fl oz) carton single cream	$\frac{2}{3}$ cup light cream
2 tablespoons grated cheese	3 tablespoons grated cheese
1 teaspoon chopped parsley	1 teaspoon chopped parsley
1 egg, beaten	1 egg, beaten
salt and freshly ground black pepper	salt and freshly ground black pepper

Peel and chop the courgettes. Cook in slightly salted boiling water for 5 minutes. Drain well then return to the saucepan with 50 g/2 oz (U.S. $\frac{1}{4}$ cup) of the butter, the cream, half the grated cheese, the parsley and the beaten egg. Stir gently, taking care not to break up the courgettes. Pour into a greased casserole, season and sprinkle on remaining cheese. Dot with remaining butter.

Bake in a moderately hot oven (200°C, 400°F, Gas Mark 6) for 5 minutes. Serve at once.

Cheesy Potato Cakes

SERVES 8–10

METRIC/IMPERIAL	AMERICAN
450 g/1 lb mashed potatoes	2 cups mashed potatoes
1 tablespoon melted margarine	1 tablespoon melted margarine
1 egg, beaten	1 egg, beaten
salt and freshly ground black pepper	salt and freshly ground black pepper
2 tablespoons flour	3 tablespoons flour
75 g/3 oz cheese, grated	$\frac{3}{4}$ cup grated cheese
flour for coating	flour for coating
fat for frying	fat for frying
beaten egg for glazing	beaten egg for glazing

Place the mashed potatoes in a mixing bowl, add the melted margarine, the beaten egg and seasoning. Stir in the cheese and the flour.

Shape into round flat cakes, about 7.5 cm × 1 cm/3 inches × $\frac{1}{2}$ inch and coat with flour. Fry in shallow fat until golden brown on both sides. Alternatively, place on a well-greased baking sheet, brush the top with beaten egg and bake in a hot oven (220°C, 425°F, Gas Mark 7) for about 20 minutes.

Curried Eggs

SERVES 4

METRIC/IMPERIAL	AMERICAN
4 eggs	4 eggs
225 g/8 oz long-grain rice	1 cup long-grain rice
1 small onion	1 small onion
1 medium cooking apple	1 medium baking apple
25 g/1 oz butter or margarine	2 tablespoons butter or margarine
1 tablespoon flour	1 tablespoon flour
2 teaspoons curry powder	2 teaspoons curry powder
300 ml/$\frac{1}{2}$ pint milk (see note)	1$\frac{1}{4}$ cups milk (see note)
1 teaspoon lemon juice	1 teaspoon lemon juice
salt and white pepper	salt and white pepper

Hard-boil the eggs and keep hot. Cook and drain the rice. Peel and finely chop the onion. Peel, core and chop the apple. Melt the butter in a saucepan, add the chopped onion and apple and fry until lightly browned. Stir in the flour and curry powder and gradually add the milk. Stir until boiling, then simmer gently for 10 minutes. Add the lemon juice and season to taste.

Shell and halve the eggs and place on a hot serving dish. Pour over the sauce and serve with the boiled rice.

Note Vegetable or meat stock can be used instead of milk when making the sauce.

Eggs with Spinach

SERVES 3 OR 6

METRIC/IMPERIAL	AMERICAN
1 (340-g/12-oz) packet frozen chopped spinach	1 (12-oz) package frozen chopped spinach
salt and freshly ground black pepper	salt and freshly ground black pepper
6 eggs	6 eggs
For the sauce	*For the sauce*
15 g/½ oz butter	1 tablespoon butter
15 g/½ oz flour	2 tablespoons flour
300 ml/½ pint milk	1¼ cups milk
salt and freshly ground black pepper	salt and freshly ground black pepper
juice of ½ lemon	juice of ½ lemon
225 g/8 oz cheese, grated	2 cups grated cheese
pinch of dry mustard	dash of dry mustard

Cook the spinach, following the instructions on the packet, drain and season with salt and pepper. Place in a shallow casserole and keep warm. Put the eggs on to poach and while they are cooking make the sauce.

Melt the butter in a small thick-based saucepan. Add the flour and mix well with a wooden spoon. Cook over a gentle heat for a minute or two without browning. Remove the pan from the heat and add the milk gradually, mixing well between each addition. Bring to the boil over a gentle heat, stirring continuously until it boils and thickens. Add salt and pepper and simmer for 5 minutes. Remove from the heat, add the lemon juice and stir in 175 g/6 oz (U.S. 1½ cups) of the cheese and a pinch of dry mustard.

Arrange the poached eggs on the spinach, cover with the cheese sauce and sprinkle with the remaining cheese. Place under a very hot grill for 2–3 minutes to brown. Serve hot.

Wurst and Eggs

SERVES 4–6

METRIC/IMPERIAL	AMERICAN
6 eggs	6 eggs
3 tablespoons water	¼ cup water
salt and freshly ground black pepper	salt and freshly ground black pepper
2 tablespoons oil	3 tablespoons oil
350 g/12 oz frying wurst, sliced	¾ lb frying wurst, sliced

Break the eggs into a jug, add the water and the seasoning and whisk well. Heat the oil in a large frying pan and place the slices of wurst side by side. Turn the wurst when the slices begin to brown and pour on the egg mixture. Fry without stirring until the eggs are just set and the underneath is brown. Slide on to a warmed serving dish and serve immediately.

Cheese Toast

SERVES 4–6

METRIC/IMPERIAL	AMERICAN
75 g/3 oz long-grain rice	½ cup long-grain rice
2 large fresh or canned tomatoes	2 large fresh or canned tomatoes
50 g/2 oz margarine	¼ cup margarine
100 g/4 oz cheese, grated	1 cup grated cheese
salt and freshly ground black pepper	salt and freshly ground black pepper
1 teaspoon vegetable extract	1 teaspoon vegetable extract

Boil the rice until tender and then drain well. Chop the tomatoes. Melt the margarine in a saucepan, add the tomatoes and cook gently for 2–3 minutes. Add the cheese, rice, salt, pepper and vegetable extract. Heat thoroughly and serve on slices of toast or fried bread.

Savoury Egg Cutlets

✡

METRIC/IMPERIAL	AMERICAN
3 hard-boiled eggs	3 hard-cooked eggs
2 tablespoons cooked long-grain rice	3 tablespoons cooked long-grain rice
2 tablespoons fresh breadcrumbs	3 tablespoons fresh bread crumbs
2 tablespoons grated cheese	3 tablespoons grated cheese
1 egg, separated	1 egg, separated
½ teaspoon curry powder	½ teaspoon curry powder
salt	salt
cayenne	cayenne pepper
milk (optional – see method)	milk (optional – see method)
dried brown bread-crumbs for coating	dry brown bread crumbs for coating
oil for frying	oil for frying

Shell and finely chop the hard-boiled eggs. Add the rice, fresh breadcrumbs, cheese, egg yolk, curry powder, salt and cayenne and mix well. If the mixture is dry, add a little milk. Form into cutlets, brush with lightly beaten egg white and coat with brown crumbs. Shallow fry until golden brown on both sides.

Rice Dishes

Of the several kinds of rice available long-grain rice is the most suitable for cooking savoury dishes and short-grain for puddings and moulds.

Both these types of rice are polished white grain with the husks removed. Brown unpolished rice, which is richer in protein and roughage, is available from health food shops and some of the larger supermarkets. It is a useful alternative to white and adds body and flavour to vegetable casseroles and other vegetarian type dishes.

The 'instant' rices have been partly cooked, and if you are not skilled at cooking rice, the final result is usually more successful.

An alternative to using rice in most savoury recipes is a cereal which originated in Eastern Europe called buckwheat, used in many Jewish recipes and referred to as kasha. This has a rich nutty flavour and cooks in less time than rice.

Allow approximately 50–75 g/2–3 oz (U.S. ¼–⅓ cup) uncooked rice per person. An average cup when full holds about 225 g/8 oz rice which when cooked would serve 3–4 people.

To wash rice

Place the rice in a strainer, place the strainer in a bowl of cold water and wash the rice well, changing the water two or three times, then drain.

To cook rice

If the grains of rice are to be kept separate, as in rice to accompany curry, then the rice must be boiled quickly on top of the cooker, but when this is not required rice can be cooked quite satisfactorily in the oven. Some kinds of rice absorb water more quickly than others, so examine the rice after it has been cooking for 15 minutes, and if necessary, add a little more boiling water.

Boiled Rice

SERVES 4–6

METRIC/IMPERIAL	AMERICAN
225 g/8 oz long-grain rice	1 cup long-grain rice
2.25 litres/4 pints water	5 pints water
1 tablespoon salt	1 tablespoon salt

Wash the rice. Pour the water into a saucepan, add the salt and bring to the boil. When it is boiling rapidly, sprinkle the rice in slowly keeping the water on the boil. Boil rapidly for 15–20 minutes until the grains feel tender if pinched between finger and thumb.

Strain the rice through a coarse sieve or colander and pour boiling water through to separate the grains. Dry in a hot oven (220°C, 425°F, Gas Mark 7) for 5 minutes.

Boiled Rice in the Oven

SERVES 4

METRIC/IMPERIAL	AMERICAN
100 g/4 oz long-grain rice	½ cup long-grain rice
1 teaspoon salt	1 teaspoon salt
600 ml/1 pint boiled water	2½ cups boiled water

Wash the rice well and place in a greased casserole. Add the salt and the water. Cover with a lid and bake in a moderately hot oven (200°C, 400°F, Gas Mark 6) for about 30 minutes. If necessary, add more water during cooking. When the rice is tender, drain off any excess water and return to the oven for 5 minutes to dry before serving.

Stuffed Peppers

SERVES 4

METRIC/IMPERIAL	AMERICAN
4 green peppers	4 green peppers
For the filling	*For the filling*
½ onion	½ onion
olive oil for frying	olive oil for frying
225 g/8 oz minced lamb or beef	1 cup ground lamb or beef
100 g/4 oz long-grain or short-grain rice	½ cup long-grain or short-grain rice
1 small clove garlic, crushed	1 small clove garlic, crushed
300 ml/½ pint chicken stock	1¼ cups chicken stock
½ teaspoon freshly grated nutmeg	½ teaspoon freshly grated nutmeg
salt and freshly ground black pepper	salt and freshly ground black pepper
For the sauce	*For the sauce*
2 tablespoons olive oil	3 tablespoons olive oil
1 (425-g/15-oz) can tomatoes, reduced to a pulp	1 (15-oz) can tomatoes, reduced to a pulp
salt and freshly ground black pepper	salt and freshly ground black pepper

Remove the tops of the peppers and reserve. Discard the seeds and pith. Place the peppers and reserved tops in a saucepan, cover with boiling salted water and simmer for 3–4 minutes. Drain well. Peel and finely chop the onions and fry in the oil until soft. Add the meat and fry until it changes colour. Then add the rice, garlic, stock, nutmeg, salt and pepper. Bring to the boil, cover and simmer gently for about 10 minutes until the rice has absorbed all the water. Remove from the heat and cool.

Place the peppers in a baking tin or flat casserole and fill with the rice mixture. Replace the tops. Pour the olive oil and tomato pulp around the peppers and season with salt and pepper. Cover the peppers tightly with a lid or with foil tucked under the rim of the dish and bake in a moderate oven (180°C, 350°F, Gas Mark 4) for 40–50 minutes until the peppers are softened. If necessary, add a little liquid during cooking.

Pilaff of Chicken Livers

✡

SERVES 4

METRIC/IMPERIAL	AMERICAN
For the rice mixture	*For the rice mixture*
225 g/8 oz long-grain rice	1 cup long-grain rice
1 tablespoon chicken fat	1 tablespoon chicken fat
1 tablespoon olive oil	1 tablespoon olive oil
1 tablespoon chopped onion	1 tablespoon chopped onion
50 g/2 oz fresh or frozen peas	$\frac{1}{3}$ cup fresh or frozen peas
25 g/1 oz mushrooms, chopped	$\frac{1}{4}$ cup chopped mushrooms
900 ml/1$\frac{1}{2}$ pints boiling chicken stock	3$\frac{3}{4}$ cups boiling chicken stock
2 tablespoons tomato sauce	3 tablespoons tomato sauce
salt and freshly ground black pepper	salt and freshly ground black pepper
For the chicken livers	*For the chicken livers*
225 g/8 oz chicken livers (see note)	$\frac{1}{2}$ lb chicken livers (see note)
1 tablespoon chicken fat	1 tablespoon chicken fat
4 spring onions (if available)	4 scallions (if available)
$\frac{1}{2}$ tablespoon ground allspice	2 teaspoons ground allspice

Wash the rice and leave to drain. Melt the chicken fat with the oil in a heavy saucepan, add the chopped onion, cover and cook gently for 5 minutes. Add the rice, peas and mushrooms, and stir for 1–2 minutes over a gentle heat. Add the boiling stock, tomato sauce and seasoning. Cover and cook gently for 20–30 minutes, stirring frequently until the rice is soft and the stock has been absorbed.

Meanwhile fry the chicken livers. Melt the chicken fat in a frying pan, add the chicken livers and cook quickly on both sides until just coloured. Lift out on to a hot plate and season with salt, pepper and allspice. In the same fat fry the spring onions for a few minutes to soften them.

When the rice mixture is nearly cooked, return the chicken livers to the frying pan and heat quickly with the spring onions. Arrange the rice mixture in a round on a hot serving dish. Make a depression on top and fill with the chicken liver mixture.

Note If chicken livers are not available substitute calf's liver or make the dish with cold veal which can be cut into dice and mixed with the rice 10 minutes before serving – just long enough to heat through.

Meat Kedgeree

✡

SERVES 4

METRIC/IMPERIAL	AMERICAN
100 g/4 oz long-grain or short-grain rice	$\frac{1}{2}$ cup long-grain or short-grain rice
150 g/6 oz cooked meat	6 oz cooked meat
1 hard-boiled egg	1 hard-cooked egg
1 small onion	1 small onion
$\frac{1}{2}$ green pepper	$\frac{1}{2}$ green pepper
50 g/2 oz margarine	$\frac{1}{4}$ cup margarine
salt and freshly ground black pepper	salt and freshly ground black pepper
$\frac{1}{2}$ teaspoon curry powder	$\frac{1}{2}$ teaspoon curry powder
1 tablespoon chopped parsley for garnish	1 tablespoon chopped parsley for garnish

Cook the rice in boiling salted water and drain well. Mince the meat. Separate the yolk and white of the hard-boiled egg, chop the white and sieve the yolk for garnish. Peel and finely chop the onion. Seed and finely chop the green pepper.

Melt the margarine in a saucepan and fry the onion and pepper until the onion is soft and lightly browned. Add the rice and the meat, season with salt, pepper and curry powder and stir over a gentle heat until thoroughly hot. Mix in the chopped white of egg and transfer the mixture to a hot serving dish. Garnish with sieved egg yolk and chopped parsley.

Pasta Dishes

All pasta is basically dried dough made into traditional shapes and sizes which are useful additions to the store cupboard because they keep well and are extremely versatile. They can be used to garnish soups, to accompany fish or meat main dishes, with fruit as a dessert or in salads. Most pasta bought in packs is dried and will keep many months but fresh pasta sold in some areas should be used within 2–3 days. Pasta alone can be too bland for most palates but it combines well with herbs, spices and other strong flavourings.

Dried pasta swells as it cooks. 50 g/2 oz dried pasta becomes about 150 g/6 oz when cooked. For a main course, allow 100 g/4 oz cooked pasta per person.

To boil macaroni or spaghetti

Allow 600 ml/1 pint (U.S. 2½ cups) water and ½ teaspoon salt for each 50 g/2 oz pasta. Cook in fast boiling water with the pan uncovered.

Spaghetti should be boiled without being broken. Lean the strands against the side of the pan and let them slide gradually into the boiling water. Cooking time will be between 12–20 minutes, depending on the quantity being cooked.

Unless cut macaroni is being used, break it into shorter lengths. Quick-cooking macaroni generally needs only 7 minutes boiling; follow the packet instructions carefully. The stick or thicker varieties will take 15–25 minutes.

Basic Recipe for Cooking Macaroni or Spaghetti in the Oven

METRIC/IMPERIAL	AMERICAN
100 g/4 oz pasta	¼ lb pasta
600 ml/1 pint boiling water	2½ cups boiling water
1 teaspoon salt	1 teaspoon salt

Place the pasta in a large casserole. Add the water and salt, cover and cook in a moderately hot oven (190°C, 375°F, Gas Mark 5) until tender. This will take between 15–40 minutes depending on the type used. The 'quick cooking' packet macaroni softens very quickly. Drain off any excess water and reserve for sauces or soups.

Meat and Apple Macaroni

✡

SERVES 3–4

METRIC/IMPERIAL	AMERICAN
175 g/6 oz minced cooked meat	¾ cup ground cooked meat
300 g/10 oz cooked macaroni	2½ cups cooked macaroni
300 ml/½ pint thick gravy	1¼ cups thick gravy
salt and freshly ground black pepper	salt and freshly ground black pepper
350 g/12 oz cooking apples	¾ lb baking apples
1 teaspoon sugar	1 teaspoon sugar
fresh brown breadcrumbs for topping	fresh brown bread crumbs for topping
15 g/½ oz margarine	1 tablespoon margarine

Mix together the meat, macaroni and gravy. Season and turn into a casserole. Peel, core and finely chop the apples and place on top. Sprinkle with the sugar and brown breadcrumbs and dot with margarine.

Bake in a moderate oven (180°C, 350°F, Gas Mark 4) for 30–40 minutes until heated through.

Macaroni Cheese

SERVES 3–4

METRIC/IMPERIAL	AMERICAN
150 g/6 oz macaroni	1½ cups macaroni
50 g/2 oz margarine	¼ cup margarine
75 g/3 oz cheese, grated	¾ cup grated cheese
salt and freshly ground black pepper	salt and freshly ground black pepper
25 g/1 oz fresh brown breadcrumbs	½ cup fresh brown bread crumbs
For the sauce	*For the sauce*
25 g/1 oz margarine	2 tablespoons margarine
25 g/1 oz flour	¼ cup flour
300 ml/½ pint milk and macaroni water	1¼ cups milk and macaroni water
salt and freshly ground black pepper	salt and freshly ground black pepper
2 tablespoons grated cheese	3 tablespoons grated cheese
½ teaspoon made mustard	½ teaspoon made mustard

Cook and drain the macaroni.

To make the sauce Melt the fat in a small thick-based saucepan. Stir in the flour with a wooden spoon. Cook over a very gentle heat for 2 minutes without browning. Remove the pan from the heat and gradually add the liquid, mixing well between each addition, then stir over a gentle heat until it boils and thickens. Add the seasoning, grated cheese and the mustard. Stir over a gentle heat until the cheese has melted.

Put a layer of the cooked macaroni in a greased casserole and pour over enough of the cheese sauce to cover it. Sprinkle with salt, pepper and a little of the grated cheese. Repeat the layers, sprinkle the top with the remaining cheese mixed with the breadcrumbs and dot with margarine. Heat in a hot oven (220°C, 425°F, Gas Mark 7) for about 15 minutes until browned.

Sausages and Savoury Noodles

SERVES 4

METRIC/IMPERIAL	AMERICAN
450 g/1 lb sausages	1 lb sausages
175 g/6 oz tomatoes	6 oz tomatoes
50 g/2 oz margarine	¼ cup margarine
3 tablespoons chopped onions	¼ cup chopped onions
2 tablespoons vinegar	3 tablespoons vinegar
2 teaspoons seedless jam	2 teaspoons seedless jam
1 teaspoon sugar	1 teaspoon sugar
½ teaspoon paprika	½ teaspoon paprika pepper
1 teaspoon made mustard	1 teaspoon made mustard
100 g/4 oz cooked noodles	¼ lb cooked noodles
salt and freshly ground black pepper	salt and freshly ground black pepper

Grill the sausages under medium heat and keep hot when cooked. Meanwhile peel and slice the tomatoes. Melt the margarine in a thick-based frying pan, add the chopped onion and the tomatoes and fry until the onions are soft and lightly browned. Add the vinegar, jam, sugar, paprika and mustard. Cover and cook very gently for 5 minutes.

Add the noodles to the mixture in the pan and heat gently for 4–5 minutes, stirring frequently. Add seasoning to taste. Turn the noodles into a hot serving dish and surround with the cooked sausages.

Spaghetti Bolognese

SERVES 4–6

METRIC/IMPERIAL	AMERICAN
1 onion	1 onion
100 g/4 oz mushrooms	1 cup mushrooms
1 clove garlic	1 clove garlic
1 small green pepper	1 small green pepper
1 (425-g/15-oz) can tomatoes	1 (15-oz) can tomatoes
600 ml/1 pint stock (see method)	2½ cups stock (see method)
3 tablespoons oil	¼ cup oil
450 g/1 lb minced beef	1 lb ground beef
2 tablespoons tomato purée	3 tablespoons tomato paste
1 teaspoon sugar	1 teaspoon sugar
1 teaspoon oregano	1 teaspoon oregano
salt and freshly ground black pepper	salt and freshly ground black pepper
450 g/1 lb spaghetti	1 lb spaghetti
2 teaspoons cornflour	2 teaspoons cornstarch
chopped parsley for garnish	chopped parsley for garnish

Peel and chop the onion, rinse and chop the mushrooms, peel and crush the garlic. Seed and finely chop the green pepper. Drain the tomatoes, reserve the liquid and add to the stock to make 600 ml/1 pint (U.S. 2½ cups).

Heat the oil in a pan and fry the onion and green pepper until the onion is browned. Add the beef, mushrooms, garlic and tomatoes and cook for a further 3 minutes to brown the meat. Stir in the tomato purée, sugar and oregano. Season and add the stock. Cover and cook gently for about 40 minutes.

Meanwhile cook the spaghetti in boiling salted water and drain well. Place on a hot serving dish.

Blend the cornflour with a little cold water and stir into the meat mixture. Cook the sauce for a further 5 minutes then serve over the spaghetti. Garnish with chopped parsley.

Ravioli

SERVES 4–6

Home-made ravioli is a time-consuming dish to prepare but the special taste is very rewarding. Make up the noodle dough (see Lockshen, page 33), roll out very thinly and cut into 7.5-cm/ 3-inch squares.

Meat filling

METRIC/IMPERIAL	AMERICAN
225 g/8 oz minced cooked meat and sausagemeat	1 cup ground cooked meat and sausage meat
40 g/1½ oz fine fresh breadcrumbs	¾ cup fine fresh bread crumbs
2 teaspoons grated onion	2 teaspoons grated onion
salt and freshly ground black pepper	salt and freshly ground black pepper
1 egg	1 egg

Cheese filling

METRIC/IMPERIAL	AMERICAN
225 g/8 oz curd cheese	1 cup curd cheese
salt and freshly ground black pepper	salt and freshly ground black pepper
1 tablespoon top of the milk	1 tablespoon top of the milk
1 tablespoon chopped parsley	1 tablespoon chopped parsley

To prepare each filling, mix all the ingredients together thoroughly. Place a teaspoon of filling in the centre of each square, dampen the edges of the dough and fold the squares into triangles, pressing the edges well together. Leave on a floured board for 1 hour to dry. Drop the ravioli a few at a time into boiling salted water and cook steadily for 20 minutes. Drain thoroughly, put on a hot dish and coat the meat ravioli with thick gravy and the cheese with grated cheese.

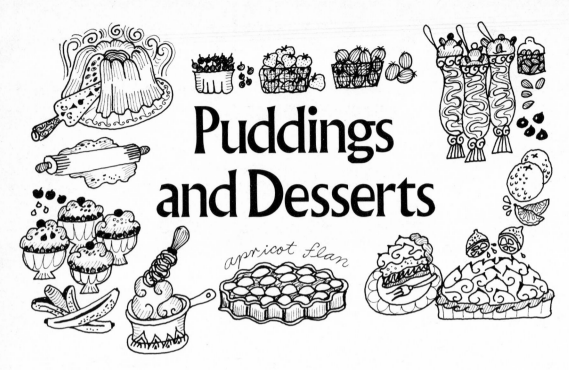

Puddings and Desserts

apricot flan

It is possible to use more imagination in the serving and decorating of desserts than perhaps any of the other courses, and for this reason many people believe that the dessert course is the most difficult to make. Most of the recipes in this chapter are uncomplicated but tasty.

The use of the liquidiser eliminates much of the hard work previously associated with baking desserts, but the one area where care and a certain amount of skill is still needed is pastry making. However, this problem can be completely overcome by simply buying the pastry. Vegetarian shortcrust and puff pastry are readily available as are the more exotic pastries. Ready frozen or fresh strudel pastry can be found in many delicatessens. Bought pastry is a very useful standby but making one's own is well worth the effort in most cases.

Overleaf are the recipes for shortcrust and biscuit crust pastries, the most used for pies and flans.

Gingerbread ring (see page 134)

Shortcrust Pastry

MAKES 225 G/8 OZ PASTRY

METRIC/IMPERIAL	AMERICAN
225 g/8 oz plain flour	2 cups all-purpose flour
pinch of salt	dash of salt
110 g/4 oz margarine	½ cup margarine
2 tablespoons water	3 tablespoons water

Sift the flour and salt into a bowl, add the margarine and cut it into the flour with a knife. Then rub it in lightly with the finger-tips until the mixture resembles fine bread-crumbs. Add the cold water and mix with a palette knife until a stiff paste is formed and the sides and base of the bowl are clean. Turn on to a lightly floured board, knead lightly until free of cracks, then roll, cut and use as required.

Biscuit Crust Pastry

MAKES 225 G/8 OZ PASTRY

For flans and pies

METRIC/IMPERIAL	AMERICAN
225 g/8 oz plain flour	2 cups all-purpose flour
1 tablespoon castor sugar	1 tablespoon sugar
150 g/5 oz butter	⅔ cup butter
1 teaspoon lemon juice	1 teaspoon lemon juice
1 teaspoon cold water	1 teaspoon cold water
1 egg yolk	1 egg yolk

Sift the flour and sugar into a bowl and make a well in the centre. Add the butter in pieces. Mix together the lemon juice and water and stir in the egg yolk with a fork. Pour on to the butter in the bowl, and then make the pastry by the same method as the shortcrust pastry.

Note Omit the sugar for a savoury flan.

Baked oranges (see page 121)

These quantities of shortcrust and biscuit crust pastry will make 15 tartlet cases or line a 18–20-cm/7–8-inch flan ring or an average sized plate pie.

The following hints may help when making pastry:

1 All the utensils should be cold and dry.

2 Use block margarine at room temperature. Block margarine is preferable to the soft tub variety which should be used straight from the refrigerator.

3 Never stretch the pastry or it will shrink away at the edges during baking.

2 Preheat the oven so that it is the correct temperature before baking the pastry.

Fruit Pies

Almost any kind of fruit – fresh, canned, frozen or bottled – may be used, or a mixture of fruits; the soft summer fruits are delicious when mixed. Large fruit should be cut into pieces. Apples are improved if grated lemon rind or one or two cloves are added.

Fill the pie dish with fruit and sugar in layers; the quantity of fruit will vary according to availability, the size of the dish and individual taste. The top layer should always be fruit as sugar is apt to make the crust sugary. Pile the fruit slightly in the centre and with certain fruit add a little water. *To cover the pie* Place a strip of pastry around the dampened edge of the pie dish. The best way to lift the pastry is to place the rolling pin on the pastry just past the centre. Fold about one third of the pastry over the pin, then lift the rolling pin with the pastry over it and roll (without stretching) over the top of the fruit. Wet the pastry on the rim of the dish, press the pastry lid down gently then cut off the pastry level with the edge of the dish. Use a sharp knife angled away from the rim. Flute or flake the edges, or using a fork or teaspoon press down around the rim to make an impression.

Cut V shapes in the pastry with a pair of kitchen scissors to let the steam escape and bake in a hot oven (220°C, 425°F, Gas Mark 7) for 15 minutes then at a slightly lower temperature until the fruit is cooked, about 40 minutes altogether.

The time will vary according to the type and degree of ripeness of the fruit. If soft fruit or cooked or bottled fruit is being used the pie should only take 30 minutes to cook.

When the pastry is half cooked, brush over the top with beaten egg white or cold water and dredge with castor sugar.

Fruit Flans

Use biscuit crust pastry and roll out to 5 mm/¼ inch thick and about 3.5 cm/1½ inches wider than the flan ring.

For baking use an 18 or 20-cm/7 or 8-inch ungreased fluted or plain flan ring on a baking sheet, or a deep sandwich tin of the same size. Line the sandwich tin with greased greaseproof paper.

Lift the pastry on to a rolling pin and transfer to the ring. Ease the pastry into the ring without breaking it. Press the pastry smoothly round the sides and bottom of the tin. Trim off the surplus pastry with a sharp knife or roll off with the rolling pin.

Bake 'blind' by lining the pastry case with a round of greaseproof paper and covering the base with crusts of bread or haricot beans kept specially for the purpose. This will prevent the base of the pastry rising. Bake in a hot oven (220°C, 425°F, Gas Mark 7) for about 15 minutes, then remove the paper and return to the oven for a few minutes to dry the bottom and finish cooking. Remove from the tin, cool on a wire tray and when cold fill as required.

Almost any kind of fruit, fresh canned, bottled or frozen, can be used for the filling.

Arrange the fruit neatly in the case and cover with thickened syrup or apricot glaze.

A layer of confectioners' custard (pastry cream) can be spread on the base and the fruit laid on top of this, if the flan is to be served with a dairy meal.

To Thicken Fruit Syrup
Take 150 ml/¼ pint (U.S. ⅔ cup) syrup from canned or freshly cooked fruit, add a little more sugar if necessary and bring to the boil. Add 1 teaspoon of arrowroot mixed with a little cold syrup, stir until boiling and simmer for 5 minutes.

Apricot Glaze
Rub 2 tablespoons (U.S. 3 tablespoons) apricot jam through a sieve into a saucepan, add 150 ml/¼ pint (U.S. ⅔ cup) fruit juice and bring to the boil. Blend 1 teaspoon arrowroot or cornflour with a little cold water and pour on the boiling syrup. Return to the pan, stir until boiling and simmer for 3–4 minutes.

The flan can be served plain or topped with meringue or whipped cream.

Syrup Glaze
For fresh fruit. Boil together 100 g/4 oz (U.S. ½ cup) sugar and 150 ml/¼ pint (U.S. ⅔ cup) water or fruit juice, flavour with a little lemon juice, boil until thick and syrupy and pour over the fruit when cold.

Confectioners' Custard

MAKES ABOUT 300 ML/½ PINT (U.S. 1¼ CUPS)

METRIC/IMPERIAL	AMERICAN
25 g/1 oz sugar	2 tablespoons sugar
15 g/½ oz cornflour	2 tablespoons cornstarch
300 ml/½ pint milk	1¼ cups milk
25 g/1 oz margarine	2 tablespoons margarine
2 egg yolks, beaten	2 egg yolks, beaten
vanilla essence	vanilla extract

Mix the sugar and cornflour to a smooth paste with 2 tablespoons (U.S. 3 tablespoons) of the milk; heat the remaining milk until warm and stir in the paste. Return the mixture to the saucepan, add the margarine, stir continuously until boiling then simmer gently for 3 minutes. Cool slightly, add the beaten egg yolks and stir over a gentle heat until the custard thickens, being careful not to let it come to the boil again. Flavour with vanilla essence.

Puddings and Desserts for Non-dairy Meals

Lemon Meringue Pie

SERVES 6

METRIC/IMPERIAL	AMERICAN
For the pastry	*For the pie dough*
200 g/8 oz plain flour	2 cups all-purpose flour
100 g/4 oz margarine	½ cup margarine
1 egg yolk	1 egg yolk
1 teaspoon castor sugar	1 teaspoon sugar
1 teaspoon lemon juice	1 teaspoon lemon juice
For the filling	*For the filling*
25 g/1 oz cornflour	¼ cup cornstarch
300 ml/½ pint water	1¼ cups water
75 g/3 oz castor sugar	6 tablespoons sugar
grated rind and juice of 1 large lemon	grated rind and juice of 1 large lemon
25 g/1 oz margarine	2 tablespoons margarine
2 large egg yolks	2 large egg yolks
For the meringue	*For the meringue*
2 large egg whites	2 large egg whites
75 g/3 oz castor sugar	6 tablespoons sugar
For decoration	*For decoration*
glacé cherries	candied cherries
angelica	angelica

Make the pastry following the instructions on page 117 and line an 18 or 20-cm/7 or 8-inch flan case. Bake and cool.

To make the filling Mix the cornflour to a thick cream with a little of the water. Heat the remaining water until boiling and stir into the creamed cornflour. Add the sugar, lemon rind and juice and return the mixture to the saucepan. Bring to the boil, stirring continuously until the mixture boils, then lower the heat and simmer for 2–3 minutes until thickened and smooth. Remove the pan from the heat, stir in the margarine and beat in the egg yolks one at a time. Pour the filling into the cooked pastry case.

To make the meringue Whisk the egg whites until very stiff, fold in the sugar and pipe or spoon over the filling, making sure to completely seal the edges. Sprinkle with a little sugar and bake in a cool oven (150°C, 300°F, Gas Mark 2) for 20–30 minutes until the meringue is crisp and very lightly coloured. Serve cold, decorated with glacé cherries and angelica.

Variation

To make a pineapple meringue pie, use a 339-g/12-oz can of pineapple pieces. Drain the pieces and make the juice up to 300 ml/½ pint (U.S. 1¼ cups) with water. Use this liquid to replace the 300 ml/½ pint (U.S. 1¼ cups) of water to make the filling. When the filling has been boiled and thickened, stir in the pineapple pieces after beating in the egg yolks.

Apricot or Plum Flan

SERVES 4–6

METRIC/IMPERIAL	AMERICAN
275 g/10 oz fruit	10 oz fruit
75 g/3 oz sugar	6 tablespoons sugar
300 ml/½ pint water	1¼ cups water
1 teaspoon arrowroot	1 teaspoon arrowroot

Make the flan case following the instructions on page 118. Halve the fruit and remove the stones. Boil the sugar and water together for 5 minutes then put in the fruit and simmer gently until just tender, but not broken. Take out the fruit and drain well.

Blend the arrowroot with 1 tablespoon cold water to a smooth paste and stir it into the fruit juice. Bring to the boil, stirring continuously, then lower the heat and simmer gently for 5 minutes. When really cold, fill the pastry case with the fruit and cover with the thickened syrup.

Syrup Tart

SERVES 6

METRIC/IMPERIAL	AMERICAN
For the pastry	*For the pie dough*
100 g/4 oz margarine	½ cup margarine
200 g/8 oz plain flour	2 cups all-purpose flour
2 tablespoons water	3 tablespoons water
For the filling	*For the filling*
4 tablespoons golden syrup	⅓ cup corn syrup
grated rind of 1 lemon or ½ teaspoon ginger	grated rind of 1 lemon or ½ teaspoon ginger
50 g/2 oz fine fresh white breadcrumbs	1 cup fresh soft bread crumbs

Make the pastry following the instructions on page 117 and line a 23-cm/9-inch oven-proof plate. Trim and decorate the edge. Measure the syrup with a warm spoon into a warm bowl. Add the lemon rind or ginger and the breadcrumbs. Spread the syrup mixture over the pastry.

Roll out the pastry trimmings, cut into narrow strips, dampen the ends and make a lattice pattern over the filling. Bake in a moderately hot oven (200°C, 400°F, Gas Mark 6) for about 30 minutes.

Note As an alternative to breadcrumbs, use 50 g/2 oz desiccated coconut (U.S. ⅔ cup shredded coconut).

Almond Fruit Tart

SERVES 4–6

METRIC/IMPERIAL	AMERICAN
For the pastry	*For the pie dough*
100 g/4 oz plain flour	1 cup all-purpose flour
50 g/2 oz margarine	¼ cup margarine
2 teaspoons castor sugar	2 teaspoons sugar
water to mix	water to mix
For the filling	*For the filling*
1 tablespoon apricot jam or marmalade	1 tablespoon apricot jam or marmalade
25 g/1 oz sliced glacé cherries	2 tablespoons sliced candied cherries
25 g/1 oz currants	3 tablespoons currants
25 g/1 oz sultanas	3 tablespoons seedless white raisins
50 g/2 oz margarine	¼ cup margarine
50 g/2 oz castor sugar	¼ cup sugar
1 egg, beaten	1 egg, beaten
40 g/1½ oz ground rice	¼ cup ground rice
40 g/1½ oz ground almonds	⅓ cup ground almonds
½ teaspoon almond essence	½ teaspoon almond extract
1 tablespoon flaked almonds	1 tablespoon flaked almonds

Make the pastry following the instructions on page 117 and line an 18-cm/7-inch flan ring. Spread the jam on the pastry and sprinkle the fruit on top. Cream together the margarine and sugar, beat in the egg and stir in the ground rice and ground almonds. Spread the mixture over the fruit and sprinkle with flaked almonds.

Bake in a moderate oven (180°C, 350°F, Gas Mark 4) for about 35 minutes. Serve hot or cold.

Baked Oranges

SERVES 6

METRIC/IMPERIAL	AMERICAN
6 oranges	6 oranges
125 g/4½ oz soft brown sugar	½ cup soft brown sugar
6 cloves	6 cloves
1 tablespoon lemon juice	1 tablespoon lemon juice
1 tablespoon curaçao or brandy	1 tablespoon curaçao or brandy

Cover the oranges with boiling water for 2–3 minutes then drain and remove the peel. By scalding them all the pith should come off with the peel. Divide the oranges into segments and take out any pips. Put the segments into an ovenproof dish with the sugar and cloves between each layer. Cover and set aside for 1 hour.

Cook in a moderately hot oven (190°C, 375°F, Gas Mark 5) for 45 minutes. Leave to cool with the lid on. When cold sprinkle with the lemon juice and curaçao or brandy. *(Illustrated on page 116)*

Apple Charlotte

SERVES 4–6

METRIC/IMPERIAL	AMERICAN
675 g/1½ lb cooking apples	1½ lb baking apples
100 g/4 oz fresh breadcrumbs	2 cups fresh soft bread crumbs
2 tablespoons golden syrup	3 tablespoons maple syrup
1 tablespoon water	1 tablespoon water
grated rind and juice of 1 lemon	grated rind and juice of 1 lemon
40 g/1½ oz soft brown sugar	3 tablespoons soft brown sugar
¼ teaspoon ginger	¼ teaspoon ginger
25 g/1 oz margarine for topping	2 tablespoons margarine for topping

Peel, core and thinly slice the apples. Grease an ovenproof dish. Place a layer of breadcrumbs in the dish then a layer of sliced apples; repeat the layers until the dish is full.

Pour the syrup, water, lemon rind and juice, sugar and ginger into a small saucepan over a gentle heat and stir until the sugar has dissolved. Pour over the apple and breadcrumbs, dot with margarine and bake in a moderate oven (180°C, 350°F, Gas Mark 4) for 1–1¼ hours.

Rhubarb Charlotte Make as above, using chopped rhubarb in place of apples.

Apple Crisp

SERVES 4–6

METRIC/IMPERIAL	AMERICAN
450 g/1 lb cooking apples	1 lb baking apples
2 tablespoons sugar	3 tablespoons sugar
50 g/2 oz margarine	¼ cup margarine
50 g/2 oz castor sugar	¼ cup sugar
25 g/1 oz ground rice	2 tablespoons ground rice
50 g/2 oz fine desiccated coconut	⅔ cup finely shredded coconut
1 teaspoon baking powder	1 teaspoon baking powder
1 large egg, beaten	1 large egg, beaten
½ teaspoon almond essence	½ teaspoon almond extract
1 tablespoon apricot or plum jam	1 tablespoon apricot or plum jam

Peel, core and slice the apples and place in a thick-based saucepan with the sugar and a little water. Cook gently until soft. Cream the margarine and sugar until soft and fluffy. Mix together the ground rice, coconut and baking powder and mix into the creamed mixture, alternately with the beaten egg.

Grease a shallow ovenproof dish, spread the base with jam then add the stewed apples and cover with the creamed mixture. Bake in a moderately hot oven (200°C, 400°F, Gas Mark 6) for 20–30 minutes.

Note This pudding can be successfully heated up: as there is no flour in the mixture it does not harden.

Baked Rice Kugel

SERVES 4–6

METRIC/IMPERIAL	AMERICAN
100 g/4 oz short or long-grain rice	½ cup short or long-grain rice
1 large egg	1 large egg
75 g/3 oz soft brown sugar	⅓ cup soft brown sugar
50 g/2 oz margarine, melted	¼ cup melted margarine
1 tablespoon marmalade	1 tablespoon marmalade
1 tablespoon ground almonds	1 tablespoon ground almonds
1 cooking apple, grated	1 baking apple, grated
50 g/2 oz sultanas	½ cup seedless white raisins
soft brown sugar for sprinkling	soft brown sugar for sprinkling

Grease a fairly deep casserole or ovenproof dish. Boil the rice until tender following the instructions on page 109. Beat the egg with the sugar and add to the rice, together with all the remaining ingredients. Pour into the greased casserole and sprinkle with a little brown sugar. Bake in a moderate oven (180°C, 350°F, Gas Mark 4) for 40 minutes – or longer if a crispy texture is preferred.

Queen of Gooseberry Pudding

SERVES 4–6

METRIC/IMPERIAL	AMERICAN
450 g/1 lb gooseberries	1 lb gooseberries
75 g/3 oz granulated sugar	⅓ cup sugar
2 large eggs, separated	2 large eggs, separated
25 g/1 oz margarine, melted	2 tablespoons melted margarine
75 g/3 oz fresh breadcrumbs	1½ cups fresh soft bread crumbs
75 g/3 oz castor sugar	⅓ cup sugar

Trim the gooseberries and place in a thick-based saucepan with the granulated sugar and just enough water to cover. Cook over a low heat until soft, then blend to a purée in a liquidiser or press through a sieve. There should be about 600 ml/1 pint (U.S. 2½ cups) of purée – if necessary, add a little water to make up the quantity.

Mix the purée with the egg yolks, margarine, and breadcrumbs and pour into a shallow greased ovenproof dish. Bake in a moderate oven (180°C, 350°F, Gas Mark 4) for 30 minutes. Whisk the egg whites until stiff and fold in the castor sugar. Pipe or spoon the meringue over the pudding and return to the oven for about 20 minutes until the meringue is set and lightly browned. Serve hot.

Lockshen Pudding

SERVES 6

METRIC/IMPERIAL	AMERICAN
100 g/4 oz medium egg noodles	¼ lb medium egg noodles
50 g/2 oz margarine	¼ cup margarine
1 large egg	1 large egg
50 g/2 oz sugar	¼ cup sugar
pinch of salt	dash of salt
1 teaspoon cinnamon	1 teaspoon cinnamon
2 tablespoons sultanas	3 tablespoons seedless white raisins
1 tablespoon marmalade	1 tablespoon marmalade
1 cooking apple, grated (optional)	1 baking apple, grated (optional)

Boil and drain the noodles and, while still warm, stir in the margarine. Beat the egg and sugar together lightly and add to the noodles, together with all the remaining ingredients. Mix thoroughly and pour into a fairly deep ovenproof dish. Bake in a moderate oven (180°C, 350°F, Gas Mark 4) for about 40 minutes until set and browned.

Plum Pudding

METRIC/IMPERIAL	AMERICAN
100 g/4 oz stale breadcrumbs	1 cup stale bread crumbs
225 g/8 oz raisins (preferably seedless)	1½ cups raisins (preferably seeded)
225 g/8 oz sultanas	1½ cups seedless white raisins
225 g/8 oz currants	1½ cups currants
25 g/1 oz blanched almonds	¼ cups whole shelled almonds
50 g/2 oz candied peel	⅓ cup candied peel
1 medium cooking apple	1 medium baking apple
1 teaspoon freshly grated nutmeg	1 teaspoon freshly grated nutmeg
175 g/6 oz margarine	¾ cup margarine
100 g/4 oz plain flour	1 cup all-purpose flour
½ teaspoon salt	½ teaspoon salt
1 teaspoon mixed spice	1 teaspoon mixed spice
225 g/8 oz dark soft brown sugar	1 cup dark soft brown sugar
grated rind and juice of 1 lemon	grated rind and juice of 1 lemon
grated rind and juice of 1 orange	grated rind and juice of 1 orange
2 eggs, well beaten	2 eggs, well beaten
2 tablespoons brandy or sherry	3 tablespoons brandy or sherry

Make the breadcrumbs in a liquidiser or food processor, or on a fine grater. Stone the raisins, if necessary, and wash and dry all the fruit. Cut the almonds into strips and slice the peel. Core and grate the apple, grate the nutmeg and melt the margarine.

Sift the flour, salt and mixed spice into a large bowl. Add all the remaining ingredients and mix thoroughly.

Grease one 1.25-litre/2-pint pudding basin or two 600-ml/1-pint basins. Fill the basin with the mixture to within 2.5 cm/1 inch of the top. Cover first with greased greaseproof paper then with foil. Tuck the foil securely round the basin rim or tie with string. Steam for 6–7 hours until firm and dark brown.

When the pudding is cooked, cool completely then remove the covering and replace with fresh greaseproof paper and foil. If stored in a cool dry place, the pudding will keep for several months and is always best made at least 2 months before it is needed.

When required, steam or boil for at least 2 hours. Uncover and leave for 2 or 3 minutes for the steam to escape. Turn on to a hot dish, sprinkle the top with sugar and serve with wine sauce (see page 86) or hard sauce (see page 88).

Baked Bread Pudding

SERVES 6–8

METRIC/IMPERIAL	AMERICAN
400 g/14 oz stale bread	¾–1 lb stale bread
25 g/1 oz mixed peel	3 tablespoons candied peel
100 g/4 oz mixed dried fruit	¾ cup mixed dried fruit
50 g/2 oz margarine, melted	¼ cup margarine, melted
2 tablespoons golden syrup	3 tablespoons corn syrup
1 teaspoon mixed spice	1 teaspoon mixed spice
1 large egg	1 large egg
1 tablespoon soft brown sugar	1 tablespoon soft brown sugar

Use any available stale bread, including crusts. Soak the bread in water until soft, then drain in a colander or sieve and squeeze by hand until very dry. Beat with a fork until free of lumps. Wash and dry the fruit, if necessary.

Place all the ingredients except the brown sugar in a bowl and mix well. Turn into a shallow greased baking dish or roasting tin and sprinkle with the sugar. Bake in a moderate oven (180°C, 350°F, Gas Mark 4) for about 1 hour.

Variations

Grated orange or lemon rind can be used instead of the mixed peel.

Add a cooking apple, 50 g/2 oz (U.S. ¼ cup) brown sugar and 1 tablespoon marmalade to make the pudding richer.

Dried Fruit Casserole

✡

SERVES 8–10

METRIC/IMPERIAL	AMERICAN
100 g/4 oz dried figs	¾ cup dried figs
100 g/4 oz dried prunes	¾ cup dried prunes
100 g/4 oz dried apricots	¾ cup dried apricots
100 g/4 oz apple rings	½ cup apple rings
50 g/2 oz seedless raisins	⅓ cup seeded raisins
50 g/2 oz flaked almonds (optional)	½ cup flaked almonds (optional)
100–225 g/4–8 oz soft brown sugar (see method)	½–1 cup soft brown sugar (see method)

Soak the dried fruit overnight in cold water in a large ovenproof dish; the mixture of dried fruits can be varied according to taste and availability. If necessary, pour off a little of the water to leave the fruit just covered. Add the nuts, if used, and enough sugar to taste. Cook in a cool oven (150°C, 300°F, Gas Mark 2) so that the fruit just simmers for about 30 minutes or until soft.

Note For added flavour, add 2 quarters of a lemon to mixtures of prunes and apricots, or 1 tablespoon of rose water to the dried fruits while they are soaking.

Apricot Meringue

✡

SERVES 4–6

METRIC/IMPERIAL	AMERICAN
225 g/8 oz dried apricots	1⅓ cups dried apricots
100 g/4 oz castor sugar	½ cup sugar
2 large eggs, separated	2 large eggs, separated
3 tablespoons sifted icing sugar	¼ cup sifted confectioners' sugar

Wash the apricots, cover with water and soak overnight. Place the apricots in a saucepan with enough of the water to cover and simmer gently until soft. Blend to a purée in a liquidiser or rub through a sieve. Add the castor sugar and egg yolks and beat lightly. Pour the mixture into an ovenproof dish and bake in a moderate oven (180°C, 350°F, Gas Mark 4) for 20 minutes.

Whisk the egg whites until stiff and fold in the icing sugar. Spoon over the pudding, dredge with a little more icing sugar and return to the oven for about 20 minutes until the meringue is set and lightly browned.

Variation

For a special occasion, add 2 tablespoons (U.S. 3 tablespoons) apricot brandy to the fruit purée.

Banana Snow

✡

SERVES 4–6

METRIC/IMPERIAL	AMERICAN
4 large ripe bananas	4 large ripe bananas
juice of 1 lemon	juice of 1 lemon
1 egg white	1 egg white
1 tablespoon castor sugar	1 tablespoon superfine sugar
glacé cherries for decoration	candied cherries for decoration

Place the peeled bananas in the bowl of an electric mixer and mash to a pulp with a fork. Add the lemon juice and egg white and beat with the mixer until thick and creamy. Add the sugar and beat for a further minute. Spoon into a large glass serving dish or into individual glasses. Decorate with glacé cherries.

Apricot-matzo pudding (see page 175)
Overleaf: *Bola (see page 151)*; *Bagels (see page 150)*;
Streusel (see page 153); *Cholla (see page 152)*;
Coffee kuchen (see page 153)

Puddings and Desserts for Dairy Meals

Cheesecake

SERVES 6

METRIC/IMPERIAL	AMERICAN
For the pastry case	*For the pie shell*
225 g/8 oz shortcrust or biscuit crust pastry (see page 117)	½ lb basic pie dough or biscuit crust pastry (see page 117)
For the first filling	*For the first filling*
50 g/2 oz margarine	¼ cup margarine
25 g/1 oz castor sugar	2 tablespoons sugar
1 large egg, beaten	1 large egg, beaten
300 g/10 oz curd cheese	1¼ cups curd cheese
25 g/1 oz candied peel (optional)	3 tablespoons candied peel (optional)
25 g/1 oz currants (optional)	3 tablespoons currants (optional)
finely grated rind of ½ lemon	finely grated rind of ½ lemon
For the second filling	*For the second filling*
350 g/12 oz curd cheese	1½ cups curd cheese
2 tablespoons plain flour	3 tablespoons all-purpose flour
2 tablespoons single cream	3 tablespoons light cream
2 large eggs, separated	2 large eggs, separated
75 g/3 oz castor sugar	6 tablespoons sugar
25 g/1 oz margarine, melted	2 tablespoons melted margarine
finely grated rind of ½ lemon	finely grated rind of ½ lemon

To make the pastry case, roll out the pastry and line a greased 20-cm/8-inch loose-bottomed flan tin or sandwich tin. Prick the base. Set aside while making the filling.
To make the first filling Cream together the margarine and sugar, add the egg, cheese, peel and currants if used and the grated lemon rind. Mix thoroughly and pour into the pastry case. Bake in a hot oven (220°C, 425°F, Gas Mark 7) for 10 minutes then reduce the heat to moderate (180°C, 350°F, Gas Mark 4) and bake for a further 20–30 minutes until the pastry is lightly browned and the filling firm. *(Illustrated opposite)*
To make the second filling Place the curd cheese in a bowl and mix in the flour and cream. Beat the egg yolks lightly with the sugar, add the melted margarine and lemon rind then stir into the cheese mixture. Whisk the egg whites until stiff and fold in. Pour into the pastry case and bake as above. *(Illustrated opposite)*

Variation

SERVES 10–12

If preferred, kuchen dough can be used in place of ordinary pastry (see page 152). Grease and line two 20-cm/8-inch loose-bottomed sandwich tins (the lining should come above the level of the tin). Roll out the dough and line the base of the tins. Leave the tins in a warm place for the dough to rise again for 30 minutes. Fill with either of the cheese mixtures and bake in a moderately hot oven (200°C, 400°F, Gas Mark 6) for about 30 minutes.

Cheesecakes (see above); Blintzes and soured cream (see page 103)

Apfel Kuchen (Applecake)

✡

SERVES 8–10

METRIC/IMPERIAL	AMERICAN
For the kuchen dough	*For the kuchen dough*
15 g/½ oz fresh yeast or 2 teaspoons dried yeast	½ cake compressed yeast or ½ package active dry yeast
sugar (see method)	sugar (see method)
50 g/2 oz margarine	¼ cup margarine
300 ml/½ pint milk	1¼ cups milk
450 g/1 lb plain flour	4 cups all-purpose flour
pinch of salt	dash of salt
50 g/2 oz castor sugar	¼ cup sugar
1 egg, beaten	1 egg, beaten
For the filling	*For the filling*
50 g/2 oz margarine, melted	¼ cup margarine, melted
450–675 g/1–1½ lb cooking apples	1–1½ lb baking apples
50 g/2 oz castor sugar	¼ cup sugar
1 teaspoon cinnamon	1 teaspoon cinnamon
50–75 g/2–3 oz sultanas	½ cup seedless white raisins

To make the dough Cream the yeast with 1 teaspoon of sugar. Melt the margarine in the milk and when just lukewarm, pour on to the creamed yeast. If using dried yeast, dissolve 1 teaspoon sugar in the warm milk and margarine and sprinkle the yeast on top.

Sift the flour and salt into a warm bowl and make a well in the centre. Pour in the yeast mixture, gradually work in the flour from the sides and knead into a smooth dough. Leave the dough in the bowl, cover with greased polythene or cling film and set aside in a warm place for 1½–2 hours for the dough to rise and double in size.

Add the sugar and beaten egg and knead thoroughly. Roll out the kuchen dough to fit the base of a 33 × 23-cm/13 × 9-inch Swiss roll tin.

Leave to prove for 10 minutes then brush with a little of the melted margarine. Peel and core the apples, cut into eighths and place on the dough in parallel lines. Sprinkle with the sugar, cinnamon, sultanas and the remaining melted margarine. Bake for 15 minutes in a moderately hot oven (200°C, 400°F, Gas Mark 6) then reduce the temperature to moderate (180°C, 350°F, Gas Mark 4) and bake for a further 15–20 minutes until the apples are soft and the pastry cooked.

Upside-down Applecake

✡

SERVES 6–8

METRIC/IMPERIAL	AMERICAN
For the cake mixture	*For the cake batter*
170 g/6 oz self-raising flour	1½ cups all-purpose flour sifted with 2½ teaspoons baking powder
1 teaspoon baking powder	
85 g/3 oz castor sugar	⅓ cup sugar
1 large egg	1 large egg
6 tablespoons milk	½ cup milk
30 g/1 oz margarine, melted	2 tablespoons melted margarine
For the topping	*For the topping*
675 g/1½ lb cooking apples	1½ lb baking apples
40 g/1½ oz margarine	3 tablespoons margarine
50 g/2 oz soft brown sugar	¼ cup soft brown sugar

To make the cake mixture Sift the flour and baking powder into a bowl and add the sugar. Beat the egg with the milk and add to the dry ingredients, together with the melted margarine. Beat well with a wooden spoon to a fairly soft consistency.

To make the topping Peel, core and slice the apples. Melt the margarine in a 20-cm/8-inch round deep cake tin, tilting the tin to cover the inside all over. Sprinkle with the brown sugar then cover the base with over-lapping apple slices. Cover with the cake mixture and bake in a moderately hot oven (200°C, 400°F, Gas Mark 6) for about 35 minutes. Reverse the tin on to a serving dish, leave for about 5 minutes in this position then remove the tin. Serve plain or with custard.

Note For a meat meal, replace the milk with 5 tablespoons (U.S. 6 tablespoons) tepid water and 1 tablespoon lemon or orange juice.

Blackcurrant Cream

SERVES 6–8

METRIC/IMPERIAL	AMERICAN
450 g/1 lb black-currants, fresh or frozen	1 lb black currants, fresh or frozen
150 ml/¼ pint water	⅔ cup water
75 g/3 oz castor sugar	⅓ cup sugar
300 ml/½ pint thick custard (see page 87)	1¼ cups thick custard (see page 87)
1 (142-ml/5-fl oz) carton double cream	⅔ cup heavy cream
chopped nuts for decoration	chopped nuts for decoration

Cook the blackcurrants with the water and sugar until soft. Blend to a purée in a liquidiser or rub through a sieve. Add the custard and blend for about 15 seconds. Whip the cream in a bowl until thick but not stiff. Fold half of the cream into the blackcurrant mixture and pour into individual glasses. Whip the remaining cream until stiff. Decorate the glasses with the whipped cream and chopped nuts.

Chestnut Cream

SERVES 6–8

METRIC/IMPERIAL	AMERICAN
450 g/1 lb chestnuts	1 lb chestnuts
75 g/3 oz plain chocolate	3 squares semi-sweet chocolate
150 ml/¼ pint milk	⅔ cup milk
25 g/1 oz castor sugar	2 tablespoons sugar
¼ teaspoon vanilla essence	¼ teaspoon vanilla extract
2 tablespoons single cream	3 tablespoons light cream

Slit the skins of the chestnuts, place in a saucepan and cover with water. Bring to the boil and boil for 15 minutes. Take out a few at a time with a draining spoon, hold with oven gloves and, while still hot, remove the outer shell and inner skin with a sharp knife. Cut the chestnuts into rough pieces and place in a liquidiser.

Grate the chocolate and add 50 g/2 oz (U.S. 2 squares) to the chestnuts, together with the milk. Blend for 30 seconds until the mixture is reduced to a purée. Pour the purée into a saucepan, add the sugar and stir over a gentle heat until the mixture boils. Add the vanilla essence and continue stirring over a gentle heat for 2–3 minutes. Set aside until cold.

Stir in the cream, pour into individual glasses and serve chilled, sprinkled with the remaining grated chocolate.

Strawberry or Raspberry Fool

SERVES 4–6

METRIC/IMPERIAL	AMERICAN
450 g/1 lb raspberries or strawberries	1 lb raspberries or strawberries
4 tablespoons water	⅓ cup water
100 g/4 oz castor sugar	½ cup superfine sugar
1 (142-ml/5-fl oz) carton double cream	⅔ cup heavy cream
1 large egg white	1 large egg white
For decoration	*For decoration*
whipped cream	whipped cream
whole fruit	whole fruit

Place the fruit in a liquidiser with the water and blend for about 30 seconds until the fruit is reduced to a purée. Pour into a bowl and stir in the sugar. Whip the cream until it stands in peaks and whisk the egg whites until stiff. Fold both into the fruit purée and spoon into individual glasses. Chill and decorate with whipped cream and fruit.

Note If using frozen fruit, defrost completely and use the juice in place of water.

Variation

Use 300 ml/½ pint (U.S. 1¼ cups) thick custard instead of the cream and egg white.

Puddings and Desserts for Dairy or Non-dairy Meals

Butter or milk may be used as an alternative, but the basic recipe is suitable for non-dairy meals.

Apple Strudel

SERVES 8–10

METRIC/IMPERIAL	AMERICAN
For the pastry	*For the pie dough*
225 g/8 oz plain flour	2 cups all-purpose flour
pinch of salt	dash of salt
1 small egg	1 small egg
2 tablespoons olive oil	3 tablespoons olive oil
150 ml/¼ pint warm water (see method)	⅔ cup warm water (see method)
For the filling	*For the filling*
450 g/1 lb cooking apples	1 lb baking apples
1 tablespoon fresh breadcrumbs	1 tablespoon fresh soft bread crumbs
margarine (see method)	margarine (see method)
3 tablespoons currants	¼ cup currants
25 g/1 oz flaked almonds	¼ cup flaked almonds
75–100 g/3–4 oz soft brown sugar	⅓–½ cup soft brown sugar
juice of 1 lemon	juice of 1 lemon
50 g/2 oz margarine, melted	¼ cup melted margarine

Sift the flour and salt into a bowl and make a well in the centre. Add the egg and oil and enough of the water to make a dough which should be soft and pliable but should not stick to the bowl or hands. Knead the dough well on a lightly floured board until smooth then cover with a warm bowl and leave on the board for 30 minutes.

To prepare the filling Peel, core and very thinly slice the apples. Fry the breadcrumbs in a little margarine until crisp and brown, then add to the apples together with the currants, flaked almonds, sugar and lemon juice.

To make the strudel Spread a cloth on a flat surface and sprinkle well with flour. Place the pastry in the centre and roll it out as thinly as possible into a large rectangle, then pull the edges gently until the dough is paper thin and transparent. Spread the filling over the pastry and sprinkle with some of the melted margarine. Lift one edge of the cloth and roll the pastry like a 'roly-poly'; seal the ends. Place the roll in a large crescent shape on a greased baking sheet and brush the surface liberally with the remaining melted margarine.

Bake in a hot oven (220°C, 425°F, Gas Mark 7) until lightly browned then reduce the heat to moderate (180°C, 350°F, Gas Mark 4) and continue to bake for a total of about 40 minutes.

Alternative fillings

Cherry filling

METRIC/IMPERIAL	AMERICAN
2 (425-g/15-oz) cans morello cherries, drained and stoned	2 (15-oz) cans morello cherries, drained and pitted
175 g/6 oz cake crumbs	3 cups cake crumbs
100 g/4 oz flaked almonds	1 cup flaked almonds
50 g/2 oz brown sugar	¼ cup brown sugar
1 teaspoon cocoa powder	1 teaspoon cocoa powder

Apricot filling

METRIC/IMPERIAL	AMERICAN
675 g/1½ lb fresh apricots, stoned	1½ lb fresh apricots, stoned
175 g/6 oz cake crumbs	3 cups cake crumbs
175 g/6 oz flaked almonds	1½ cups flaked almonds
75 g/3 oz brown sugar	⅓ cups brown sugar

Cheese filling

METRIC/IMPERIAL	AMERICAN
225 g/8 oz curd cheese	1 cup curd cheese
25 g/1 oz butter, melted	2 tablespoons melted butter
1 egg, beaten	1 egg, beaten
sugar/salt to taste	sugar/salt to taste

Chocolate Mousse

SERVES 4–6

METRIC/IMPERIAL	AMERICAN
75 g/3 oz plain chocolate	3 squares semi-sweet chocolate
3 large eggs, separated	3 large eggs, separated
whipped cream or chopped walnuts for decoration	whipped cream or chopped walnuts for decoration

Break the chocolate into a heatproof bowl and place over a saucepan of hot water until the chocolate has melted. Remove from the heat. Lightly beat the egg yolks and stir into the melted chocolate. Whisk the whites until quite stiff and fold them into the mixture.

Spoon into individual glasses and leave until cold and set. Decorate with whipped cream or chopped nuts.

Variation

Add the finely grated rind of $\frac{1}{2}$ an orange and 2 teaspoons brandy just before folding in the egg whites.

Continental Apple Tart

SERVES 6

METRIC/IMPERIAL	AMERICAN
For the pastry	*For the pie dough*
150 g/5 oz butter or margarine	$\frac{2}{3}$ cup butter or margarine
275 g/10 oz plain flour	$2\frac{1}{2}$ cups all-purpose flour
75 g/3 oz castor sugar	6 tablespoons sugar
1 egg	1 egg
For the filling	*For the filling*
675 g/1$\frac{1}{2}$ lb cooking apples	1$\frac{1}{2}$ lb baking apples
25 g/1 oz currants	3 tablespoons currants
25 g/1 oz sultanas	3 tablespoons seedless white raisins
soft brown sugar	soft brown sugar
25 g/1 oz chopped candied peel	3 tablespoons chopped candied peel
$\frac{1}{2}$ teaspoon cinnamon	$\frac{1}{2}$ teaspoon cinnamon

This tart is best made in a 20-cm/8-inch loose-bottomed flan tin.

To make the pastry Rub the butter into the flour, add the sugar and the egg and knead thoroughly to a pliable dough. Cover and place in a refrigerator for 20 minutes.

To make the filling Peel, core and chop the apples and cook very gently with the currants and sultanas and a little water until reduced to a pulp. Sweeten to taste with brown sugar and add the chopped peel. Set aside until cold.

To make the tart Roll the pastry into a long strip, fold into three and roll out again. Repeat the folding and rolling once more. Line the bottom and sides of the flan tin with the pastry, sprinkle with castor sugar and a little flour, pour the prepared filling into the pastry case and decorate with strips of any surplus pastry. Bake in a moderate oven (180°C, 350°F, Gas Mark 4) for 1 hour, keeping the tart covered with foil or an enamel plate for the first 45 minutes. Leave in the tin until it cools.

Steamed Sponge Pudding

SERVES 6–8

METRIC/IMPERIAL	AMERICAN
110 g/4 oz margarine	½ cup margarine
85 g/3 oz castor sugar	⅓ cup sugar
2 eggs, beaten	2 eggs, beaten
3 drops vanilla essence	3 drops vanilla extract
170 g/6 oz self-raising flour	1½ cups all-purpose flour sifted with 1½ teaspoons baking powder
milk or water for mixing	milk or water for mixing

Cream together the margarine and sugar until light and fluffy. Beat in the eggs, one at a time, and beat in the vanilla essence. Fold in the flour and, if necessary, add a little milk or water to make a soft dropping consistency. Turn into a greased basin, cover and steam for 1½ hours. Serve with jam sauce or custard sauce (see page 87).

Variations

Jam pudding Put 3 tablespoons (U.S. ¼ cup) jam or marmalade in the bottom of the greased basin, then add the pudding mixture.

Cherry pudding Add 50 g/2 oz (U.S. ¼ cup) halved glacé cherries to the basic mixture.

Fruit pudding Add 85 g/3 oz sultanas (U.S. ½ cup seedless white raisins) and 25 g/1 oz mixed peel (U.S. 3 tablespoons candied peel) to the basic mixture and add ½ teaspoon mixed spice to the flour before sifting.

Coffee pudding Add 50 g/2 oz (U.S. ½ cup) chopped nuts.

Banana and date pudding Add 50 g/2 oz (U.S. ¼ cup) chopped dates and 2 mashed bananas to the basic mixture.

Gingerbread Ring

SERVES 6–8

METRIC/IMPERIAL	AMERICAN
For the ring	*For the ring*
150 g/5 oz butter or margarine	⅔ cup butter or margarine
150 g/5 oz golden syrup	½ cup corn syrup
1 tablespoon water	1 tablespoon water
100 g/4 oz brown sugar	½ cup brown sugar
200 g/7 oz plain flour	1¾ cups all-purpose flour
2 teaspoons baking powder	2 teaspoons baking powder
25 g/1 oz ground almonds	¼ cup ground almonds
1 teaspoon grated lemon rind	1 teaspoon grated lemon rind
2 teaspoons ground ginger	2 teaspoons ground ginger
2 eggs, beaten	2 eggs, beaten
For the filling	*For the filling*
apple or any other fruit compote	apple or any other fruit compote

Grease a 20-cm/8-inch ring tin or Kugelhopf tin.

To make the ring Put the butter, syrup, water and sugar into a thick-based saucepan and heat gently until the butter has melted and the sugar dissolved. Sift the dry ingredients together into a mixing bowl and pour the syrup mixture into the middle. Beat well until thoroughly mixed. Beat in the egg a little at a time, then pour the mixture into the prepared tin.

Bake in a moderate oven (160°C, 325°F, Gas Mark 3) for about 1 hour until well risen and firm. Cool slightly in the tin for 10 minutes then turn out on to a serving dish. Serve hot or cold, filling the centre with the compote. *(Illustrated on page 115)*

Baking

It is easier to be judged on one's baking than on one's cooking. A creamy cheesecake or melt-in-the-mouth sponge brings forth more praise than the best-made chicken soup. The new all-in-one method of making cakes and the possibility of using a freezer to store the baking help greatly to improve the chances of success.

Before starting to bake the oven should be at the correct temperature. Heating the oven in advance will ensure this.

Unless the cake tins to be used are the non-stick variety, they should be prepared before beginning to mix the cake. Shallow tins used for larger cakes should be well greased. Using a pastry brush dipped in oil is an efficient way of doing this.

For richer cakes such as fruit cakes the tin should be lined with a layer of oiled greaseproof paper. To allow room for the cake to rise the cake tin should only be filled two-thirds full.

To test to see if a cake is cooked through before removing it from the oven, pierce with a warm skewer or knitting needle. If it is sticky, the cake should be baked a little longer.

After removing the cake from the oven, allow a large cake to stand in the tin for about 10 minutes before turning out on to the cooling tray and then leave it to cool completely before storing it in the tin.

Cakes freeze very well. They should be wrapped in foil or placed in a thick gauge polythene bag. Cakes baked in loaf tins instead of the usual round cake tins are easier to cut and make better use of freezer space. A cake mixture sufficient for an 18–20-cm/7–8-inch round tin will bake well in a 1-kg/2-lb loaf tin.

Decorated cakes can be placed in the freezer unwrapped until the icing or cream is hard, and then wrapped and stored.

Many of the recipes in this section include milk. Water or orange juice can be used as a substitute if the cake is to be served after a meat meal.

Cakes and Biscuits

Honey Cake

✡

METRIC/IMPERIAL	AMERICAN
225 g/8 oz clear honey	$\frac{2}{3}$ cup clear honey
2 large eggs	2 large eggs
110 g/4 oz castor sugar	$\frac{1}{2}$ cup sugar
3 tablespoons vegetable oil	$\frac{1}{4}$ cup vegetable oil
225 g/8 oz self-raising flour	2 cups all-purpose flour sifted with 2 teaspoons baking powder
$\frac{1}{2}$ teaspoon ground ginger	$\frac{1}{2}$ teaspoon ground ginger
$\frac{1}{2}$ teaspoon cinnamon	$\frac{1}{2}$ teaspoon cinnamon
$\frac{1}{2}$ teaspoon mixed spice	$\frac{1}{2}$ teaspoon mixed spice
$\frac{1}{2}$ teaspoon bicarbonate of soda	$\frac{1}{2}$ teaspoon baking soda
150 ml/$\frac{1}{4}$ pint warm water	$\frac{2}{3}$ cup warm water

Grease and line a 23-cm/9-inch square cake tin. Warm the honey in a thick-based saucepan until it thins.

Beat together the eggs and sugar until thick and creamy and stir in the oil and honey. Sift together the flour, ginger, cinnamon and mixed spice. Dissolve the bicarbonate of soda in the warm water.

Fold the sifted ingredients and water alternately into the beaten mixture to make a smooth fairly thick mixture. Pour into the prepared cake tin and bake in the centre of a moderate oven (160°C, 325°F, Gas Mark 3) for about 1$\frac{1}{4}$ hours.

Leave the cake in the tin for 5 minutes then turn out on to a wire tray to cool. The cake can be served plain or brushed with honey and sprinkled with shredded almonds.

Note This cake is delicious used in strudel fillings (see page 132).

Orange Drizzle Cake

✡

METRIC/IMPERIAL	AMERICAN
For the cake	*For the cake*
175 g/6 oz margarine	$\frac{3}{4}$ cup margarine
175 g/6 oz castor sugar	$\frac{3}{4}$ cup sugar
3 large eggs	3 large eggs
175 g/6 oz self-raising flour, sifted	1$\frac{1}{2}$ cups all-purpose flour sifted with 1$\frac{1}{2}$ teaspoons baking powder
2 tablespoons milk or water	3 tablespoons milk or water
grated rind of 2 oranges	grated rind of 2 oranges
For the syrup	*For the syrup*
50 g/2 oz granulated sugar	$\frac{1}{4}$ cup sugar
juice of 2 oranges	juice of 2 oranges
For the topping	*For the topping*
100 g/4 oz plain chocolate	4 squares semi-sweet chocolate
15 g/$\frac{1}{2}$ oz margarine	1 tablespoon margarine

Grease and line a 1-kg/2-lb loaf tin. Cream the margarine and sugar together until soft and fluffy. Beat in the eggs one at a time, adding a tablespoon of flour after each addition. Fold in the sifted flour and stir in the milk or water and orange rind.

Turn the mixture into the prepared tin and bake in the centre of a moderate oven (180°C, 350°F, Gas Mark 4) for about 1 hour until well risen, golden brown and firm.

Leave the cake in the tin for 5 minutes, then turn out on to a wire tray to cool.

To make the syrup Heat the sugar with the orange juice until a thin syrup is formed. Prick the surface of the cake gently in several places and drizzle the warm syrup over the cake.

To make the topping Break the chocolate into small pieces, put into a bowl with the margarine and place over a pan of hot water until it melts. Stir gently and spread over the cake. Alternatively, for special occasions, top with chocolate fudge icing (see page 148).

Mocha almond gâteau (see page 140)

Walnut Layer Cake

✡

METRIC/IMPERIAL	AMERICAN
For the cake	*For the cake*
175 g/6 oz butter or margarine	¾ cup butter or margarine
175 g/6 oz castor sugar	¾ cup sugar
3 large eggs	3 large eggs
225 g/8 oz self-raising flour, sifted	2 cups all-purpose flour sifted with 2 teaspoons baking powder
50 g/2 oz chopped walnuts	½ cup chopped walnuts
3 drops almond essence	3 drops almond extract
2 tablespoons milk	3 tablespoons milk
For the filling	*For the filling*
50 g/2 oz butter	¼ cup butter
75 g/3 oz icing sugar, sifted	¾ cup sifted confectioners' sugar
15 g/½ oz finely chopped walnuts	2 tablespoons finely chopped walnuts
For the icing	*For the frosting*
225 g/8 oz icing sugar, sifted	1¾ cups sifted confectioners' sugar
2 tablespoons warm water	3 tablespoons warm water
vanilla essence	vanilla extract
8 walnut halves	8 walnut halves

Grease and line an 18-cm/7-inch round deep cake tin.

Cream the butter and sugar together until soft and fluffy. Beat in the eggs one at a time, adding a tablespoon of flour with each. Stir in the nuts, the almond essence and milk. Lastly fold in the flour.

Transfer the mixture to the prepared tin and bake in the centre of a moderately hot oven (190°C, 375°F, Gas Mark 5) for 30 minutes, then lower the temperature to moderate (160°C, 325°F, Gas Mark 3) for a further 45 minutes until the cake is well risen, golden brown and firm.

Leave the cake in the tin for 5 minutes then turn out on to a wire tray to cool.

To make the filling Cream together the butter and icing sugar until soft and fluffy and then mix in the chopped walnuts.

To make the icing Place the icing sugar in a small saucepan, add the warm water and vanilla essence and stir over a gentle heat until just warm. It should be thick enough to coat the back of a spoon. If too thin, add more sugar; if too thick, add more water. Use at once.

To finish the cake, divide into three layers and sandwich them together with the filling. Spread the icing over the top and decorate with the walnut halves.

Variations

Ice with American icing (see page 149).

Coffee walnut cake Spread the layers and ice the top with coffee butter icing (see page 149) and decorate with walnuts.

Chocolate Cake

✡

METRIC/IMPERIAL	AMERICAN
150 g/5 oz self-raising flour, sifted	1¼ cups all-purpose flour sifted with 1 teaspoon baking powder
175 g/6 oz castor sugar	¾ cup sugar
175 g/6 oz soft margarine	¾ cup soft margarine
75 g/3 oz drinking chocolate powder	¾ cup drinking chocolate powder
3 large eggs	3 large eggs
3 tablespoons boiling water	¼ cup boiling water

Grease and line a 20–23-cm/8–9-inch cake tin. Mix all the ingredients together in one bowl. Stir gently to begin with until all the ingredients are combined. Beat for 2 minutes.

Transfer the mixture to the prepared cake tin and bake in the centre of a moderate oven (180°C, 350°F, Gas Mark 4) for about 1 hour until well risen and firm.

Leave the cake in the tin for 5 minutes then turn on to a wire tray to cool. Cut the cake through the middle and fill with fresh cream or apricot jam and top with fudge frosting or chocolate icing (see page 148).

Haman's ears; Haman taschen; Purim fritters (see page 188)

139

Mocha Almond Gâteau

METRIC/IMPERIAL	AMERICAN
For the cake	*For the cake*
1 18-cm/7-inch sponge cake (see page 142)	1 7-inch sponge cake (see page 142)
150 ml/¼ pint strong black coffee	⅔ cup strong black coffee
2 tablespoons Tia Maria or sherry	3 tablespoons Tia Maria or sherry
For the filling	*For the filling*
75 g/3 oz butter or margarine	6 tablespoons butter or margarine
75 g/3 oz icing sugar, sifted	¾ cup sifted confectioners' sugar
40 g/1½ oz cocoa powder	⅓ cup cocoa powder
1 egg yolk	1 egg yolk
50–75 g/2–3 oz ground almonds	½–¾ cup ground almonds
black coffee or milk to mix	black coffee or milk to mix
For the topping	*For the topping*
1 (142-ml/5-fl oz) carton double cream	⅔ cup heavy cream
1 egg white	1 egg white
½ teaspoon instant coffee powder	½ teaspoon instant coffee powder
½ teaspoon cocoa powder	½ teaspoon cocoa powder
1 tablespoon boiling water	1 tablespoon boiling water
25 g/1 oz icing sugar	¼ cup confectioners' sugar
2 tablespoons Tia Maria	3 tablespoons Tia Maria
flaked almonds, toasted	flaked almonds, toasted
sifted icing sugar	sifted confectioners' sugar

Lightly grease and bottom line an 18-cm/7-inch cake tin, preferably one with a loose bottom.

Cut the cake into three layers and place the first layer in the base of the tin. Mix the coffee with the Tia Maria and sprinkle one-third over the first layer of cake.

To prepare the filling Cream all the ingredients together, adding enough coffee or milk to make a soft consistency. Spread half of the filling over the first layer of cake, cover with the second cake layer and sprinkle this with half of the remaining coffee liquid. Spread over the remaining filling, top with the third cake layer and sprinkle this with the remaining coffee liquid. Put a lightly weighted plate on top of the cake to press the layers together and set aside for about 1 hour. Alternatively the cake can be refrigerated until required for up to 1 week.

To make the topping and finish the cake Whip the cream until thick and whisk the egg white until stiff. Dissolve the coffee powder in the boiling water and mix in the cocoa powder. Stir into the whipped cream and fold in the stiffly beaten egg white, icing sugar and Tia Maria. Turn the cake out of the tin on to a serving plate and spread with the cream mixture. Cover completely with flaked almonds and decorate with a little sifted icing sugar. (*Illustrated on page 137*)

Marmalade Cake

METRIC/IMPERIAL	AMERICAN
85 g/3 oz margarine	6 tablespoons margarine
85 g/3 oz castor sugar	6 tablespoons sugar
2 eggs	2 eggs
170 g/6 oz self-raising flour, sifted	1½ cups all-purpose flour sifted with 1½ teaspoons baking powder
4 tablespoons marmalade	⅓ cup marmalade
2 tablespoons milk or water	3 tablespoons milk or water

Grease a 23-cm/9-inch shallow cake tin. Cream the margarine and sugar together until soft and fluffy. Lightly beat the eggs and add one at a time with a tablespoon of flour, beating well between each addition. Stir in the marmalade and lastly fold in the flour and milk.

Transfer the mixture to the prepared tin and bake in a moderately hot oven (190°C, 375°F, Gas Mark 5) for 45–50 minutes.

Leave the cake in the tin for 5 minutes then turn on to a wire tray to cool.

Cherry Cake

METRIC/IMPERIAL	AMERICAN
225 g/8 oz plain flour	2 cups all-purpose flour
½ teaspoon baking powder	½ teaspoon baking powder
75 g/3 oz glacé cherries	¾ cup candied cherries
175 g/6 oz butter or margarine	¾ cup butter or margarine
150 g/5 oz castor sugar	⅔ cup sugar
3 eggs	3 eggs
3 drops lemon essence	3 drops lemon extract
25 g/1 oz chopped candied peel ,	3 tablespoons chopped candied peel
2 tablespoons milk	3 tablespoons milk

Grease and line a 15–18-cm/6–7-inch round deep cake tin.

Sift the flour and baking powder together. Chop the cherries. Cream the butter and sugar together until soft and fluffy. Lightly beat the eggs and add one at a time, with a tablespoon of flour, beating lightly between each addition. Add the lemon essence, the cherries, peel, remaining flour and the milk. Stir gently.

Transfer the mixture to the prepared cake tin and bake in the centre of a moderately hot oven (190°C, 375°F, Gas Mark 5) for 30 minutes then lower the temperature to moderate (160°C, 325°F, Gas Mark 3) for a further 45 minutes–1 hour until the cake is well risen, golden brown and firm.

Leave the cake in the tin for 10 minutes and then turn on to a wire tray to cool.

Variations

Seed cake Omit the lemon essence, cherries and peel and add 1 tablespoon caraway seeds.

Ginger cake Omit the cherries, lemon essence and peel, use only 1 tablespoon milk and add 100 g/4 oz (U.S. 1⅓ cups) chopped preserved ginger and 1 tablespoon of the preserved ginger syrup.

Sultana cake Use 100 g/4 oz sultanas (U.S. ¾ cup seedless white raisins) in place of the cherries.

Walnut cake Add 50 g/2 oz (U.S. ½ cup) roughly chopped walnuts in place of the cherries and peel, and flavour with a few drops of almond essence in place of the lemon essence.

Small cakes Put 2 teaspoons of the mixture into greased bun tins and bake on the second shelf of a moderately hot oven (200°C, 400°F, Gas Mark 6) for 20–25 minutes. This makes 18–24 cakes.

Coconut Cake

METRIC/IMPERIAL	AMERICAN
110 g/4 oz butter or margarine	½ cup butter or margarine
110 g/4 oz castor sugar	½ cup sugar
3 large eggs	3 large eggs
170 g/6 oz self-raising flour, sifted	1½ cups all-purpose flour sifted with 1½ teaspoons baking powder
50 g/2 oz desiccated coconut	⅔ cup shredded coconut
grated rind and juice of 1 lemon	grated rind and juice of 1 lemon

Grease and line an 18-cm/7-inch deep cake tin. Cream the butter and sugar together until soft and fluffy. Beat in each egg separately then fold in the flour, coconut, lemon rind and juice.

Transfer the mixture to the prepared cake tin and bake in the centre of a moderately hot oven (190°C, 375°F, Gas Mark 5) for 30 minutes then lower the temperature to moderate (160°C, 325°F, Gas Mark 3) and cook for a further 45 minutes until the cake is well risen, golden brown and firm.

Leave the cake in the tin for 5 minutes then turn out on to a wire tray to cool.

Hazelnut Cake

METRIC/IMPERIAL	AMERICAN
110 g/4 oz self-raising flour, sifted	1 cup all-purpose flour sifted with 2 teaspoons baking powder
1 teaspoon baking powder	
110 g/4 oz castor sugar	½ cup sugar
110 g/4 oz soft margarine	1 cup margarine
2 large eggs	2 large eggs
50 g/2 oz ground hazelnuts	½ cup ground hazelnuts
2 teaspoons instant coffee powder dissolved in 1 tablespoon hot water	2 teaspoons instant coffee powder dissolved in 1 tablespoon hot water

Grease and line a 1-kg/2-lb loaf tin or a 20–23-cm/8–9-inch round cake tin. Place all the ingredients in a mixing bowl and beat with a wooden spoon for about 2 minutes until smooth and well mixed. Turn into the prepared tin and bake in the centre of a moderate oven (160°C, 325°F, Gas Mark 3) for 1 hour until well risen, golden brown and firm.

Leave the cake in the tin for 5 minutes then turn out on to a wire tray to cool. The cake can be iced with thin coffee icing when cold (see page 148)

Victoria Sandwich

METRIC/IMPERIAL	AMERICAN
175 g/6 oz self-raising flour, sifted	1½ cups all-purpose flour sifted with 1½ teaspoons baking powder
175 g/6 oz margarine	¾ cup margarine
175 g/6 oz castor sugar	¾ cup sugar
3 eggs	3 eggs
2 tablespoons warm water	3 tablespoons warm water

Grease two 20-cm/8-inch sandwich tins and dredge them with flour and castor sugar.

Cream the margarine and sugar until soft and fluffy. Beat in the eggs one at a time adding a tablespoon of flour after each addition. Fold in the remaining flour and the water.

Divide the mixture evenly between the prepared tins and bake in the centre of a moderate oven (160°C, 325°F, Gas Mark 3) for about 20–25 minutes, until well risen, golden brown and firm.

Leave the cakes in the tins for 5 minutes and then turn on to a wire tray to cool. When cold, sandwich the cakes together with jam, lemon curd or any other preferred filling. Sprinkle the top with castor sugar or icing sugar or spread with butter icing (see page 148).

Plava (Sponge Cake)

METRIC/IMPERIAL	AMERICAN
110 g/4 oz plain flour	1 cup all-purpose flour
25 g/1 oz butter	2 tablespoons butter
4 eggs, separated	4 eggs, separated
1 teaspoon lemon juice	1 teaspoon lemon juice
¼ teaspoon grated lemon rind	¼ teaspoon grated lemon rind
170 g/6 oz castor sugar	¾ cup sugar

Grease and line an 18-cm/7-inch round deep cake tin. Sift the flour twice. Melt the butter and set aside to cool. Beat the egg yolks in a bowl until thick and creamy. Add the lemon juice and rind and beat again until very thick. Whisk the egg whites until they are stiff, then whisk in the sugar a little at a time.

Fold the egg whites into the beaten yolks and gradually fold in the sifted flour and the melted butter. Pour the mixture into the prepared tin and bake in the centre of a moderate oven (180°C, 350°F, Gas Mark 4) for 1¼–1½ hours.

Invert the tin on to a wire tray and leave for 1 hour before turning out.

Sponge Layer Cake

METRIC/IMPERIAL	AMERICAN
75 g/3 oz self-raising flour	¾ cup all-purpose flour sifted with ¾ teaspoon baking powder
3 eggs, separated	3 eggs, separated
75 g/3 oz castor sugar	6 tablespoons sugar

Grease and bottom line one 23-cm/9-inch sandwich tin or two 15-cm/6-inch sandwich tins or grease and flour 12–15 bun tins.

Sift the flour. Beat the egg yolks and sugar together until pale and creamy. Whisk the egg whites to a stiff froth and fold into the egg yolk and sugar mixture. Carefully fold in the flour with a metal spoon. Pour into the prepared tins and bake in the centre of a moderate oven (180°C, 350°F, Gas Mark 4) for 30–35 minutes for the larger cake, 20–25 minutes for the two smaller cakes.

Eggless Fruit Cake

METRIC/IMPERIAL	AMERICAN
225–275 g/8–10 oz mixed dried fruit	1½–2 cups mixed dried fruit
25 g/1 oz chopped candied peel	¼ cup chopped candied peel
75 g/3 oz margarine	6 tablespoons margarine
75 g/3 oz sugar	6 tablespoons sugar
150 ml/¼ pint water	⅔ cup water
225 g/8 oz self-raising flour	2 cups all-purpose flour sifted with 2 teaspoons baking powder
1 teaspoon mixed spice	1 teaspoon mixed spice
½ teaspoon bicarbonate of soda	½ teaspoon baking soda

Grease and line an 18-cm/7-inch deep cake tin. If dates are being used as part of the mixed fruit, cut them into small rough pieces.

Put the fruit, candied peel, margarine, sugar and water in a thick-based saucepan and bring slowly to the boil. Simmer for 3 minutes then leave until nearly cold.

Sift the flour and spice into a bowl. Add the bicarbonate of soda to the cooled mixture and pour into the flour. Mix thoroughly with a wooden spoon and turn into the prepared tin. Smooth the surface with the back of a wet metal spoon.

Bake in a moderately hot oven (190°C, 375°F, Gas Mark 5) for 1 hour and then reduce the heat to 180°C, 350°F, Gas Mark 4 and cook for a further 30 minutes.

Leave in the tin for 5 minutes then turn on to a wire tray to cool. Leave at least 2 days before cutting. Eat plain or buttered.

Stuffed Monkey

METRIC/IMPERIAL	AMERICAN
170 g/6 oz flour	1½ cups all-purpose flour
½ teaspoon cinnamon	½ teaspoon cinnamon
110 g/4 oz butter or margarine	½ cup butter or margarine
1 egg, separated	1 egg, separated
110 g/4 oz soft brown sugar	½ cup soft brown sugar
For the filling	*For the filling*
40 g/1½ oz margarine	3 tablespoons margarine
50 g/2 oz chopped candied peel	⅓ cup chopped candied peel
25 g/1 oz castor sugar	2 tablespoons sugar
50 g/2 oz ground almonds	½ cup ground almonds
1 egg yolk	1 egg yolk

Grease a 20-cm/8-inch sandwich tin. Sift the flour and cinnamon into a bowl and rub in the butter or margarine. Add the egg yolk and the sugar and knead into a pliable dough. Divide in half and roll out into two 20-cm/ 8-inch rounds.

To make the filling Melt the margarine, add all the remaining ingredients and mix well.

Put one of the rounds on the base of the sandwich tin and cover with the filling. Place the second round on top. Brush with lightly beaten egg white and bake in a moderately hot oven (190°C, 375°F, Gas Mark 5) for about 30 minutes. Allow to cool in the tin.

Coffee Crisps

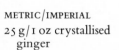

METRIC/IMPERIAL	AMERICAN
175 g/6 oz butter or margarine	¾ cup butter or margarine
85 g/3 oz icing sugar	¾ cup confectioners' sugar
2 teaspoons instant coffee granules	2 teaspoons instant coffee granules
175 g/6 oz plain flour	1½ cups all-purpose flour
icing sugar for dusting	confectioners' sugar for dusting

Cream the butter and sugar together until soft and fluffy. Add the coffee granules and the flour and mix well. Place in teaspoon quantities on a greased baking sheet, allowing a little space between each one for spreading. Flatten gently with a fork.

Bake in a moderate oven (160°C, 325°F, Gas Mark 3) for 20–25 minutes. The biscuits are rather fragile to handle when warm and should be left to cool a little before lifting from the baking sheet on to a wire tray to cool. When cool, dust the biscuits lightly with icing sugar.

Ginger Biscuits

METRIC/IMPERIAL	AMERICAN
25 g/1 oz crystallised ginger	4 pieces candied ginger
75 g/3 oz butter or margarine	6 tablespoons butter or margarine
75 g/3 oz castor sugar	6 tablespoons sugar
1 egg yolk	1 egg yolk
100 g/4 oz plain flour, sifted	1 cup sifted all-purpose flour
2 teaspoons ground ginger	2 teaspoons ground ginger
3–4 tablespoons crushed cornflakes	⅓ cup crushed cornflakes

Chop the crystallised ginger. Cream the butter and sugar until soft and fluffy. Add the egg yolk and beat well. Stir in the chopped ginger and fold in the flour with the ground ginger to make a dough consistency.

Form into small balls and roll in the crushed cornflakes, pressing them in lightly to make them stick.

Place on greased baking sheets allowing room for the biscuits to spread. Bake in a moderately hot oven (190°C, 375°F, Gas Mark 5) for about 20–25 minutes until the biscuits are lightly browned. Cool on the baking sheet for 2–3 minutes then transfer to a wire tray to cool.

Teiglech

METRIC/IMPERIAL	AMERICAN
225 g/8 oz flour	2 cups all-purpose flour
pinch of salt	dash of salt
1½ teaspoons ground ginger	1½ teaspoons ground ginger
2 large eggs	2 large eggs
450 g/1 lb golden syrup	1⅓ cups corn syrup

Sift the flour with the salt and ½ teaspoon of the ginger into a bowl. Lightly beat the eggs and add to the flour. Mix thoroughly and knead to a smooth dough. Roll out on a lightly floured surface until 1-cm/½-inch thick and cut into 2.5-cm/1-inch squares.

Warm the syrup in a saucepan, add the remaining ginger and when the syrup boils add the squares of dough a few at a time. Boil the squares gently until a pale biscuit colour – this will take about 20 minutes. Lift the squares out of the syrup with a preheated spoon and place on a moistened board. Smooth the surface of the squares using a wet spoon.

Variations

For special occasions use honey instead of syrup.

The dough can be rolled into tiny balls and after being removed from the syrup rolled in chopped nuts or desiccated coconut.

Date and Honey Buns

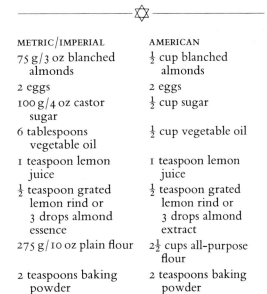

METRIC/IMPERIAL	AMERICAN
75 g/3 oz margarine	6 tablespoons margarine
25 g/1 oz castor sugar	2 tablespoons sugar
50 g/2 oz honey	3 tablespoons honey
1 egg	1 egg
175 g/6 oz self-raising flour	1½ cups all-purpose flour sifted with 1½ teaspoons baking powder
milk or water to mix	milk or water to mix
50 g/2 oz chopped dates	⅓ cup chopped dates

Grease some patty tins or arrange some paper cases on a baking sheet. Cream the margarine, sugar and honey until soft. Beat in the egg then fold in the flour with enough milk or water at room temperature to give a soft dropping consistency. Add the dates and mix lightly.

Half-fill the prepared patty tins or paper cases and bake in a moderately hot oven (200°C, 400°F, Gas Mark 6) for about 20 minutes. Cool on a wire tray.

Mandelbrot

METRIC/IMPERIAL	AMERICAN
75 g/3 oz blanched almonds	½ cup blanched almonds
2 eggs	2 eggs
100 g/4 oz castor sugar	½ cup sugar
6 tablespoons vegetable oil	½ cup vegetable oil
1 teaspoon lemon juice	1 teaspoon lemon juice
½ teaspoon grated lemon rind or 3 drops almond essence	½ teaspoon grated lemon rind or 3 drops almond extract
275 g/10 oz plain flour	2½ cups all-purpose flour
2 teaspoons baking powder	2 teaspoons baking powder
pinch of salt	dash of salt

Coarsely chop the almonds. Beat the eggs and sugar lightly, add the oil and lemon juice and the grated lemon rind or almond essence.

Sift the flour, baking powder and salt into a bowl. Add the egg mixture and the almonds and mix to a dough. With floured hands shape into rolls about 7.5 cm/3 inches wide. Place the rolls on a well-greased and floured baking sheet and bake in a moderate oven (180°C, 350°F, Gas Mark 4) for 30–40 minutes until very lightly browned.

Leave the strips until almost cold then cut across obliquely into slices about 1 cm/½ inch thick and return to the oven until a deeper brown.

Biscuit Cake

METRIC/IMPERIAL	AMERICAN
225 g/8 oz biscuits (morning coffee or rich tea type)	½ lb plain cookies
100 g/4 oz margarine	½ cup margarine
40 g/1½ oz cocoa powder	⅓ cup cocoa powder
2 tablespoons golden syrup	3 tablespoons maple syrup
25 g/1 oz castor sugar	2 tablespoons sugar
25 g/1 oz sultanas (optional)	3 tablespoons seedless white raisins (optional)
finely grated rind of 1 orange	finely grated rind of 1 orange

Grease a 20-cm/8-inch loose bottomed cake tin or line the base of an ordinary 20-cm/8-inch sandwich tin.

Coarsely crush the biscuits. Put the margarine, cocoa powder, syrup, sugar and sultanas if used in a thick-based saucepan over a moderate heat. Stir gently until the ingredients are well mixed. Stir in the biscuits and orange rind.

Press the mixture firmly and evenly into the prepared tin. Chill in the refrigerator until firm, then turn out and cut into pieces.

For special occasions, spread the mixture with melted chocolate before placing it in the refrigerator.

Basic Kichal (Biscuit) Recipe

METRIC/IMPERIAL	AMERICAN
150 g/5 oz margarine	⅓ cup margarine
150 g/5 oz castor sugar	⅔ cup sugar, firmly packed
1 egg yolk	1 egg yolk
flavouring (see variations)	flavoring (see variations)
225 g/8 oz self-raising flour	2 cups, all-purpose flour sifted with 2 teaspoons baking powder

Cream the margarine and sugar until soft and fluffy. Beat in the egg yolk and chosen flavouring, then fold in the flour. Mix thoroughly and knead to a pliable dough. Roll out to 5 mm/¼ inch thick on a lightly floured surface and cut into rounds or crescent shapes with a biscuit cutter.

Place on a greased baking sheet and bake in a hot oven (220°C, 425°F, Gas Mark 7) for 10–15 minutes or until the biscuits are lightly browned.

Variations

Lemon biscuits Add 3 drops lemon essence to the finely grated rind of ½ lemon.

Cinnamon biscuits Add 1 teaspoon ground cinnamon to the flour.

Spiced biscuits Add ¼ teaspoon each of mixed spice, ground cinnamon and ground ginger to the flour.

Jaffa biscuits Sandwich together two biscuits with seedless jam or lemon curd.

Coconut biscuits Add 1 tablespoon desiccated (shredded) coconut and 15 g/½ oz (U.S. 1½ tablespoons) finely chopped glacé cherries (candied cherries) to the basic mixture.

Wine biscuits

1 Flavour the basic mixture with lemon or vanilla essence then decorate the top of the biscuits. First brush over the surface with lightly beaten egg white, then sprinkle with chopped almonds, desiccated coconut or caraway seeds, or put a small piece of glacé cherry in the centre of each.

2 Take small pieces of the dough, roll them on a flat surface with the palm of the hand into pencil-shaped strips about 10 cm/4 inches long and shape into scrolls, twirls or rings. Brush over with lightly beaten egg white and dredge with castor sugar. Place on a greased baking sheet – not too close together – and bake in a moderately hot oven (200°C, 400°F, Gas Mark 6) for 10–15 minutes until very pale brown.

Plain Kichals

METRIC/IMPERIAL	AMERICAN
2 eggs	2 eggs
1 tablespoon castor sugar	1 tablespoon sugar
pinch of salt	dash of salt
2 tablespoons vegetable oil	3 tablespoons vegetable oil
self-raising flour (see method)	all-purpose flour sifted with 1 teaspoon baking powder to 1 cup (see method)
castor sugar for dredging	superfine sugar for dredging

Lightly beat the eggs with the castor sugar and salt. Add the vegetable oil and sufficient flour to make a pliable dough. Knead lightly, then roll out thinly on a floured surface – about 5 mm/$\frac{1}{4}$ inch thick is best. Cut into shapes and dredge lightly with castor sugar.

Place on a greased baking sheet and bake in a moderately hot oven (200°C, 400°F, Gas Mark 6) for about 20 minutes or until a light golden colour. Cool on a wire tray.

Ginger Nuts

METRIC/IMPERIAL	AMERICAN
50 g/2 oz margarine	$\frac{1}{4}$ cup margarine
2 tablespoons golden syrup	3 tablespoons corn syrup
100 g/4 oz self-raising flour	1 cup all-purpose flour sifted with 1 teaspoon baking powder
1 teaspoon ground ginger	1 teaspoon ground ginger
$\frac{1}{2}$ teaspoon ground cinnamon	$\frac{1}{2}$ teaspoon ground cinnamon
$\frac{1}{2}$ teaspoon bicarbonate of soda	$\frac{1}{2}$ teaspoon baking soda

Grease two or three baking sheets. Melt the margarine and syrup in a thick-based saucepan over moderate heat. Sift the dry ingredients into a mixing bowl, add the melted mixture and mix well. Put teaspoons of the mixture on the prepared baking sheets, leaving room around each spoonful for it to spread a little.

Bake in a moderately hot oven (190°C, 375°F, Gas Mark 5) for 12–15 minutes. Cool on a wire tray.

Viennese Fancies

METRIC/IMPERIAL	AMERICAN
40 g/1$\frac{1}{2}$ oz icing sugar	$\frac{1}{3}$ cup confectioners' sugar
100 g/4 oz margarine	$\frac{1}{2}$ cup margarine
75 g/3 oz plain flour	$\frac{3}{4}$ cup all-purpose flour
25 g/1 oz cornflour	$\frac{1}{4}$ cup cornstarch
2–3 drops vanilla or almond essence	2–3 drops vanilla or almond extract
red jam	red jam

Sift the icing sugar into a bowl. Add the margarine and beat together until creamy. Add the flour, cornflour and flavouring and beat very thoroughly.

Place 8 paper cases on a baking sheet. Put the biscuit mixture into a forcing bag with a large rose nozzle and pipe two rounds of the mixture into each paper case, leaving a small space in the centre. Bake in a moderately hot oven (190°C, 375°F, Gas Mark 5) for about 20 minutes until firm but still pale.

When cold, dredge with icing sugar and place a little jam in the centre of each.

Glacé Icing

METRIC/IMPERIAL	AMERICAN
225 g/8 oz icing sugar, sifted	1¾ cups sifted confectioners' sugar
2 tablespoons warm water	3 tablespoons warm water
flavouring (vanilla, coffee or almond essence, or 1 teaspoon lemon juice)	flavoring (vanilla, coffee or almond extract, or 1 teaspoon lemon juice)

Put the sifted icing sugar in a small saucepan, add the water and a few drops of flavouring essence or the lemon juice. Stir over a gentle heat until just warm, being careful that it does not get too hot.

It should be thick enough to coat the back of a spoon. If too thin add more sugar; if too thick, more water. Use immediately.

Chocolate Fudge Frosting

METRIC/IMPERIAL	AMERICAN
75 g/3 oz icing sugar	¾ cup confectioners' sugar
25 g/1 oz cocoa powder	¼ cup cocoa powder
2–3 teaspoons instant coffee powder	2–3 teaspoons instant coffee powder
40 g/1½ oz butter or margarine	3 tablespoons butter or margarine
2 tablespoons water	3 tablespoons water
50 g/2 oz castor sugar	¼ cup sugar

Sift the icing sugar, cocoa and coffee into a mixing bowl. Put the butter, water and sugar into a saucepan over a low heat and stir until the butter is melted and the sugar dissolved. When just boiling pour on to the sifted ingredients and beat with a wooden spoon until the icing is smooth. Allow the mixture to stand until it thickens. Use immediately for a filling; for an icing chill in the refrigerator a little while.

Butter Icing

METRIC/IMPERIAL	AMERICAN
100 g/4 oz butter or margarine	½ cup butter or margarine
175 g/6 oz icing sugar, sifted	1⅓ cups sifted confectioners' sugar
vanilla essence	vanilla extract

Cream the butter or margarine and add the sifted sugar. Beat until smooth and creamy, adding a few drops of vanilla essence.

Chocolate Butter Icing

METRIC/IMPERIAL	AMERICAN
25 g/1 oz plain chocolate, grated	1 square semi-sweet chocolate, grated
1 tablespoon milk	1 tablespoon milk
75 g/3 oz butter or margarine	6 tablespoons butter or margarine
175 g/6 oz icing sugar, sifted	1⅓ cups sifted confectioners' sugar
vanilla essence	vanilla extract

Dissolve the chocolate in the milk by slightly warming it. Cream the butter, add the sifted icing sugar and dissolved chocolate and a few drops of vanilla essence. Beat hard until thoroughly blended.

Butter Cream Filling

✡

Butter icing is also used as a butter cream filling for cakes.

Variations

Chocolate filling Melt 50 g/2 oz plain chocolate (U.S. 2 squares semi-sweet chocolate) in a basin over hot water, add to the creamed fat and sugar and mix thoroughly.

Coffee filling Add 1 tablespoon coffee essence (extract).

Coconut filling Add 2 tablespoons desiccated coconut (U.S. 3 tablespoons shredded coconut).

Ginger filling Add 25 g/1 oz chopped preserved ginger and 1 teaspoon ginger syrup.

Orange or lemon filling Add 2 teaspoons orange or lemon juice and a little grated rind in place of the vanilla essence (extract).

Nut filling Add 2 tablespoons (U.S. 3 tablespoons) finely chopped toasted almonds.

Walnut filling Add 2 tablespoons (U.S. 3 tablespoons) chopped walnuts to the coffee filling.

Cream Fillings

✡

METRIC/IMPERIAL	AMERICAN
150 ml/¼ pint double cream	⅔ cup heavy cream
1 egg white	1 egg white
2 tablespoons sifted icing sugar	3 tablespoons sifted confectioners' sugar
flavouring	flavoring

The flavouring can be vanilla or a little coffee essence. Chopped nuts, crushed burnt almonds or peanut brittle can also be added.

Whip the cream until thick and light. Whisk the egg white to a stiff froth and fold it into the cream, together with the sugar and chosen flavouring.

Nut and Apricot Filling

✡

METRIC/IMPERIAL	AMERICAN
3 tablespoons apricot jam	¼ cup apricot jam
1 tablespoon finely chopped walnuts	1 tablespoon finely chopped walnuts
3 tablespoons ground almonds	¼ cup ground almonds
flavouring (1 teaspoon lemon or orange juice, or ¼ teaspoon vanilla essence)	flavoring (1 teaspoon lemon or orange juice, or ¼ teaspoon vanilla extract)

Warm and sieve the jam and mix all the ingredients with the flavouring. This filling is very good for sandwich cakes or biscuits.

American Icing

✡

METRIC/IMPERIAL	AMERICAN
450 g/1 lb granulated sugar	2 cups sugar
150 ml/¼ pint water	⅔ cup water
pinch of cream of tartar	dash of cream of tartar
vanilla essence	vanilla extract
2 egg whites	2 egg whites

Put the sugar and water into a thick-based saucepan. Let it stand for an hour or two, then place over a very gentle heat until the sugar has dissolved. Add the cream of tartar, bring slowly to the boil then boil steadily without stirring for 7 minutes after it has reached boiling point (if you have a sugar thermometer continue boiling until the temperature reaches 115°C/240°F).

Meanwhile whisk the egg whites until stiff. Remove the syrup from the heat and add a few drops of vanilla. Pour the syrup over the egg whites and beat continuously until the mixture is thick enough to coat the back of a spoon. Then pour very quickly over the cake.

The icing sets very quickly, so if decorations are being used have them ready prepared.

Breads

When making bread use either fresh or dried yeast – both are equally good. Where the recipe asks for 25 g/1 oz yeast (U.S. 1 cake compressed yeast) use 4 teaspoons dried yeast (U.S. 1 package active dry yeast). If you prefer to use fresh yeast this can be bought in a block from the bakers and frozen.

To freeze yeast, divide into portions suitable for use in one recipe, e.g. 25 g/1 oz (U.S. 1 cake), wrap the small cubes in foil or polythene and stack in a rigid container. For immediate use, grate the frozen yeast or leave at room temperature for 30 minutes to defrost.

To prevent a crust forming on the rising dough, grease a polythene sheet (a split polythene bag will do) with oil and press it over the surface of the dough.

A food mixer with dough hook can take a lot of the effort out of yeast cookery and also reduce the time. Check the manufacturer's instructions for kneading times.

Bagels
☆

METRIC/IMPERIAL	AMERICAN
15 g/½ oz fresh yeast or 2 teaspoons dried yeast	½ cake compressed yeast or 2 teaspoons active dry yeast
25 g/1 oz castor sugar	2 tablespoons sugar
50 g/2 oz margarine	¼ cup margarine
scant 300 ml/½ pint milk or water	1¼ cups milk or water
1 teaspoon salt	1 teaspoon salt
450 g/1 lb flour	4 cups flour
1 egg yolk	1 egg yolk

Cream the fresh yeast with a teaspoon of the sugar. Put the margarine, milk, remaining sugar and salt into a saucepan over very gentle heat until the margarine has melted. Cool to lukewarm then pour in the creamed yeast. If using dried yeast, sprinkle into the warm liquid.

Sift the flour into a large warm bowl and pour the yeast mixture into the centre. Add the egg yolk and mix thoroughly by hand or in an electric mixer to a firm dough. Knead on a lightly floured surface until smooth then place in the bowl, cover with a cloth and leave in a warm place for about 1 hour until the dough is just beginning to rise.

Knead again then roll into small pieces, the thickness of a finger and about 13 cm/5 inches long. Shape into rings, pinching the ends well together. Leave on a floured surface in a warm place for about 10 minutes until just beginning to rise.

Drop the rings one at a time into a saucepan half-full of simmering water. Cook very gently until the rings rise to the top. Remove with a perforated spoon and place on a greased baking sheet. Bake the rings in a preheated moderately hot oven (200°C, 400°F, Gas Mark 6) for 20–30 minutes until crisp and golden brown. *(Illustrated on pages 126–127)*

Variations

The bagels can be sprinkled with caraway seeds or salt before baking.

3 tablespoons (U.S. ¼ cup) vegetable oil may be used in place of the margarine.

Bola

METRIC/IMPERIAL	AMERICAN
For the dough	*For the dough*
15 g/½ oz fresh yeast or 2 teaspoons dried yeast	½ cake compressed yeast or 2 teaspoons active dry yeast
1 teaspoon castor sugar	1 teaspoon sugar
300 ml/½ pint warm milk	1¼ cups warm milk
450 g/1 lb flour	4 cups all-purpose flour
225 g/8 oz butter or margarine	1 cup butter or margarine
2 large eggs	2 large eggs
For the filling	*For the filling*
175 g/6 oz candied peel	1 cup candied peel
125 g/4 oz preserved ginger	½ cup preserved ginger
25 g/1 oz soft brown sugar	2 tablespoons soft brown sugar
125 g/4 oz ground almonds	1 cup ground almonds
2 teaspoons ground cinnamon	2 teaspoons ground cinnamon
For the syrup	*For the syrup*
125 g/4 oz castor sugar	½ cup sugar
3 tablespoons water	¼ cup water
1 tablespoon preserved ginger syrup	1 tablespoon preserved ginger syrup

Grease two 20-cm/8-inch sandwich tins and leave in a warm place. Cream the fresh yeast with a teaspoon of castor sugar, then add the lukewarm milk. If using dried yeast, dissolve the sugar in the warm milk and sprinkle the yeast on top. Leave the liquid for 10 minutes until frothy. Sift the flour into a warm bowl and rub in 50 g/2 oz (U.S. ¼ cup) of the butter. Make a well in the centre. Pour in the dissolved yeast mixture and leave to stand for 15 minutes.

Add the lightly beaten eggs and mix to a soft dough. Knead well on a floured surface and place the dough in a bowl. Cover with a piece of greased polythene and leave in a warm place for 1 hour to rise.

Meanwhile, to make the filling, cut up the peel and ginger and mix with the sugar, ground almonds and cinnamon.

When the dough has risen, knead lightly on a floured surface and roll it out to a large oblong. Spread half of the butter over the surface. Fold the dough in half to enclose the butter and roll out to an oblong again. Spread the remaining butter over the surface and fold and roll again, finishing with a large thin square which is big enough to cut out four rounds of dough the same size as the sandwich tins.

Line each of the prepared tins with a round of dough, spread each one with half of the filling and cover with another round of dough. Cover the tins with greased polythene and leave for 30 minutes in a warm place to rise.

Bake in a hot oven (220°C, 425°F, Gas Mark 7) for 30 minutes.

Boil all the ingredients for the syrup together for about 10 minutes. Brush the syrup over the partly cooked bola then reduce the heat to moderate (180°C, 350°F, Gas Mark 4) and continue cooking for a further 20–30 minutes. When cooked, brush over again with syrup and when partly cooled turn out on to a wire tray. *(Illustrated on pages 126–127)*

Cholla

✡

METRIC/IMPERIAL	AMERICAN
1.6 kg/3½ lb plain flour	3½ lb all-purpose flour
2 teaspoons salt	2 teaspoons salt
25 g/1 oz fresh yeast or 15 g/½ oz dried yeast	1 cake compressed yeast or 1 package active dry yeast
1 teaspoon castor sugar	1 teaspoon sugar
1 litre/1¾ pints warm water	4¼ cups warm water
poppy seeds	poppy seeds

Sift the flour and salt into a large warm mixing bowl and make a well in the centre. Cream the fresh yeast and sugar together and stir in about 300 ml/½ pint (U.S. 1¼ cups) of the warm water. If using dried yeast, dissolve the sugar in about 300 ml/½ pint (U.S. 1¼ cups) of the warm water and sprinkle the yeast on top. Leave the liquid for 10 minutes until frothy. Pour this liquid into the centre of the flour and sprinkle the surface with a little flour from the sides of the bowl. Cover the bowl with a cloth and leave in a warm place for 20 minutes.

Work in all the flour by hand, adding as much of the warm water as is necessary to make a firm dough. Then knead for about 5–10 minutes by hand or in an electric mixer using the dough hook. Replace the dough in the bowl, cover and leave in a warm place until doubled in size. This usually takes about 1½ hours.

Turn on to a lightly floured surface and knead until the dough is smooth and elastic. Divide the dough in half and then each half into three. With the palm of the hand roll each piece into a long thin roll and form into two plaits. Place on a floured baking sheet and leave in a warm place for 15 minutes.

Brush with beaten egg and sprinkle with poppy seeds. Bake for 15 minutes towards the top of a hot oven (220°C, 425°F, Gas Mark 7) and then reduce the temperature to moderate (180°C, 350°F, Gas Mark 4) and bake for a further 35–40 minutes. Cool on a wire tray. *(Illustrated on pages 126–127)*

Kuchen Dough

✡

METRIC/IMPERIAL	AMERICAN
15 g/½ oz fresh yeast or 2 teaspoons dried yeast	½ cake compressed yeast or 2 teaspoons active dry yeast
50 g/2 oz castor sugar	¼ cup sugar
50 g/2 oz margarine	¼ cup margarine
300 ml/½ pint warm milk	1¼ cups warm milk
450 g/1 lb flour	4 cups flour
pinch of salt	dash of salt
1 egg	1 egg

Cream the fresh yeast with one teaspoon of the sugar. Melt the margarine in the warm milk and pour into the creamed yeast. Leave for 10 minutes until frothy. If using dried yeast, add the sugar to the warm milk and margarine and sprinkle the yeast on top. Leave until frothy.

Sift the flour and salt into a large warm mixing bowl. Make a well in the centre and pour in the yeast mixture. Gradually work in the flour from the sides and mix to a smooth dough either by hand or using the dough hook of an electric mixer. Cover the bowl and leave in a warm place to rise for 1½–2 hours.

Knead the dough in the bowl and add the remaining sugar and the beaten egg and continue to knead thoroughly until smooth and elastic. Use as the basis for the recipe below.

Plain Coffee Kuchen

Roll out the risen dough to about 1 cm/½ inch thick. Place in a greased 20-cm/8-inch sandwich tin and leave in a warm place for 30 minutes until doubled in size. Pour a little melted butter over the top and sprinkle with castor sugar, cinnamon and chopped nuts. Bake in a moderately hot oven (190°C, 375°F, Gas Mark 5) for about 30 minutes. Cool on a wire tray.

Note The kuchen dough can also be used as a base for cheesecake (see page 129).

Bun ring

Divide the risen kuchen dough into three equal pieces. Roll each piece by hand into a long strand, then form the three into a plait. Place in a circle on a well-greased baking tin and leave in a warm place for 30 minutes until doubled in size. Brush the top with melted margarine, sprinkle with castor sugar and chopped nuts and bake in a moderately hot oven (190°C, 375°F, Gas Mark 5) for about 20 minutes. Cool on a wire tray.

Streusel

Roll out the risen dough to 1 cm/$\frac{1}{2}$ inch thick, place in a shallow buttered tin and leave in a warm place for 30 minutes until doubled in size. Meanwhile, prepare the streusel topping (see below) and when the dough has risen sprinkle it over the top. Bake in a moderately hot oven (190°C, 375°F, Gas Mark 5) for 30 minutes. Cool on a wire tray. *(Illustrated on pages 126–127)*

Coffee Kuchen
✡

METRIC/IMPERIAL	AMERICAN
20 g/$\frac{3}{4}$ oz fresh yeast or 3 teaspoons dried yeast	$\frac{3}{4}$ cake compressed yeast or 3 teaspoons active dry yeast
300 ml/$\frac{1}{2}$ pint warm milk and water or warm water alone	1$\frac{1}{4}$ cups warm milk and water or warm water alone
575 g/1$\frac{1}{4}$ lb plain flour	4$\frac{1}{4}$ cups all-purpose flour
$\frac{1}{2}$ teaspoon salt	$\frac{1}{2}$ teaspoon salt
75 g/3 oz butter or margarine	6 tablespoons butter or margarine
75 g/3 oz castor sugar	6 tablespoons sugar
1 egg, beaten	1 egg, beaten
100 g/4 oz sultanas	$\frac{2}{3}$ cup seedless white raisins
50 g/2 oz currants	$\frac{1}{3}$ cup currants
50 g/2 oz chopped candied peel	$\frac{1}{3}$ cup chopped candied peel
For the topping	*For the topping*
melted margarine and castor sugar	melted margarine and sugar

Cream the fresh yeast with one teaspoon of the sugar and add the warm liquid. If using dried yeast, dissolve the sugar in the warm liquid and sprinkle the yeast on top. Leave the liquid for 10 minutes until frothy. Sift the flour and salt into a large warm mixing bowl and rub in the butter until the mixture resembles fine breadcrumbs. Mix in the remaining sugar and add the frothy yeast liquid and the egg and mix thoroughly. Knead to a smooth, elastic dough on a lightly floured surface then replace the dough in the bowl. Cover with a cloth and leave in a warm place for about 1$\frac{1}{2}$ hours until doubled in size.

Turn the dough on to a floured surface and sprinkle with the dried fruit. Knead lightly until it is evenly distributed.

Warm and grease two 1-kg/2-lb loaf tins or 18-cm/7-inch cake tins. Half fill the tins with the kuchen mixture and leave in a warm place for 30 minutes until doubled in size. Pour a little melted margarine over the top, sprinkle with castor sugar and bake in a moderately hot oven (190°C, 375°F, Gas Mark 5) for 15 minutes. Reduce the heat to moderate (180°C, 350°F, Gas Mark 4) and cook for a further 30 minutes until brown and well risen. *(Illustrated on pages 126–127)*

Variation

For a richer recipe, brush the uncooked kuchen with melted butter and sprinkle with streusel topping (see following recipe).

Streusel Topping
✡

METRIC/IMPERIAL	AMERICAN
50 g/2 oz flour	$\frac{1}{2}$ cup all-purpose flour
$\frac{1}{2}$ teaspoon cinnamon	$\frac{1}{2}$ teaspoon cinnamon
75 g/3 oz sugar	$\frac{1}{3}$ cup sugar
50 g/2 oz butter	$\frac{1}{4}$ cup butter
few chopped almonds	few chopped almonds

Sift the flour and cinnamon into a bowl. Mix in the sugar, then rub in the butter until the mixture resembles fine breadcrumbs. Add a few chopped almonds. Brush the top of the kuchen dough quite liberally with melted butter then sprinkle over the streusel topping.

Quick Kuchen

METRIC/IMPERIAL	AMERICAN
175 g/6 oz butter or margarine	¾ cup butter or margarine
225 g/8 oz castor sugar	1 cup sugar
2 eggs	2 eggs
450 g/1 lb self-raising flour, sifted	4 cups all-purpose flour sifted with 4 teaspoons baking powder
50 g/2 oz raisins	⅓ cup raisins
grated rind of 1 lemon (optional)	grated rind of 1 lemon (optional)
200 ml/8 fl oz hot milk	1 cup hot milk

Cream the butter and sugar together until soft and fluffy. Beat in the eggs one at a time, then add the sifted flour, raisins and lemon rind if used. Add half of the hot milk at this stage as the mixture will be fairly stiff. Mix well together, then add the remainder of the milk to form a loose mixture.

Pour the mixture into two greased and lined 1-kg/2-lb loaf tins and bake in a moderate oven (180°C, 350°F, Gas Mark 4) for 45 minutes until well risen and golden brown. Cool slightly then turn out and cool on a wire tray.

This cake can be served on its own or buttered.

Spice Loaf

METRIC/IMPERIAL	AMERICAN
50 g/2 oz margarine	¼ cup margarine
100 g/4 oz dark brown sugar	½ cup dark brown sugar
225 g/8 oz mixed fruit	1⅓ cups mixed fruit
1 teaspoon cinnamon	1 teaspoon cinnamon
1 teaspoon mixed spice	1 teaspoon mixed spice
1 teaspoon bicarbonate of soda	1 teaspoon baking soda
150 ml/¼ pint boiling water	⅔ cup boiling water
1 large egg	1 large egg
225 g/8 oz self-raising flour	2 cups all-purpose flour sifted with 2 teaspoons baking powder
½ teaspoon vanilla essence	½ teaspoon vanilla extract
50 g/2 oz chopped walnuts (optional)	½ cup chopped walnuts (optional)

Grease and line a 1-kg/2-lb loaf tin. Place the margarine, sugar, dried fruit, spices and bicarbonate of soda in a mixing bowl. Pour on the boiling water and mix until the margarine is melted. Beat the egg and add to the mixture with the flour and vanilla essence. Stir well.

Transfer to the prepared tin, sprinkle with the walnuts if used, and bake in the centre of a moderate oven (180°C, 350°F, Gas Mark 4) for 45 minutes. Cool in the tin for a few minutes then turn out on to a wire tray.

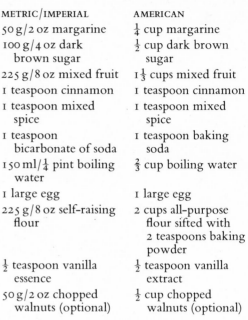

Honeyed chicken (see page 62)

Overleaf: Open sandwich (see page 160); Green salad (see page 91); Frankfurter and bean casserole (see page 161); Vegetable soup with frankfurters (see page 161)

Cooking for One

When it comes to cooking for one, whatever the situation – in a house, a flat or a bedsitter – and regardless of age too, it seems that the main problem is time. Time to do the shopping so that there is always food available, and time to prepare a meal. When there is no regular meal pattern expected by other people the tendency is to start to make a meal when overcome by feelings of hunger – and that doesn't provide much incentive for preparing complicated menus.

Associated with this lack of time and the need to produce something quickly is nutrition. Those living alone tend to be at either end of the age spectrum; young people leaving home for the first time and attending university or tackling their first job, or people whose families have left home. For both these age groups good nutrition is important and quick meals can tend to contain a large proportion of carbohydrate.

Fish and meat are more expensive, especially when only small quantities are needed, and also have a short storage life. Therefore when choosing recipes shopping and storage are important considerations.

There are three pieces of equipment which though not essential will go a long way towards making life simpler and in the long run more economical:

A refrigerator which reduces waste and enables shopping trips to be carried out weekly not daily.

A pressure cooker which cuts down the time for making soups, stocks and casseroles to a bare minimum.

A small freezer. This final item may initially appear to be an extravagance but there are models small enough to go on top of a work surface or refrigerator. It provides the facility to buy large economical packs of food or joints of meat, of cooking large quantities when time is available and freezing small portions for use later, and of avoiding waste. Items cooked and not eaten, or bought and not cooked, can be kept for a later date instead of being thrown away.

Stocking the larder is worth some careful thought. A few basic items will help to improve the flavour of food and will increase the variety of dishes that can be made quickly. Buying kosher convenience food may prove difficult as it is not readily found in all areas. However, the choice available when it can be found is so considerable that it is worth stocking up with non-perishable items when a good source is located.

Listed here are possible items from which to choose:

Canned foods: fish, including gefillte fish, beans, fruit and beef-burgers. There is a great variety of soups – chicken with or without kneidlech, mushroom and oxtail – and an interesting range of fruit soups imported from Israel. Full meals include braised meat with rice, meatballs in tomato sauce, beef stews with vegetables, ravioli and spaghetti. Though more expensive than home prepared foods, these can provide a quick and tasty meal.

Packaged foods: provide a choice of cake mixes, cheese spreads, jellies, fruit pies, lockshen noodles and macaroni.

Standard store cupboard items should include chrane, pickled cucumbers, custard powder, flavourings, gravy powder, mayonnaise and salad cream, olive and vegetable oils, jams and spreads. Soup cubes are a must – they are so useful for flavouring soups, sauces and stews. Beef, chicken and vegetable cubes are available.

Add to this list instant puddings, milk shakes, skimmed milk powders, peanut butter and anchovy paste. Even a kosher kitchen can take advantage of a great variety of prepared items to make cooking both quick and tasty.

If a freezer is available it will be possible to store fruit, ready-prepared pastry, ice cream, fruit pies and vegetables. It is also an advantage to be able to keep really basic items such as packaged homogenised milk, butter, bread and beaten egg whites or egg yolks against a real emergency.

When time for cooking and shopping are at a premium, having fresh herbs on hand can be a great help. Most herbs grow well from seeds and are quite hardy – they can be planted in a sunny spot in the garden or in pots near the kitchen window. The result will be an improvement in the flavour of the food and could also be the beginning of a very satisfying hobby.

When there is time available – say at a weekend – it is worth filling the oven entirely. The dishes could include a roast, a casserole, cooked fruit, beans or rice, and soup can be made in the oven too. This food, properly packed and refrigerated when cool, will keep for a minimum of 3 days. Used imaginatively these dishes can provide the basis for several different needs.

Soups

With additions soup can make a quick and nourishing meal in itself. Use packaged, canned or home-made soup or that made from a cube.

Below are some ideas for ringing the changes with bought convenience foods or basic dishes prepared at home.

Milk soups

Add one or more of the following:

Yogurt added just before serving. This goes well with tomato soup or borsht.
Grated cheese in onion or vegetable soup.
Egg can be poached in the soup as you would in water.
Toast cut into cubes and added to the soup just before serving.
Spaghetti in vegetable soups.
Frozen vegetables heated in the soup as you would in water.
Milk or cream added just before serving. Make sure the soup does not boil afterwards.
Fresh herbs home grown or bought.

Meat soups

Rice pre-cooked and stored in the refrigerator. Spoon in as much as is needed and make sure it is heated through in the soup.
Sausages sliced frankfurter or wurst. Allow time for thorough cooking.
Kneidlech made from packet mix. Use just as much mixture as is needed.
Lockshen, noodles, kreplech, ravioli all bought in packs. Use as much as necessary.
Butterbeans, kidney beans add these from a can or soak and cook in bulk in advance.
Meatballs See following recipe.

To make this way of serving a basic soup most effective only heat up each time the quantity of soup needed. For example, if a large quantity of vegetable soup has been stored in the refrigerator, measure out the portion needed and then add one of the items in the list.

Meatballs for Soup

METRIC/IMPERIAL	AMERICAN
100 g/4 oz raw minced beef	$\frac{1}{4}$ lb raw ground beef
50 g/2 oz breadcrumbs or matzo meal	$\frac{3}{4}$ cup bread crumbs or matzo meal
1 teaspoon grated onion	1 teaspoon grated onion
2 teaspoons chopped parsley	2 teaspoons chopped parsley
salt, pepper and nutmeg	salt, pepper and nutmeg
grated rind of 1 lemon	grated rind of 1 lemon
1 egg, beaten	1 egg, beaten

Place the minced meat in a bowl and mix in the remaining ingredients. Roll into balls the size of large marbles and cook in boiling soup for 15–20 minutes.

Meat Dishes

Roast

It is well worth buying a roast for one. Though the cooking time is quite long, preparation is minimal. The traditional way of using a roast is ideal. The first day the meat can be eaten hot, the second day cold in a large sandwich (see following recipe), and after that, depending on the quantity left, use it in curry, Cornish Pasties (see following page) or an omelette filling. For a tasty filling, fry onions with minced or finely chopped cold meat, green peppers, aubergines (eggplants) and fresh or canned tomatoes, and add chilli powder, garlic or fresh herbs for flavouring.

Filling Meat Sandwich

Use rye bread or brown bread, if possible, spread with soft margarine and horseradish sauce, lay the slices of meat on top and cover with sliced olive or pickled cucumber. Serve with lemon tea.

Cornish Pasties

MAKES 4

METRIC/IMPERIAL	AMERICAN
1 (368-g/13-oz) packet frozen puff or shortcrust pastry, defrosted	1 (13-oz) package frozen puff paste or basic pie dough, defrosted
1 large potato	1 large potato
225 g/8 oz cooked meat, diced	1 cup diced cooked meat
1 small onion	1 small onion
1 tablespoon chopped parsley	1 tablespoon chopped parsley
salt and freshly ground black pepper	salt and freshly ground black pepper
2 tablespoons gravy	3 tablespoons gravy
beaten egg for glazing	beaten egg for glazing

Roll out the pastry to 3 mm/⅛ inch thick, and cut into 4 rounds using a saucer. Peel and parboil the potato and cut into cubes about the same size as the meat. Peel and chop the onion. Mix all the ingredients together and place heaped tablespoons of the mixture in the centre of each round of pastry. Dampen the edges, fold over in half, press the pastry layers well together and crimp with the fingers. Brush with beaten egg and cut a small hole in the centre for the steam to escape.

Bake in a hot oven (220°C, 425°F, Gas Mark 7) for 15 minutes then reduce the heat to moderate (160°C, 325°F, Gas Mark 3) and bake for a further 30 minutes. Eat hot or cold.

Chicken

When making chicken dishes such as casseroles or stews, buy one or two chicken pieces and reduce the other ingredients accordingly.

As with meat, it is worth roasting a whole chicken even for one and buying a bird of reasonable size – the flavour is usually better and there are many ways of using the remaining meat. Cold chicken sandwiches are popular and using chicken pieces in a salad is a good way of serving the cold meat, as the following recipe shows.

Chicken Salad

Remove the skin and bone from cooked chicken and cut into neat pieces. Put a layer of cooked green peas into a salad dish, cover with sliced tomatoes and lay the chicken on top. Coat with mayonnaise. Any of the following may be added to diced chicken before mixing with mayonnaise: diced tongue, diced pineapple, spring onions (scallions), diced celery or peeled grapes.

Casseroles

Having eaten one portion, refrigerate the remainder and reheat in portions as required. Do not reheat the entire casserole each time.

To each portion add one of the following:
Frozen vegetables
Wine
Cooked butter beans or kidney beans
Spaghetti
Cooked rice or kasha.

Sausages

Frankfurters, Viennas and wurst keep well in the refrigerator and can be used in a variety of ways.

Frankfurters

In a sandwich filling Cut the hot sausage and place between 2 slices of rye bread. Add sweet and sour cucumber and mustard.
As an open sandwich Put a lettuce leaf on a slice of rye bread and arrange on it slices of frankfurter and gherkin (sweet dill pickle), with spring onion (scallion) and watercress to garnish. (*Illustrated on page 156*)

In a casserole See the frankfurter and bean casserole, below.
Omelette filling Cook sliced with onions and herbs.
In soup Slice and heat in meat or vegetable soups. *(Illustrated on page 156)*
With canned sauerkraut Heat the sauerkraut and sausages separately and serve together.

Wurst

Depending on the variety, use in:
Rice salad See page 94.
A sandwich with salad vegetables.
Wurst and eggs See page 107.
Soup Slice and heat in meat or vegetable soups.

Frankfurter and Bean Casserole

METRIC/IMPERIAL	AMERICAN
1 small onion	1 small onion
1 stick celery	1 stalk celery
1 tablespoon oil or margarine	1 tablespoon oil or margarine
175 g/6 oz frankfurters	6 oz frankfurters
1 (213-g/7¾-oz) can baked beans	1 (7¾-oz) can baked beans
1 teaspoon mustard seed	1 teaspoon mustard seed
salt and freshly ground black pepper	salt and freshly ground black pepper
chopped parsley for garnish	chopped parsley for garnish

Peel and slice the onion, wash and slice the celery. Fry the vegetables in oil in a flameproof casserole until soft. Add the remaining ingredients, cover and cook in a moderate oven (180°C, 350°F, Gas Mark 4) for 30–40 minutes.

Garnish with chopped parsley and serve with toast. *(Illustrated on page 156)*

Eggs

Eggs are a favourite standby and many of the recipes in the lunch and supper dishes chapter would be useful to make.

In addition, use eggs in soups: break an egg into the soup, either whole or beaten, and wait just long enough for the egg to cook. Pancakes, omelettes and soufflés are also quick ways of making meals from eggs. Try making the following sweet omelette.

Sweet Omelette

METRIC/IMPERIAL	AMERICAN
3 eggs, separated	3 eggs, separated
1 tablespoon castor sugar	1 tablespoon sugar
2 tablespoons warm water	3 tablespoons warm water
25 g/1 oz butter	2 tablespoons butter
icing sugar	confectioners' sugar

Beat up the yolks until they are quite pale in colour, then add the sugar and the water and beat together. Whisk the egg whites to a stiff froth – they should be stiff enough to stay in the bowl when it is inverted.

Melt the butter in an omelette pan over a gentle heat. Fold the egg whites into the yolks and turn the mixture into the pan. Cook over a moderate heat until the omelette is lightly browned underneath and the surface is full of breaking air bubbles. Then place under a moderately hot grill until the omelette is cooked on top. Loosen the edge and underneath with a palette knife, mark down the middle and double it over. Turn carefully on to a hot dish and serve at once, dusted with icing sugar.

Sweet fillings

Add with the yolks: grated orange or lemon rind, or melted chocolate, or instant coffee.

Add warm before the omelette is doubled over: orange and ginger marmalade, or fruit purée.

Vegetables

The following suggestions are for frozen or canned vegetables which require no preparation and little cooking.

Soup To make a quick soup, boil one or more varieties of vegetables together with some herbs, add a stock cube or vegetable extract and then rub through a sieve or blend in a liquidiser. At this stage use any of the additions suggested in the soup section.

Casseroles Add vegetables to a basic casserole mixture when reheating.

Vegetable Casserole Make this with fresh vegetables or a mixture of frozen and fresh: cauliflower, sprouts, cabbage, carrots, parsnips, celery and tomatoes. Prepare the vegetables according to kind and cut into very small pieces. Allow 100 g/4 oz (U.S. ½ cup) margarine to every 1 kg/2 lb of vegetables and melt it slowly in a small pan. Put the vegetables into a casserole, and add a good seasoning of salt and pepper. Pour over the melted margarine and stir until all the vegetables are coated. Add 150 ml/¼ pint (U.S. ⅔ cup) of hot water, cover tightly and cook in a moderate oven (160°C, 325°F, Gas Mark 3) for 1½ hours.

Fruit

Stewed fruit can form the basis of many different dishes. Some of them are associated with breakfast or are often suggested as a dessert, but if a reasonable quantity is made stewed fruit could be the.main lunch or supper dish.

Stew whatever fruit is in season – if there is a shortage of fresh fruit use frozen. Buy the free-flow variety and use just as much as you need.

Add to the fruit any of the following:

Curd cheese or cottage cheese Curd cheese is possibly the best because it is smoother. Mash the cheese and fruit together and eat with brown bread. Add a little honey for extra flavour.

Raisins and nuts On their own or add yogurt as well.
Cereal Many brands of cereal can be used. Make up the cereal with a minimum quantity of milk so that the consistency is quite thick and stir in the fruit.
Muesli Delicious sprinkled with chopped nuts.
Omelettes Use as a filling for sweet omelettes (see page 161).

Using a Freezer

If you decide to invest in a freezer, here are some extra ideas which may prove useful. Packaging is very important – all food should be packed in quantities which are correct for serving.

Cut cakes and pies into slices and wrap each slice separately.

Turn casseroles or soups into containers which hold only one serving.

Portion raw meat, cut for casseroles, into 225-g/8-oz packages. Pack minced meat in similar quantities.

Buy free-flow packs of fruit and vegetables so that small quantities can be used at a time. Reseal the pack carefully to avoid freezer burn.

Passover Cookery

Passover is perhaps the best loved of the festivals, especially by the children as it gives them a chance to stay up to the Seder table, to see and touch the special Pesach dishes, to read the Haggadah and to hear the lovely songs.

The Seder Table

For the traditional Seder table (*illustrated on pages 166–167*) the following are required:

Three matzot, placed separately in the folds of a special matzot cover. If there is no special cover, a large table napkin can be folded into four and one matzo placed in each of the three folds, making sure that the matzot do not touch each other. Then the cover or table napkin is put on a large plate. The middle matzo will be broken during the Seder service, and part of it will become the 'Afikomen' which is hidden and searched for by the children after the meal.

A roast shankbone of lamb, representing the Paschal Lamb which the Jews were told to sacrifice. A chicken bone is often used instead of the lamb.

One roasted egg, representing the Festival offering.

Maror, bitter herbs symbolising the bitterness of the life of the Jews as slaves in Egypt. Some small pieces of horseradish or coarsely grated horseradish root are usually used.

Charoseth, representing the mortar which the Jews used to build the cities of the pharaohs (see recipe, page 169).

A green herb, symbolising the 'spring-time' of hope when the Jews left for the promised land. Parsley, lettuce or watercress are most used.

The shankbone, roasted egg, maror, charoseth and green herb are all arranged on a special pesach plate which is placed near the Afikomen.

A bowl of salt water, into which the green herb is dipped, symbolises the tears shed while the Jews were in captivity. Some communities also traditionally have a bowl of hard-boiled eggs in salt water on the Seder table.

Wine Sufficient wine should be provided for four full glasses for each person present.

Elijah's cup This is a spare goblet of wine which though placed on the table is not used during the ceremony.

The table is set with the candles, the special foods and the wine, but the crockery and cutlery for the meal are set aside until that part of the Seder service is reached.

Just before the Seder begins, a basin, a jug of fresh water and a hand towel should be placed on a small table near the seat of the head of the house, and cushions provided for the men at the table.

Passover Cookery
During Passover matzot are eaten instead of bread and no wheat flour is used. Fine matzo meal or potato flour should be used for thickening soups and sauces. When frying fish, first coat with fine matzo meal, then dip in beaten egg. Or if to be served hot, dip the fish first in the egg then coat with fine or medium meal and fry in a pan with sufficient oil to cover the fish. For veal stuffing, substitute mashed potato for breadcrumbs. Cutlets should be brushed over with beaten egg and then coated with matzo meal.

Note Some of the ingredients used in the recipes may not always be available as supervised products in every country, every year. Also, if cake meal is not available, fine matzo meal can be substituted.

Eingemacht (beetroot jam) (see page 183); Fried matzot (see page 171)
Overleaf: *The Seder table*

Charoseth

METRIC/IMPERIAL	AMERICAN
50 g/2 oz mixed almonds and walnuts	½ cup mixed almonds and walnuts
1 large dessert apple	1 large dessert apple
1 generous teaspoon cinnamon	1 generous teaspoon cinnamon
wine (see method)	wine (see method)

Chop the nuts finely. Peel, core and coarsely grate or chop the apple. Add the nuts, cinnamon and enough wine to bind the ingredients together.

Almond Balls (for Soup)

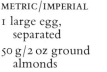

METRIC/IMPERIAL	AMERICAN
1 large egg, separated	1 large egg, separated
50 g/2 oz ground almonds	½ cup ground almonds
grated rind of ½ lemon	grated rind of ½ lemon
pinch of salt	dash of salt
oil for deep frying	oil for deep frying

Mix together the egg yolk, almonds, lemon rind and salt. Whisk the egg white to a stiff froth and fold into the other ingredients. Drop a little from the end of a small spoon into very hot fat and when puffed up and brown drain well on absorbent kitchen paper. Stir into the soup just before serving.

Cinnamon balls; Coconut pyramids; Almond macaroons (see page 182)

Matzo Meal Noodles

SERVES 3–4

METRIC/IMPERIAL	AMERICAN
2 large eggs	2 large eggs
½ teaspoon salt	½ teaspoon salt
2 tablespoons matzo meal	3 tablespoons matzo meal
chicken fat for frying	chicken fat for frying

Whisk the eggs with the salt, add the matzo meal and mix thoroughly.

Melt a little chicken fat in a frying pan and pour in enough of the mixture to cover the bottom. When cooked on one side, turn and cook the other. Roll up each pancake and cut across into noodles 5 mm/¼ inch wide. Drop into boiling soup and cook for 2–3 minutes.

Matzo Kleis (1) (Kneidlech)

METRIC/IMPERIAL	AMERICAN
250 ml/8 fl oz boiling water	1 cup boiling water
110 g/4 oz medium matzo meal	1 cup medium matzo meal
1 egg	1 egg
2 tablespoons chicken fat	3 tablespoons chicken fat
1 teaspoon chopped parsley	1 teaspoon chopped parsley
salt and freshly ground black pepper	salt and freshly ground black pepper
pinch of nutmeg and ginger	dash of nutmeg and ginger

Pour the boiling water over the meal and stir well. Add the egg, chicken fat, parsley and all the seasonings. Mix thoroughly and place in a refrigerator or very cold place for at least 1 hour.

With wet hands, roll into tiny balls. Drop into boiling soup and simmer gently for 15 minutes with the saucepan uncovered.

Matzo Kleis (2)

METRIC/IMPERIAL	AMERICAN
2 matzot	2 matzot
1 onion	1 onion
2 tablespoons chicken or vegetable fat	3 tablespoons chicken or vegetable fat
salt and freshly ground black pepper	salt and freshly ground black pepper
pinch of ground ginger	dash of ground ginger
2 eggs, well beaten	2 eggs, well beaten
fine matzo meal (see method)	fine matzo meal (see method)

These are best made in advance and left for a few hours in a cool place or refrigerator before cooking.

Soak the matzot in cold water until soft, then drain and squeeze dry. Put in a bowl and break up with a fork.

Peel and finely chop the onion and fry in the chicken fat until golden brown. Remove from the heat and add the soaked matzot, salt, pepper, ginger, eggs and sufficient fine meal to bind the mixture to a stiff consistency.

With wet hands roll into tiny balls and coat with fine meal. Drop into hot boiling soup or stew, 20 minutes before serving.

Savoury Matzo Pudding

SERVES 3–4

METRIC/IMPERIAL	AMERICAN
6–8 matzot	6–8 matzot
65 g/2½ oz margarine	5 tablespoons margarine
3 large eggs, well beaten	3 large eggs, well beaten
salt and freshly ground black pepper	salt and freshly ground black pepper
1 medium onion, peeled and grated	1 medium onion, peeled and grated
little margarine for topping	little margarine for topping

Break the matzot into small pieces and place in a colander. Pour on boiling water to soften the pieces, then allow them to drain quickly. Place the softened pieces in a mixing bowl. Melt 50 g/2 oz (U.S. ¼ cup) of the margarine in a saucepan and place the remainder in a casserole in a warm oven to melt. Add the 50 g/2 oz (U.S. ¼ cup) of melted margarine and the egg to the matzot and mix well. Season with salt and pepper and stir in the grated onion. Spread the melted margarine round the casserole and pour in the matzo pudding mixture. Dot the top with margarine and bake in a moderate oven (180°C, 350°F, Gas Mark 4) for 40–50 minutes.

Note The pudding can be covered with foil for the first 30 minutes then uncovered to allow the top to crisp.

Fried Matzot (1)

Break some matzot into neat equal-sized pieces, soak in milk until slightly soft but not soggy. Drain, dip in beaten egg and fry until golden brown on both sides. Serve sprinkled with cinnamon, sugar and grated lemon or orange rind.

Fried Matzot (2)

SERVES 3–4

METRIC/IMPERIAL	AMERICAN
4 matzot	4 matzot
3 eggs, lightly beaten	3 eggs, lightly beaten
salt and freshly ground black pepper	salt and freshly ground black pepper
50 g/2 oz butter or vegetable oil	¼ cup butter or vegetable oil

Break the matzot into small pieces, place in a colander, pour boiling water over and drain quickly. They should be moist but not soggy. Add to the eggs and season with salt and pepper.

Melt the butter or heat the oil in a frying pan, add the egg mixture and cook over a gentle heat, stirring frequently until just set. *(Illustrated on page 165)*

Potato Pancakes

MAKES 10–12

METRIC/IMPERIAL	AMERICAN
450 g/1 lb potatoes, peeled	1 lb potatoes, peeled
2 eggs, well beaten	2 eggs, well beaten
about 25 g/1 oz fine matzo meal	¼ cup fine matzo meal
salt and freshly ground black pepper	salt and freshly ground black pepper
oil for frying	oil for frying

Grate the potatoes into cold water, then drain very well. Add the eggs and enough matzo meal to form a fairly thick batter. Season with salt and pepper.

Heat a little oil or fat in a thick-based frying pan and add the mixture in tablespoonfuls. Fry until golden brown on both sides. Drain on absorbent kitchen paper and serve hot.

These can be served with a meat course or as a sweet. If the latter, omit the pepper and serve with jam or stewed fruit.

Meat Blintzes

MAKES 12–14

METRIC/IMPERIAL	AMERICAN
For the blintzes	*For the blintzes*
225 g/8 oz potato flour	1¾ cups potato flour
2 eggs	2 eggs
450–600 ml/¾–1 pint water	2–2½ cups water
chicken fat for frying	chicken fat for frying
For the meat filling	*For the meat filling*
2 small onions	2 small onions
chicken fat for frying	chicken fat for frying
225 g/8 oz minced cooked meat	1 cup ground cooked meat
salt and freshly ground black pepper	salt and freshly ground black pepper
1 egg, beaten	1 egg, beaten

To make the blintzes, sift the potato flour into a bowl, make a well in the centre and break in the eggs. Mix to a thin batter using as much of the cold water as is necessary.

Heat a 15–18-cm/6–7-inch frying pan or omelette pan and pour in enough batter to make a thin pancake. Tilt the pan to cover the base completely. Cook on one side only until the pancake is set, then turn on to a plate and keep warm. Continue until all the mixture has been used.

To make the filling Peel and chop the onions and fry in a little chicken fat until golden brown. Add the meat, seasoning and egg and mix well.

Spread the uncooked side of each pancake with a spoonful of the meat filling. Fold in half and then in half again into three-cornered pieces and fry on both sides in hot chicken fat until golden brown.

Matzo Fritters (1) Beolas
✡

SERVES 4

METRIC/IMPERIAL	AMERICAN
For the clarified sugar syrup	*For the clarified sugar syrup*
100 g/4 oz sugar	½ cup sugar
150 ml/¼ pint water	⅔ cup water
2–3 strips lemon rind	2–3 strips lemon rind
For the fritters	*For the fritters*
3 eggs	3 eggs
3 tablespoons fine matzo meal	¼ cup fine matzo meal
vegetable oil for deep frying	vegetable oil for deep frying
ground cinnamon	ground cinnamon
clarified sugar syrup (see above)	clarified sugar syrup (see above)

To make the clarified sugar syrup Heat the sugar, water and lemon rind together in a small thick-based saucepan until boiling. Boil for 5 minutes then strain and cool.

To make the fritters Beat the eggs until light and frothy, then add the meal and beat for 5 minutes. Drop teaspoonfuls of the mixture into deep hot oil and when lightly browned on one side turn and brown the other side. Drain well on absorbent kitchen paper and when cold place in a glass dish, pour over the clarified sugar syrup and serve cold.

Matzo Fritters (2)
✡

MAKES 10–12

METRIC/IMPERIAL	AMERICAN
75 g/3 oz fine matzo meal	¾ cup fine matzo meal
1 tablespoon castor sugar	1 tablespoon sugar
2 large eggs, separated	2 large eggs, separated
150 ml/¼ pint milk or water	⅔ cup milk or water
For serving	*For serving*
jam or sugar and lemon juice	jam or sugar and lemon juice

Mix together the meal and sugar. Whisk the egg yolks lightly with the milk or water. Add the meal and sugar and mix thoroughly. Whisk the egg whites until stiff and fold in.

Thoroughly grease a thick-based frying pan. Place over a moderate heat and when hot pour in the mixture a tablespoon at a time, leaving plenty of space between each one. When each fritter becomes full of bubbles, turn with a broad knife and brown the other side.

Serve hot with jam or sprinkled with sugar and lemon juice.

Grimslich
✡

MAKES 14–16

METRIC/IMPERIAL	AMERICAN
2 matzot	2 matzot
2 eggs, separated	2 eggs, separated
50 g/2 oz fine matzo meal	½ cup fine matzo meal
50 g/2 oz ground almonds	½ cup ground almonds
¼ teaspoon cinnamon	¼ teaspoon cinnamon
100 g/4 oz mixed dried fruit	⅔ cup mixed dried fruit
50 g/2 oz sugar	¼ cup sugar
50 g/2 oz melted fat or margarine	¼ cup melted fat or margarine
oil for frying	oil for frying
castor sugar for serving	superfine sugar for serving

Soak the matzot in cold water until soft, then squeeze very dry and break up with a fork. Whisk the egg whites until stiff. Add the egg yolks to the matzot with the remaining ingredients and mix well. Then fold in the egg whites.

Drop heaped teaspoonfuls of the mixture into hot shallow oil and fry until golden brown on both sides. Sprinkle with sugar and serve hot.

Carrot Candy (Ingber)

MAKES ABOUT 1 KG/2 LB

METRIC/IMPERIAL	AMERICAN
450 g/1 lb carrots, peeled	1 lb carrots, peeled
450 g/1 lb sugar	2 cups sugar
1 teaspoon ground ginger	1 teaspoon ground ginger
25 g/1 oz ground almonds	$\frac{1}{4}$ cup ground almonds
50–100 g/2–4 oz chopped nuts	$\frac{1}{2}$–1 cup chopped nuts

Grate the carrots on a fine grater. Place in a thick-based saucepan with the sugar, and place on an asbestos mat over a very gentle heat. Stir until the sugar has dissolved and continue cooking very slowly, stirring continuously, until all the moisture has been absorbed by the carrot and the mixture becomes very thick.

Stir in the ginger and ground almonds, keeping the sides of the pan clear of the mixture. Test a little on a plate and if it sets stir in the nuts and remove the pan from the heat. Spread quickly on a damp board or in a flat tin and, when cool, mark into squares. When cold, break into pieces and allow to dry before storing in a tin.

Carrot Pudding (1)

SERVES 4–6

METRIC/IMPERIAL	AMERICAN
50 g/2 oz margarine	$\frac{1}{4}$ cup margarine
50 g/2 oz castor sugar	$\frac{1}{4}$ cup sugar
2 eggs, separated	2 eggs, separated
50 g/2 oz potato flour, sifted	$\frac{1}{2}$ cup sifted potato flour
pinch of salt	dash of salt
1 teaspoon cinnamon	1 teaspoon cinnamon
25 g/1 oz chopped walnuts	$\frac{1}{4}$ cup chopped walnuts
4 tablespoons wine	$\frac{1}{3}$ cup wine
grated rind and juice of 1 lemon	grated rind and juice of 1 lemon
225 g/8 oz carrots, peeled and grated	$\frac{1}{2}$ lb carrots, peeled and grated
25 g/1 oz chopped dates or sultanas (optional)	$\frac{1}{4}$ cup chopped dates or seedless white raisins (optional)

Cream the margarine and sugar together until soft and fluffy. Beat in the egg yolks one at a time then fold in the sifted potato flour, salt, cinnamon, nuts, wine, lemon rind and juice, grated carrot and chopped fruit if used. Whisk the egg whites until stiff and fold into the pudding mixture. Spoon into a greased baking dish and bake in a moderate oven (180°C, 350°F, Gas Mark 4) for about 45 minutes.

Carrot Pudding (2)

SERVES 4–6

METRIC/IMPERIAL	AMERICAN
100 g/4 oz margarine	½ cup margarine
90 g/3½ oz soft brown sugar	⅓ cup soft brown sugar
1 large egg, beaten	1 large egg, beaten
3 tablespoons potato flour	¼ cup potato flour
8 tablespoons wine	⅔ cup wine
50 g/2 oz seedless raisins or chopped dates	⅓ cup seeded raisins or chopped dates
1 teaspoon cinnamon	1 teaspoon cinnamon
450 g/1 lb carrots, grated	1 lb carrots, grated
pinch of salt	dash of salt
8 tablespoons fine matzo meal	⅔ cup fine matzo meal
1 teaspoon baking powder	1 teaspoon baking powder

Cream the margarine and sugar together until soft and fluffy and beat in the egg. Mix the potato flour with the wine and stir into the creamed mixture together with the raisins, cinnamon, carrot and salt. Finally fold in the matzo meal sifted with the baking powder. Spoon the mixture into a greased ovenproof dish and bake in a moderate oven (180°C, 350°F. Gas Mark 4) for 1 hour.

Meringue Pudding

SERVES 4–6

METRIC/IMPERIAL	AMERICAN
350 g/12 oz cooking apples	¾ lb baking apples
2 large eggs, separated	2 large eggs, separated
125 g/5 oz castor sugar	⅔ cup sugar
grated rind and juice of 1 lemon	grated rind and juice of 1 lemon
100 g/4 oz fine matzo meal	1 cup fine matzo meal
2 bananas	2 bananas

Peel, core and grate the apples. Lightly beat the egg yolks and stir into the grated apple, together with 75 g/3 oz (U.S. ⅓ cup) of the sugar and the rind and juice of the lemon. Stir in the matzo meal. Beat lightly, turn into a greased, shallow ovenproof dish and bake in a moderately hot oven (190°C, 375°F, Gas Mark 5) for 40 minutes. Remove from the oven.

Cover the top of the pudding with thinly sliced banana. Whisk the egg whites until stiff, fold in the remaining sugar and spoon or pipe over the banana. Return to a cool oven (140°C, 275°F, Gas Mark 1) for 15–20 minutes until the meringue is set and lightly browned.

Apple Pudding

SERVES 4–6

METRIC/IMPERIAL	AMERICAN
450 g/1 lb cooking apples	1 lb baking apples
3 eggs, separated	3 eggs, separated
100 g/4 oz castor sugar	½ cup sugar
3 tablespoons fine matzo meal	¼ cup fine matzo meal
1 tablespoon ground almonds	1 tablespoon ground almonds
grated rind and juice of 1 lemon	grated rind and juice of 1 lemon
½ teaspoon cinnamon	½ teaspoon cinnamon

Peel, core and grate the apples. Whisk the egg whites until stiff. Beat the egg yolks lightly with the sugar. Add the grated apple, matzo meal, almonds, lemon rind and juice and the cinnamon. Mix thoroughly, then fold in the egg whites. Turn into a greased, fairly deep ovenproof dish and bake in a moderately hot oven (190°C, 375°F, Gas Mark 5) for about 1 hour.

Almond Pudding

SERVES 4

METRIC/IMPERIAL	AMERICAN
4 eggs, separated	4 eggs, separated
125 g/5 oz castor sugar	⅔ cup sugar
100 g/4 oz ground almonds	1 cup ground almonds

Whisk the egg whites until stiff. Beat the egg yolks and sugar together until very light. Add the ground almonds and beat for 2–3 minutes. Then fold in the egg whites. Turn into a greased, fairly deep baking dish and bake in a moderate oven (180°C, 350°F, Gas Mark 4) for about 50 minutes. Serve chilled, sprinkled with castor sugar.

Matzo Pudding

SERVES 4–6

METRIC/IMPERIAL	AMERICAN
2 matzot	2 matzot
mixed spice	mixed spice
150 g/6 oz mixed dried fruit	1 cup mixed dried fruit
75 g/3 oz soft brown sugar	⅓ cup soft brown sugar
2 tablespoons fine matzo meal	3 tablespoons fine matzo meal
50 g/2 oz melted margarine	¼ cup melted margarine
2 large eggs	2 large eggs

Break up the matzot and soak in cold water until soft, then drain and squeeze very dry. Put in a mixing bowl and break up with a fork. Add mixed spice to taste and all the remaining ingredients except 25 g/1 oz (U.S. 2 tablespoons) of the sugar. Mix thoroughly and turn into a greased fairly shallow baking dish. Sprinkle with the remaining sugar and bake in a moderately hot oven (200°C, 400°F, Gas Mark 6) for 50 minutes. Serve with rum sauce (see page 89).

Apricot-matzo Pudding

SERVES 6

METRIC/IMPERIAL	AMERICAN
1.5 kg/3 lb fresh apricots or 2 (566-g/1¼-lb) cans apricots	3 lb fresh apricots or 2 (20-oz) cans apricots
450 ml/¾ pint water and 275 g/10 oz granulated sugar, or 450 ml/¾ pint syrup from the apricots	2 cups water and 1½ cups sugar, or 2 cups syrup from the apricots
6 matzot	6 matzot
175 g/6 oz margarine	⅔ cup margarine
3 eggs	3 eggs
For the decoration	*For the decoration*
12 fresh strawberries	12 fresh strawberries
1½ tablespoons castor sugar	2 tablespoons superfine sugar

Halve the fresh apricots and remove the stones. Place in a saucepan with the water and sugar. Simmer gently over low heat for 2–3 minutes. Drain and retain the syrup. Alternatively, drain the syrup from the canned apricots and retain the amount required in the recipe.

Dip the matzot into the syrup and place in alternate layers with the apricots in a greased casserole, finishing with a layer of apricots. Melt the margarine, whisk in the eggs and the remaining syrup and pour the mixture over the apricots and matzot.

Decorate with the fresh strawberries rolled in the sugar. Bake in a cool oven (150°C, 300°F, Gas Mark 2) for 30 minutes, or until the egg mixture is fairly firm and golden brown. Serve warm or cold. (*Illustrated on page 125*)

Coffee Chocolate Cream

SERVES 4–6

METRIC/IMPERIAL	AMERICAN
25 g/1 oz cocoa powder	$\frac{1}{4}$ cup cocoa powder
50 g/2 oz sugar	$\frac{1}{4}$ cup sugar
25 g/1 oz potato flour	$\frac{1}{4}$ cup potato flour
600 ml/1 pint strong black coffee	$2\frac{1}{2}$ cups strong black coffee
2 eggs, well beaten	2 eggs, well beaten
chopped almonds for topping	chopped almonds for topping

Mix together the cocoa, sugar and potato flour with a little of the cold coffee in the top of a double saucepan or in a bowl over a saucepan of hot water. Heat the remaining coffee until warm and stir into the cocoa mixture. Add the beaten egg and place over hot but not boiling water, stirring continuously until the mixture thickens. Set aside to cool, whisking from time to time, and serve cold sprinkled with chopped almonds.

Chocolate Truffles

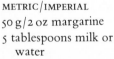

METRIC/IMPERIAL	AMERICAN
50 g/2 oz margarine	$\frac{1}{4}$ cup margarine
5 tablespoons milk or water	6 tablespoons milk or water
60 g/2$\frac{1}{2}$ oz sugar	$\frac{1}{3}$ cup sugar
5 tablespoons medium matzo meal	6 tablespoons medium matzo meal
75 g/3 oz desiccated coconut	1 cup shredded coconut
2 tablespoons cocoa powder	3 tablespoons cocoa powder
1 tablespoon wine or strong black coffee	1 tablespoon wine or strong black coffee
extra coconut, cocoa powder or ground almonds for coating	extra coconut, cocoa powder or ground almonds for coating

Melt the margarine with the milk or water. Stir in the sugar then cool the mixture slightly. Add all the other ingredients, mix well to a firm mixture and roll into small balls. Coat with coconut, cocoa powder or ground almonds and keep refrigerated until needed.

Hazelnut Sponge

METRIC/IMPERIAL	AMERICAN
4 large eggs, separated	4 large eggs, separated
110 g/4 oz castor sugar	$\frac{1}{2}$ cup sugar
110 g/4 oz ground hazelnuts or walnuts	1 cup ground hazelnuts or walnuts
grated rind and juice of $\frac{1}{2}$ lemon	grated rind and juice of $\frac{1}{2}$ lemon
15 g/$\frac{1}{2}$ oz fine matzo meal	2 tablespoons fine matzo meal

Whisk the egg whites until stiff. Beat together the egg yolks and sugar until thick and creamy. Stir in the nuts, lemon rind and juice and meal, and fold in the egg whites.

Turn into a greased and lined 15–18-cm/ 6–7-inch round deep cake tin and bake in a moderately hot oven (190°C, 375°F, Gas Mark 5) for 50 minutes–1 hour. Leave the cake in the tin for 5 minutes then turn out on to a wire tray to cool.

Chocolate Matzo Cake

METRIC/IMPERIAL	AMERICAN
225 g/8 oz plain chocolate	8 squares semi-sweet chocolate
75 g/3 oz margarine	⅓ cup margarine
75 g/3 oz castor sugar	⅓ cup sugar
50 g/2 oz desiccated coconut	⅔ cup shredded coconut
4 matzot	4 matzot
6 tablespoons wine or	½ cup wine

Grease a 28 × 18-cm/11 × 7-inch Swiss roll tin and line with silicone or waxed paper. Melt half of the chocolate and spread over the lined base of the prepared tin.

Melt the margarine in a saucepan then remove from the heat and slowly stir in the sugar and coconut.

Break the matzot into small pieces and soak for 1–2 minutes in the wine. Add this to the melted mixture and press evenly over the chocolate base, using a large wet palette knife or wet hands. Melt the remaining chocolate and spread over the mixture in the tin. Leave to set and harden, then turn upside down, remove the paper and cut the cake into squares.

Store in the refrigerator until needed.

Orange and Almond Sponge Cake

METRIC/IMPERIAL	AMERICAN
3 large eggs, separated	3 large eggs, separated
170 g/6 oz castor sugar	¾ cup sugar
grated rind and juice of 1 orange	grated rind and juice of 1 orange
2 tablespoons cake meal, sifted	3 tablespoons sifted cake meal
2 tablespoons potato flour, sifted	3 tablespoons sifted potato flour
60 g/2 oz ground almonds	½ cup ground almonds
icing sugar	icing sugar

Beat the egg yolks with half of the sugar until the mixture is thick and creamy. Beat in the juice and rind of the orange. Whisk the whites until very stiff then whisk in the remainder of the sugar to make a stiff meringue. Fold the egg white mixture into the egg yolk mixture then fold in the sifted cake meal, potato flour and ground almonds.

Pour the mixture into a greased and lined 18–20-cm/7–8-inch round deep cake tin and bake in a moderate oven (180°C, 350°F, Gas Mark 4) for about 45 minutes. Leave in the tin for 5 minutes then turn out on to a wire tray to cool. Dust with sifted icing sugar before serving.

Wine and Nut Cake

METRIC/IMPERIAL	AMERICAN
7 eggs, separated	7 eggs, separated
200 g/7 oz castor sugar	⅔ cup sugar
3 tablespoons sweet wine	¼ cup sweet wine
50 g/2 oz fine matzo meal	½ cup fine matzo meal
100 g/4 oz chopped hazelnuts or walnuts	1 cup chopped hazelnuts or walnuts

Whisk the egg whites until stiff. Beat together the egg yolks and sugar until thick and creamy; add the wine and beat well. Fold in the matzo meal and nuts and lastly the egg whites.

Pour into an ungreased 23–25-cm/9–10-inch round deep cake tin or use a 20-cm/8-inch square roasting tin and bake in a moderate oven (160°C, 325°F, Gas Mark 3) for about 1¼ hours until firm and golden brown. When baked, invert the tin over a wire cooling tray but do not remove until cold.

Sponge Cake

METRIC/IMPERIAL	AMERICAN
170 g/6 oz butter or margarine	3/4 cup butter or margarine
60 g/2 oz fine matzo meal	1/2 cup fine matzo meal
110 g/4 oz potato flour	1 cup potato flour
3 large eggs, separated	3 large eggs, separated
170 g/6 oz castor sugar	3/4 cup sugar

Grease and line a 20-cm/8-inch round deep cake tin. Whisk the egg whites until stiff. Place the butter or margarine over a very gentle heat until just melted. Sift together the matzo meal and potato flour. Beat together the egg yolks and sugar until very light. Stir in the melted butter, the potato flour and matzo meal and fold in the egg whites.

Pour into the prepared tin and bake in a moderately hot oven (190°C, 375°F, Gas Mark 5) for about 1¼ hours. When baked invert on a cooling rack and leave until nearly cold before turning out of the tin.

Note This cake can be flavoured with vanilla sugar or grated orange or lemon rind.

Pesach Sponge

METRIC/IMPERIAL	AMERICAN
4 large eggs, separated	4 large eggs, separated
50 g/2 oz castor sugar	1/4 cup sugar
grated rind and juice of 1 lemon	grated rind and juice of 1 lemon
1 tablespoon sifted cake meal	1 tablespoon sifted cake meal
2 tablespoons sifted potato flour	3 tablespoons sifted potato flour

Beat the egg yolks with half of the sugar until they are thick and creamy, then fold in the juice and rind of the lemon. Whisk the whites until very stiff, and beat in the remainder of the sugar.

Fold the egg whites into the yolks then fold in the sifted cake meal and potato flour. Pour the mixture into a greased and lined 23-cm/9-inch cake tin and bake in a moderately hot oven (190°C, 375°F, Gas Mark 5) for about 30 minutes. Leave in the tin for 5 minutes then turn out on to a wire tray to cool.

Rout Cakes

METRIC/IMPERIAL	AMERICAN
225 g/8 oz castor sugar	1 cup sugar
225 g/8 oz ground almonds	2 cups ground almonds
3 egg yolks	3 egg yolks
icing sugar	confectioners' sugar
For the royal icing	*For the royal icing*
225 g/8 oz icing sugar	1¾ cups confectioners' sugar
1 egg white, lightly beaten	1 egg white, lightly beaten
1 teaspoon lemon juice	1 teaspoon lemon juice

Mix the sugar and almonds together, then add enough of the egg yolk to form a pliable paste. Dredge a flat surface with icing sugar and roll out the paste to 8 mm/⅓ inch thick. Leave in a cool place for 1 hour.

Form the paste into any preferred shape – it can be cut into diamonds or fingers or rolled into pencil-shaped pieces and formed into rings, scrolls and twirls.

Place on a well-greased baking sheet and bake in a moderate oven (160°C, 325°F, Gas Mark 3) for 45–50 minutes until firm. Cool on a wire tray and decorate with royal icing.

To make the icing Sift the sugar into a mixing bowl, make a well in the centre and add enough of the lightly beaten egg white and lemon juice to make a thick coating consistency. Beat vigorously with a wooden spoon until the icing is very smooth. Spread the icing over the biscuits and leave until set.

Passover Pastry

MAKES 225 G/8 OZ

METRIC/IMPERIAL	AMERICAN
100 g/4 oz fine matzo meal or cake meal	1 cup fine matzo meal or cake meal
100 g/4 oz castor sugar	½ cup sugar
25–50 g/1–2 oz ground almonds	¼–½ cup ground almonds
100 g/4 oz potato flour	1 cup potato flour
100 g/4 oz soft margarine	½ cup soft margarine
1 egg, beaten	1 egg, beaten

Place all the ingredients in a mixing bowl and work together by hand or with a fork until the mixture forms a dough. Chill for at least 1 hour and if the mixture is difficult to roll it can be pressed into a tin.

This quantity is enough to line two 18-cm/7-inch tins. It will make enough for the base of Almond Bakewell Pudding (see below) and Apple Flan (see right).

Almond Bakewell Pudding

SERVES 4–6

METRIC/IMPERIAL	AMERICAN
For the pastry base	For the pastry base
100 g/4 oz Passover pastry (see above)	¼ lb Passover pastry (see above)
For the filling	For the filling
50 g/2 oz margarine	¼ cup margarine
50 g/2 oz castor sugar	¼ cup sugar
1 egg	1 egg
50 g/2 oz ground almonds	½ cup ground almonds
1 teaspoon potato flour	1 teaspoon potato flour

Make the pastry and line an 18-cm/7-inch flan tin.

Place all the ingredients for the filling in a mixing bowl and mix well. Spread over the pastry base. Bake in a moderate oven (180°C, 350°F, Gas Mark 4) for 30–40 minutes.

Apple Flan

SERVES 4–6

METRIC/IMPERIAL	AMERICAN
For the pastry base	For the pastry base
100 g/4 oz Passover pastry (see left)	¼ lb Passover pastry (see left)
For the filling	For the filling
1 kg/2 lb cooking apples	2 lb baking apples
100–150 g/4–6 oz sugar	½–¾ cup sugar
1 tablespoon ground cinnamon	1 tablespoon ground cinnamon
sugar and chopped walnuts for topping	sugar and chopped walnuts for topping

Make up the pastry and line an 18-cm/7-inch flan tin.

To make the filling Peel and grate the apples and mix with the sugar and cinnamon. Put the filling into the flan case and sprinkle with the sugar and nuts. Bake in a moderately hot oven (190°C, 375°F, Gas Mark 5) for 15 minutes then reduce the heat to moderate (180°C, 350°F, Gas Mark 4) and cook for a further 20 minutes.

Apple Amber

✡

SERVES 4

METRIC/IMPERIAL	AMERICAN
675 g/1½ lb apples	1½ lb apples
50 g/2 oz margarine	¼ cup margarine
50–75 g/2–3 oz brown sugar	4–6 tablespoons brown sugar
grated rind and juice of 1 lemon	grated rind and juice of 1 lemon
2 egg yolks	2 egg yolks
For the meringue topping	*For the meringue topping*
2 egg whites	2 egg whites
25 g/1 oz castor sugar	2 tablespoons sugar

Peel and slice the apples and put in a saucepan with the margarine, brown sugar and grated lemon rind and juice. Cover and cook gently until the apples are tender. Reduce the apples to a pulp with a potato masher or pass through a sieve. Add the egg yolks and beat lightly then pour into a deep ovenproof dish.

Whisk the egg whites until stiff. Beat in half of the castor sugar, then fold in the remainder. Spoon or pipe the meringue on top of the apple, making sure to seal the sides. Place in a preheated moderate oven (160°C, 325°F, Gas Mark 3) for about 10 minutes until the meringue is set and lightly browned.

Apple Anna

✡

SERVES 4–6

METRIC/IMPERIAL	AMERICAN
3 large cooking apples	3 large baking apples
65 g/2½ oz soft brown sugar	5 tablespoons soft brown sugar
1 banana	1 banana
25 g/1 oz butter or margarine	2 tablespoons butter or margarine

Peel and slice one apple and place in a shallow casserole. Sprinkle with about 2 tablespoons (U.S. 3 tablespoons) of the brown sugar. Slice the banana over the apple and then peel and slice the remaining apples into the dish. Sprinkle with the remaining sugar and dot with butter.

Cover with a lid or foil and bake in a moderately hot oven (190°C, 375°F, Gas Mark 5) for 20 minutes. Uncover and bake for a further 15 minutes until the fruit is tender. Serve hot with cream.

Jordan Cakes

✡

MAKES 18–24

METRIC/IMPERIAL	AMERICAN
100 g/4 oz butter or margarine	½ cup butter or margarine
100 g/4 oz castor sugar	½ cup sugar
2 eggs, well beaten	2 eggs, well beaten
100 g/4 oz potato flour, sifted	1 cup sifted potato flour
50 g/2 oz ground almonds	½ cup ground almonds

Grease and line a 28 × 18-cm/11 × 7-inch Swiss roll tin. Beat together the butter or margarine and sugar until soft and fluffy. Add the egg, a little at a time, beating well between each addition, then fold in the sifted potato flour and the ground almonds.

Spread the mixture evenly in the prepared tin and bake in a moderately hot oven (200°C, 400°F, Gas Mark 6) for about 15 minutes. Cut into 18 or 24 pieces before removing from the tin, then cool on a wire tray.

Prelatoes

MAKES ABOUT 20

METRIC/IMPERIAL	AMERICAN
40 g/1½ oz fine matzo meal	6 tablespoons fine meal
25 g/1 oz potato flour	¼ cup potato flour
2 eggs, separated	2 eggs, separated
75 g/3 oz castor sugar	6 tablespoons sugar

Line two greased baking tins with greased greaseproof or silicone paper. Sift together the meal and potato flour. Whisk the egg whites to a stiff froth. Beat together the yolks and sugar until light and creamy, then stir in the meal and potato flour. Mix lightly and fold in the stiffly beaten egg whites.

Place large teaspoonsfuls of the mixture on the prepared tins, well apart, and bake in a moderately hot oven (190°C, 375°F, Gas Mark 5) for 20–25 minutes until set and lightly browned. Cool on a wire tray and when cold dredge with castor sugar.

Fruit and Nut Meringues

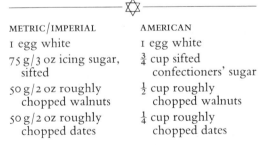

METRIC/IMPERIAL	AMERICAN
1 egg white	1 egg white
75 g/3 oz icing sugar, sifted	¾ cup sifted confectioners' sugar
50 g/2 oz roughly chopped walnuts	½ cup roughly chopped walnuts
50 g/2 oz roughly chopped dates	¼ cup roughly chopped dates

Whisk the egg white until very stiff and glossy. Beat in the icing sugar a tablespoon at a time, then fold in the nuts and dates. Drop in small heaps on a greased baking sheet.

Bake in a cool oven (150°C, 300°F, Gas Mark 2) for 25–30 minutes until the meringues are crisp and a pale golden colour.

Note Use silicone paper to line the baking sheet if possible – this makes the meringues easier to remove without the possibility of their breaking.

Almond Bars

MAKES 9

METRIC/IMPERIAL	AMERICAN
50 g/2 oz whole blanched almonds	½ cup whole blanched almonds
65 g/2½ oz castor sugar	5 tablespoons granulated sugar
65 g/2½ oz icing sugar	½ cup confectioners' sugar
100 g/4 oz ground almonds	1 cup ground almonds
1 teaspoon lemon juice	1 teaspoon lemon juice
1 egg yolk	1 egg yolk
For the icing	*For the frosting*
1 teaspoon egg white icing sugar	1 teaspoon egg white confectioners' sugar
2 teaspoons water	2 teaspoons water
strong black coffee (optional)	strong black coffee (optional)

Reserve nine almond halves for decoration; chop the remainder finely. Sift the two sugars together into a bowl, add the ground almonds, lemon juice and chopped almonds. Stir in enough of the egg yolk to make a stiff dough then knead until smooth. Turn on to a board sprinkled with icing sugar and shape into a bar about 6–7.5 cm/2½–3 inches wide and about 1 cm/½ inch thick. Roll gently to smooth the top and pat the sides with a knife to keep the shape.

Place on a baking sheet lined with greased greaseproof or silicone paper and bake in a moderate oven (180°C, 350°F, Gas Mark 4) for 40–45 minutes or until set. While still warm cut across into nine bars about 2.5 cm/1 inch wide and leave on the baking sheet until cold.

To make the meringue icing Put the egg white in a small bowl and stir in sifted icing sugar with a wooden spoon until the mixture stiffens; then stir in the water. Stand the bowl in a container of warm water and continue adding the icing sugar, beating all the time until the mixture thickens again. Beat in a few drops of strong black coffee to colour, if liked.

Spread the icing on to the bars and top with half an almond.

Almond Macaroons

✡

METRIC/IMPERIAL	AMERICAN
2 large egg whites	2 large egg whites
100 g/4 oz ground almonds	1 cup ground almonds
3 tablespoons fine matzo meal	¼ cup fine matzo meal
200 g/8 oz castor sugar	1 cup sugar
split almonds for topping	split almonds for topping

Whisk the egg whites very slightly. Mix together the ground almonds, matzo meal and sugar. Add the egg whites and mix thoroughly. Cover a greased baking sheet with silicone paper or rice paper and place teaspoons of the mixture on to it (or use a forcing bag and plain pipe) leaving room for the mixture to spread.

Place a split almond on each macaroon and bake in a moderate oven (180°C, 350°F, Gas Mark 4) for about 35 minutes until the macaroons are set and a pale golden brown. Leave on the baking sheet to cool. *(Illustrated on page 168)*

Cinnamon Balls

✡

MAKES ABOUT 40

METRIC/IMPERIAL	AMERICAN
3 egg whites	3 egg whites
150 g/5 oz castor sugar	⅔ cup sugar
2 teaspoons cinnamon	2 teaspoons cinnamon
225 g/8 oz ground almonds	2 cups ground almonds
2 teaspoons desiccated coconut (optional)	2 teaspoons shredded coconut (optional)
icing sugar	confectioners' sugar

Beat the egg whites to a stiff froth. Add the sugar, cinnamon, ground almonds and coconut, if used, and mix thoroughly. Roll into small balls and place on a greased baking sheet. Bake in a moderate oven (180°C, 350°F, Gas Mark 4) for 20–25 minutes until set.

Put some icing sugar in a polythene bag and while the cinnamon balls are still warm shake them in the bag, one at a time, to coat them. *(Illustrated on page 168)*

Note The addition of the coconut to the recipe keeps the cinnamon balls soft.

Coconut Pyramids

✡

METRIC/IMPERIAL	AMERICAN
225 g/8 oz desiccated coconut	2⅓ cups shredded coconut
150 g/5 oz castor sugar	⅔ cup sugar
2 small eggs	2 small eggs
little grated rind of orange or lemon	little grated rind of orange or lemon

Mix together all the ingredients thoroughly. With hands dipped in cold water, form into pyramids and place on a greased baking sheet. Bake in a moderately hot oven (190°C, 375°F, Gas Mark 5) until lightly browned. *(Illustrated on page 168)*

Note This recipe can be made with 4 egg yolks instead of 2 whole eggs if these are surplus from other baking.

Wafer Biscuits

MAKES 12–15

METRIC/IMPERIAL	AMERICAN
50 g/2 oz butter or margarine	$\frac{1}{4}$ cup butter or margarine
1 egg	1 egg
50 g/2 oz castor sugar	$\frac{1}{4}$ cup sugar
little grated lemon rind	little grated lemon rind
25 g/1 oz fine matzo meal	$\frac{1}{4}$ cup fine matzo meal
25 g/1 oz potato flour	$\frac{1}{4}$ cup potato flour

Melt the butter or margarine but do not let it boil. Beat together the egg and sugar until light and frothy. Add the melted fat and lemon rind and whisk again. Stir in the matzo meal and potato flour.

Place teaspoonfuls of the mixture well apart on a thoroughly greased baking sheet. Bake in a preheated hot oven (230°C, 450°F, Gas Mark 8) until the mixture has set and the edges are lightly browned.

Remove the biscuits from the tin immediately and cool on a wire tray.

Eingemacht (Beetroot Jam)

MAKES ABOUT 3.5 KG/8 LB

METRIC/IMPERIAL	AMERICAN
1.75 kg/4 lb beetroot	4 lb raw beets
2.25 litres/4 pints water	5 pints water
1.5 kg/3$\frac{1}{2}$ lb preserving or granulated sugar	3$\frac{1}{2}$ lb sugar
juice of 6 lemons	juice of 6 lemons
4 teaspoons ground ginger	4 teaspoons ground ginger
50 g/2 oz chopped walnuts	$\frac{1}{2}$ cup chopped walnuts
50 g/2 oz chopped almonds	$\frac{1}{2}$ cup chopped almonds

Peel the beetroot then place in a large saucepan and cover with water. Bring to the boil and boil for 10 minutes. Then drain, cool and cut into match-like strips or grate on a coarse grater.

Place the beetroot in a preserving pan with the water, sugar and the lemon juice. Stir well until the sugar has dissolved then bring to the boil. Lower the heat and cook gently for 2–3 hours until the mixture is thick and brown. Add the ginger and the nuts. Test the jam on a cold saucer to see if it will set and when ready place in warm jars and cover with cellophane jam discs and tops. *(Illustrated on page 165)*

Festival Fare

Menus for Shabbat and the Festivals

Shabbat

Friday evening

The eve of Shabbat is an important family occasion. However busy each member is with his own affairs, on Friday evening the family sits together for the Shabbat meal. The food is probably the most traditional, and although it is served every week any of the items would be missed if they did not appear.

Shabbat Dinner

Chopped liver

Chicken soup with lockshen and kneidlech

Roast chicken with stuffing

Stuffed helzel

Roast potatoes

Vegetables in season

Gingerbread ring and stewed fruit or Dried fruit casserole

Lemon tea and kichals

Shabbat Lunch

This is the meal the family comes home to from the synagogue. No food may be cooked on the Sabbath and all dishes have to be prepared in advance. In the summer when the weather is warm a cold meal may be acceptable, such as cold borsht followed by cold roast meat and salad. The more traditional lunch is served hot, the cholent having been in the oven since before the Sabbath.

Gefillte fish

Lentil soup

Cholent

Continental apple tart

Pesach

The Festival of Freedom from Slavery
Nissan 14–22 : April

Seder Night

✡

The Passover meal is served in the middle of the Seder service. All the crockery and cutlery should be prepared and placed on one side as the table is only set when the time comes for the meal to be served.

The coffee and pesach sponge cake will be served at the table as no food is eaten after the Afikomen, i.e. the piece of matzo eaten at the end of the meal.

Chopped liver

Chicken soup and almond balls

Roast chicken
Savoury matzo pudding
New potatoes and carrots
Green salad

Coffee chocolate cream
Pesach sponge

Coffee

The chapter on Passover Cookery is to be found on page 163.

Shevuoth

The Feast of Weeks
Sivan 6, 7 : May

Shevuoth was originally a harvest festival celebrating the beginning of the wheat harvest. Every man took the first fruits of his crop as an offering to the Temple.

To celebrate the festival the synagogue and home are decorated with seasonal flowers and plants.

Shevuoth is also remembered as the birthday of the Torah.

Milk, cheese and honey are the symbolic foods of this festival, resulting in delicious dairy dishes such as cheese blintzes and cheesecakes.

Shevuoth Lunch

Cucumber salad with soured cream

Fried fish, cold
New potatoes
Tomato salad
Green salad with French dressing

Cheese blintzes or
Dried fruit casserole with cream

Rosh Hashanah

New Year
Tishri 1, 2: September/October

At New Year only sweet foods are eaten, symbolising the hope for sweetness and happiness during the year. No bitter or sour foods are included in any meal and the cholla is baked in a round instead of the usual plait to symbolise the promise of a full rich year.

Apple is the fruit traditionally associated with Rosh Hashanah and it is served sliced next to a dish of honey. Before the meal begins each person dips a slice of apple in the honey and wishes for a sweet New Year.

Rosh Hashanah Dinner

Cherry soup

Honeyed chicken

Meatless carrot tzimmas

Roast potatoes

Upside-down applecake

Honey cake and Teiglech

Yom Kippur

The Day of Atonement
Tishri 10: September/October

On this day of atonement, Jews fast for 25 hours from sunset of the evening before until the following sunset. The meal served before the fast is important because after it is finished not even a drink may be taken until the following evening. It is therefore customary not to serve highly spiced or highly seasoned foods.

The contents of this pre-fast meal vary – families have their own preferences but many prefer to begin the fast using the same menu as for a Friday evening meal.

Breaking the fast is gradual. On returning from synagogue it is usual to serve a hot drink first, often milk tea, with sponge cake and biscuits, followed by a light fish dish with salads.

Smoked salmon or Chopped herring

Fried fish
Halibut with egg and lemon sauce

Tomato salad
Avocado salad
Potato salad

Chocolate mousse

Succoth

The Feast of Tabernacles
Tishri 15–23 : October

Succoth is the Jewish festival of thanksgiving. It lasts seven days and Jews commemorate the protection of God during the forty years wandering in the wilderness by building a succah or small makeshift hut in the garden. The succah has no roof but is covered with leaves and branches through which the stars can be seen, and the hut is festooned with fruit and vegetables.

Succoth Dinner

Avocado dip

Holishkes (stuffed cabbage leaves)
Minced meat with kasha in pastry
Fresh vegetables in season

Apple strudel
Fresh fruit salad

Chanukah

The Feast of Lights
Kislev 25–Tebet 2 : December

During Chanukah Jews remember the battle of the Maccabees to save the Temple. This is a time of parties and celebrating and the children enjoy it greatly. They are given presents, often in the form of money known as Chanukah 'gelt'.

The only really traditional food eaten at this time is potato latkes, but as Chanukah comes in December when the nights are cold a warm filling meal is most appropriate.

Chanukah Dinner

Lentil soup

Salt beef
Potato latkes
Pickled cucumber
Chips (French fries) or roast potatoes

Almond fruit tart

Purim

The Feast of Lots
Adar 14: February/March

Sometimes called the Feast of Esther, Purim celebrates the downfall of Haman – who planned a massacre of the Jewish population of Persia – through the efforts of the King's favourite Queen, Esther, and her uncle Mordecai.

There is no particular special menu for a Purim meal but the traditional cake is Haman taschen. This small cake is made in a triangle or three-cornered shape. There are two versions of the origin of the shape – one that Haman wore a three-cornered hat, the other that his ears were long and pointed.

Haman Taschen

Make a kuchen dough (see page 152). Roll it out about 5 mm/¼ inch thick, cut into 4 rounds and brush the edges with melted margarine or oil. Spread with the chosen filling and fold the edges to form three-cornered cakes. Brush the tops with warm honey and leave in a warm place to rise until doubled in volume. Bake in a moderately hot oven (200°C, 400°F, Gas Mark 6) until golden brown. *(Illustrated on page 138)*

Fillings

Cream cheese filling Add a little sugar and a few currants to soft cream cheese.

Prune filling Stone and chop 225 g/ 8 oz cooked prunes and add the grated rind and juice of ½ lemon.

Poppy seed filling

METRIC/IMPERIAL	AMERICAN
100 g/4 oz poppy seeds	1 cup poppy seeds
150 ml/¼ pint water	⅔ cup water
50 g/2 oz margarine	¼ cup margarine
50 g/2 oz chopped nuts	½ cup chopped nuts
50 g/2 oz raisins, chopped	⅓ cup chopped raisins
1 tablespoon golden syrup	1 tablespoon corn syrup
25 g/1 oz sugar	2 tablespoons sugar
25 g/1 oz chopped peel	3 tablespoons chopped peel

Put all the ingredients in a saucepan and cook over a gentle heat until thick.

Purim Fritters

Cut stale bread into 1-cm/½-inch slices and shape into rounds with a biscuit cutter. Lightly beat 2 egg yolks with 4 tablespoons (U.S. ⅓ cup) water and sweeten to taste. Dip the bread in this, drain and fry in shallow fat until golden brown on both sides. Drain and sprinkle with castor sugar and cinnamon before serving. *(Illustrated on page 138)*

Haman's Ears

Beat up 2 eggs and stir in 3 tablespoons (U.S. ¼ cup) oil. Then mix in sufficient flour to make a soft dough. Knead very thoroughly, break off small pieces and roll out on a floured board as thin as possible, to about the size of a meat to dry for an hour or longer. Fry in hot oil until a very light brown. Drain and, if liked, sprinkle with castor sugar. Handle very carefully as they break easily. *(Illustrated on page 138)*

Index